Father-Daughter Relationships

In this fully revised second edition, *Father-Daughter Relationships: Contemporary Research and Issues*, Nielsen summarizes the most relevant research to have emerged since the publication of the first edition and provides a panoramic view in a crisp, clear, engaging format. This book aims to break down the persistent misconceptions about fatherhood and father-daughter relationships and guides readers to a more objective, analytical approach.

The research is enlivened with compelling personal stories from fathers and daughters, including well-known celebrities and politicians. Quizzes and questionnaires show readers how to apply the research to their own lives and how to identify their own biases and misconceptions. Nielsen's scope reaches far beyond white middle-class families to include racial minorities, divorced and separated parents, immigrant families, gay fathers, and lesbian daughters. The book also covers fathers affected by poverty, incarceration, substance abuse, military service, and terminal illnesses, amongst other issues. *Father-Daughter Relationships: Contemporary Research and Issues* goes on to explore the father's impact on his daughter's cognitive, academic, social, psychological, and physical well-being at various stages of her life, as well as his impact on her vocational choices and relationships with men.

This book is essential reading for college students in education, psychology, sociology, women's studies, and counseling courses. It is also an indispensable resource for practitioners working with families as teachers, social workers, or mental health and family court professionals.

Linda Nielsen is a Professor of Education at Wake Forest University in Winston Salem, North Carolina. A member of the faculty for over 40 years, she is a nationally recognized expert on father-daughter relationships.

Textbooks in Family Studies

Series Editor, Robert Milardo

The Textbooks in Family Studies Series is an interdisciplinary series that offers cutting edge textbooks in family studies and family psychology. Volumes can be complete textbooks and/or supplementary texts for the undergraduate and/or graduate markets. Both authored and edited volumes are welcome. Please contact the series editor, Robert Milardo at rhd360@maine.edu, for details in preparing a proposal that should include the goal of the book, table of contents, an overview of competing texts, the intended market including course name(s) and level, and suggested reviewers.

Father-Daughter Relationships
Contemporary Research and Issues
by Linda Nielsen (2012)

Stepfamilies
A Global Perspective on Research, Policy and Practice
by Jan Pryor (2014)

Serving Military Families
Theories, Research, and Application, Second Edition
by Karen Rose Blaisure, Tara Saathoff-Wells, Angela Pereira, Shelley MacDermid Wadsworth, and Amy Laura Dombro (2016)

Evidence-based Approaches to Relationship and Marriage Education
edited by James J. Ponzetti, Jr. (2016)

Evidence-based Parenting Education
A Global Perspective
edited by James J. Ponzetti, Jr. (2016)

Evidence-based Approaches to Sexuality Education
A Global Perspective
edited by James J. Ponzetti, Jr. (2016)

Father-Daughter Relationships
Contemporary Research and Issues, Second Edition
by Linda Nielsen (2019)

Father-Daughter Relationships

Contemporary Research and Issues

Second edition

Linda Nielsen

Routledge
Taylor & Francis Group

NEW YORK AND LONDON

Second edition published 2019
by Routledge
711 Third Avenue, New York, NY 10017

and by Routledge
2 Park Square, Milton Park, Abingdon, Oxon OX14 4RN

Routledge is an imprint of the Taylor & Francis Group, an informa business

[First edition published by Routledge in 2012]

Library of Congress Cataloging-in-Publication Data
Names: Nielsen, Linda, author.
Title: Father-daughter relationships : contemporary research and issues /
   Linda Nielsen.
Description: Second edition. | New York, NY : Routledge, 2019.
Identifiers: LCCN 2019004477 (print) | LCCN 2019006438 (ebook) | ISBN
   9780429279133 (Ebook) | ISBN 9780367232863 (hardback : alk. paper) |
   ISBN 9780367232870 (pbk. : alk. paper)
Subjects: LCSH: Fathers and daughters. | Communication in families. |
   Parent and child.
Classification: LCC HQ755.85 (ebook) | LCC HQ755.85 .N5284 2019
   (print) | DDC 306.874/2–dc23
LC record available at https://lccn.loc.gov/2019004477

ISBN: 978-0-367-23286-3 (hbk)
ISBN: 978-0-367-23287-0 (pbk)
ISBN: 978-0-429-27913-3 (ebk)

Typeset in Sabon
by Taylor & Francis Books

Contents

Boxes

Preface

Why devote an entire book to the research on father-daughter relationships? Why encourage professors to create college courses exclusively focused on fathers and daughters? And why should professionals who work with daughters and their parents—especially teachers, mental health professionals, social workers, and health care providers—read this book?

The most important reason is that as a society, as researchers, and as professionals who work with families, we pay much less attention to father-daughter relationships than to other parent-child relationships in the family. Why does this matter? It matters because half of the children in this country are daughters—and the nature of their relationships with their fathers has a profound and far-reaching impact on their lives. As we will see throughout this book, the father's impact begins during his daughter's infancy and reaches far beyond her childhood. Her physical health, emotional and psychological well-being, academic and vocational success, drug and alcohol use, teenage pregnancy, and the quality of her romantic relationships and marriage are among the many aspects of her life that are linked to the kind of relationship she has with her father as she is growing up.

Moreover, the quality of the father-daughter relationship, especially if he is largely or completely absent, has an impact on many of the most widespread problems currently facing American girls and women. For example, fathers have an impact on whether their daughters become obese—a problem that has reached epidemic proportions and poses lifelong health problems not only for obese daughters. Daughters whose fathers are absent from their lives are also the most likely to grow up living in poverty—a problem that is more prevalent in the U.S. than in any other industrialized nation in the world.

Father-daughter relationships also merit more attention because they are generally more distant and more fragile than other parent-child relationships. Compared to mothers, fathers generally do not have as close a relationship with their children, especially with their daughters. This is not only a loss for daughters, but for fathers as well. Father-daughter relationships also tend to be more damaged and more likely to end than father-son relationships if the parents separate—or if the parents never lived together. The fragility of their relationship has become even more likely in recent years since almost 40% of the children are born to parents who are not married or living together, and nearly 40% of married parents divorce well before their children turn 18. Since father-son relationships typically receive more attention and more support in families and in society, daughters are at greater risk of having a damaged, weakened, or ruined relationship with their fathers. Throughout this book we will be examining the many factors that contribute to creating, maintaining, and strengthening fathers' relationships with their daughters—as well as factors that weaken, undermine, or destroy them.

Audience

This book is intended for upper level undergraduate and for graduate students, as well as for professionals working with families. The book is especially relevant for courses in psychology, sociology, women's studies, and counseling. The book will help prepare students for their future work with families from diverse backgrounds—for example, immigrant families, gay and lesbian families, and families in the military. The book also offers the most recent research and current issues for professionals in the fields of mental health, social work, health care, family services, and education.

On a more personal level, the book is beneficial for anyone who wants a better understanding of father-daughter relationships in their own families—fathers, daughters, stepparents, and mothers. It will also benefit brothers, husbands, or boyfriends who are wondering how the father-daughter relationship has influenced the women they love. The book is also a valuable resource for men who someday hope to become fathers.

Aims and Distinctive Features of the Book

Having been a professor for 45 years, I designed this book with teachers in mind. I present the research in ways that male and female students in my Fathers and Daughters course have found intriguing and engaging. I also hope the book will inspire professors to create a course exclusively focused on fathers and daughters in their own departments. On request, I am happy to provide the 15-page syllabus and supplemental materials that I have created for my course.

The primary aim of this book is to provoke readers into re-examining many of their beliefs and assumptions about fathers and about father-daughter relationships. I want readers to become acutely aware of the misconceptions or false beliefs that limit or damage many father-daughter relationships. I also want readers to learn how to interpret research more carefully and how to approach controversial issues more analytically, more objectively, and more critically—in short, to be less likely to be duped or misled by research that is seriously flawed or misrepresented.

In order to help readers apply the research to their own families or to their work with families, each chapter includes several unique features. Personal stories from fathers and from daughters, including well-known celebrities, Olympic athletes, and politicians, illustrate various aspects of the research. Quizzes and questionnaires lead readers to assess and to reconsider their own beliefs about fathers and father-daughter relationships—beliefs which at certain points will be refuted by the research and the statistical facts. Hopefully, this disconnect between beliefs and data will lead to change in the readers' own lives or in the work they do with families. Boldfaced terms and questions for "review" will help readers focus on the most important concepts and major conclusions from the research. (Hint: the material that professors are most likely to include on the tests.) Each chapter ends with controversial and personal "questions for discussion and debate" to provoke discussions with classmates, friends, colleagues, and family members.

While students and practitioners are reading this research book, I recommend reading my other book as well: *Between Fathers and Daughters: How to enrich or rebuild your adult relationship*. The two books are designed to be read together. *Between Fathers and Daughters* is a practical guidebook with specific recommendations, detailed activities, and self-assessment quizzes designed for fathers and their adolescent or adult daughters. The book is a detailed roadmap for how to apply the research in our professional work with families or in our own lives. For example, in the present book we will be exploring the research showing *why* most fathers and daughters find it more difficult than mothers and daughters to talk about personal or emotional issues. But the research does not show us *how* fathers and daughters can learn to communicate more openly, more honestly, and more comfortably. To improve their communication and enrich their relationship, exactly what do the father and the daughter need to start doing—and what do they each need to *stop* doing? *Between Fathers and Daughters* answers practical, specific questions such as these.

In the present book, the emphasis is on the most recent research and statistics. Presenting research or statistics that are more a decade old can be extremely misleading when it comes to drawing conclusions about contemporary father-daughter relationships. Similarly, the research in this book focuses only on American studies. No single book can present the research from several countries in a detailed or extensive way. My aim is not to present a brief, cursory overview of research from many countries or to compare father-daughter relationships in various countries. My goal is to present a more in-depth summary of the contemporary research on American fathers' relationships with their daughters.

One of the unique features of the book is the inclusion of personal comments from fathers, daughters, and stepmothers about the father-daughter relationships in their family. These are included in boxed inserts throughout the book. You will note that there are no references cited for these commentaries. The reason is that these comments are excerpts from the thousands of conversations and email correspondence I have had with fathers, daughters, and stepmothers over the past 30 years. To protect their privacy, I have changed the names and any other identifying information.

Overview of the Book

This book begins by examining how we are tricked or "woozled" into accepting research and statistics as true, when in fact they are false or only partially true. By understanding these "woozling" techniques, we reduce the odds of being duped or mislead by research studies and statistics that are seriously flawed or misrepresented. Then we examine eight of the most popular myths or woozles that can damage or undermine father-daughter relationships. This chapter also describes the most common mistakes that we make in processing information—mistakes that lead to inaccurate memories, faulty beliefs, and skewed perceptions.

Chapter 2 considers how fathers are often ignored, demeaned, or marginalized by researchers, policy makers, the media, mental health and medical professionals, advertisers, authors, and filmmakers. We then examine the specific components of "good" fathering and of high quality father-daughter relationships. We also explore several factors that create the greatest obstacles for most men as parents. In that light, we consider whether children would benefit more if we put less emphasis on fathers' incomes and more emphasis on fathering time. Then we explore how fatherhood affects men physiologically, financially, and emotionally. The chapter closes by zeroing in on some of the specific ways that daughters impact their fathers' opinions and behavior.

Chapter 3 summarizes the research on the father's impact on his daughter's cognitive, academic, vocational, social, and emotional development. What impact does he have on her development as an infant and toddler? What aspects of her life does he influence as she moves through childhood, adolescence, and early adulthood? Among the many topics discussed are his impact on her early language development and ability to regulate her own emotions, her social relationships with teachers and peers, academic success and vocational interests, dating and sexual behavior, depression and suicide, and identity development.

Chapter 4 is entirely devoted to a question that typically is overlooked in academic books: How does the father influence his daughter's physical well-being? Her physical well-being includes more than her overall physical fitness, eating and sleeping habits, participation in sports, and success as an elite athlete. It also includes the many serious and lifelong health problems for the 40% of daughters who are obese—a national epidemic that is linked to several aspects of father-daughter relationships. But fathers also influence their daughters' health in respect to her smoking, vaping, drinking, using drugs, contracting sexually transmitted diseases, becoming pregnant as a teenager, and being physically or sexually abused when she starts dating.

Chapter 5 explores the mother's impact on the father's relationship with their daughter. We begin with a brief overview of three theories that highlight the mother's influence over father-child relationships: psychoanalytic theories, attachment theories, and family systems theories. Next, we consider how the daughter's relationship with her mother and father generally differ in respect to closeness, conflict, and communication. Then the focus shifts to the specific ways that mothers influence the father-daughter relationship: gatekeeping, the quality of the co-parenting relationship, and the quality of the parents' marriage or relationship with one another.

Chapter 6 delves into the specific ways that divorce or separation often have a negative impact on fathers' relationships with their daughters. What accounts for these changes and how could we reduce their negative impact? How do each of these factors damage the relationship: divorce woozles, sole physical custody, role reversals, enmeshment, parental alienation, and gatekeeping? Finally, we consider how and why the father remarrying generally complicates, strains, or damages his relationship with his daughter.

Chapter 7 explores the similarities and differences in father-daughter relationships in various racial groups. What aspects of their relationships are unique? What problems are more likely to arise between fathers and daughters in some racial groups than in others? How might we reduce those problems? What is "colorism" and how can fathers help their daughters cope with it? Finally, how are father-daughter relationships in first generation or undocumented immigrant families unique?

Chapter 8 is a compilation of family situations that pose special challenges—or extremely serious problems—for fathers' relationships with their daughters. As the chapter demonstrates, the most damaging situations are extreme poverty and the father's incarceration, alcoholism, drug abuse, or incestuous behavior. Far less damaging, but still challenging, are the father-daughter relationships in families where fathers are in the military, where either the father or the daughter is not heterosexual, where the daughter was conceived through sperm donation, or where the father has a terminal illness.

Unfortunately, a number of intriguing questions cannot be addressed in this book because there is too little research to answer them. For example, how do father-daughter relationships change after the daughter marries or after she becomes a mother? How does growing up with an extremely wealthy or famous father help or hinder their relationship? How are adopted, or biracial, or twin daughters' relationships with their fathers unique? I hope the younger generation of researchers will address questions such as these. In the meantime, we will embark on a fascinating journey into the research presently at hand and into controversial issues affecting father-daughter relationships in America today.

Acknowledgements

This book has been shepherded along the way by several dedicated and talented professionals. I appreciate the feedback provided by the reviewers, Dr. Joyce Endendijk and Professor Kari Adamsons. I am also grateful for the support of Helen Pritt, editor, Charlotte Mapp, editorial assistant, and Sarah Fish, my copy-editor.

Dr. Linda Nielsen
Professor of Education
Wake Forest University, Winston Salem NC
nielsen@wfu.edu

Chapter 1

Fathers, Facts, and Fictions

Before embarking on our exploration of the hundreds of research studies presented in the following chapters, we need a basic understanding of how research data is sometimes misrepresented or distorted. Without this knowledge, we can easily be duped and deceived into adopting beliefs that are not true—or that are only partially true. Social scientists use a variety of terms to refer to the false beliefs or half-truths that arise when data are misreported or misrepresented—terms such as factoids, scholarly rumors, pseudoscience, and voodoo science. Throughout this book, I use the term "woozling" and "woozles" to describe the duping process and the falsehoods and partial truths that subsequently arise.

What's a Woozle?

Nearly forty years ago, the sociologist Richard Gelles popularized the concept of the "**woozle effect**."[1,2] Given his expertise on domestic violence studies, Gelles became concerned about how the data were frequently misrepresented and misused by advocacy groups for their own political purposes. He was troubled because only those studies that supported a particular advocacy position—many of which were seriously flawed—were being presented to the public and to policy makers as "the" research, while all the studies refuting the advocates' position were ignored. As a result, the public and policy makers were embracing many false beliefs about the prevalence and seriousness of domestic violence—beliefs that Gelles referred to as "**woozles**."

What is a woozle? Gelles and his colleague, Beverly Houghton, coined the term "woozle effect" based on the children's story *Winnie the Pooh*.[3] In the story Winnie the Pooh, an adorable but not especially bright little bear, dupes himself and his friends into believing that they are being followed by a scary beast—a beast that Winnie calls a woozle. Although they never actually see the woozle, Winnie convinces his friends that it exists because they see its footprints alongside theirs as they walk in circles around a tree. The footprints are, of course, their own. But gullible Pooh and his friends are confident that they are onto something really big. In fact, their foolhardy behavior is based on faulty "data." In the same way, Gelles realized that the public was being deceived into believing woozles about domestic violence that were based on only a small sample of very flawed studies.

As defined by Gelles, a woozle is a belief or a claim that is not supported—or is only partially or tentatively supported—by the empirical data. But because the claim is repeatedly cited and frequently presented in misleading ways, the public and policy makers come to believe it. As a result, data that are not accurate or that are only partially accurate come to be accepted as the "scientific evidence" on a particular topic. Put differently, a woozle is a definitive statement based on data that are very limited, flawed, ambiguous, or erroneous. Through a number of different "woozling" techniques, these flawed, scanty, or inaccurate data become widely disseminated and widely believed, overshadowing data that would challenge it. Certain aspects of a woozle might be partially true in that some studies can be interpreted in ways that lend partial support to portions of the woozle. There might be a small grain of truth buried in a bushel of untruths. This is one reason why woozles are so hard to dismantle. Often a woozle has an inherent appeal to people's existing beliefs or to their personal feelings about a particular topic, which makes it even more difficult to dismantle the woozle.

Eventually the processes that have promoted the woozle are successful enough that the flawed, limited, or exaggerated data come to have an impact on public opinion and public policy. Like Winnie the Pooh and his friends who are led astray by their own footprints, we are led astray by the questionable, weak, or contradictory evidence underlying the woozle. Describing the woozling process in the field of physics in his book, *Voodoo Science*, professor Robert Park puts it simply: we have been bamboozled.[4]

How Are Woozles Born and Raised?

How do studies or statistical data become part of a woozle? How do data from a study morph into something that barely resembles the researchers' original findings? As we will see, no one person or no one event can be held accountable for creating or for promoting a woozle. The woozle itself arises from a pattern of events and circumstances, not from any single factor or isolated event. Academicians have identified a constellation of factors that interact with one another in ways that create woozles.[5-8] Consider the following information to be a "woozle warning" guide.

Evidence by Citation

Woozles often begin when one or two studies are frequently and repeatedly cited in academic articles, at conferences, or to the media—while the bulk of the research is ignored or rarely mentioned. The more frequently the study is cited, the more credible it becomes. In other words, people naively assume that just because a particular study is widely cited and repeatedly discussed, its conclusions are valid and reliable. Gelles referred to this woozling process as "evidence by citation."

Misrepresenting Other Researchers' Data

Woozles can also arise when professionals are discussing and writing about a study's findings without ever having actually read the study—or having only read a synopsis or an abstract. The sociologist Janet Johnston calls these misrepresentations "scholarly rumors" because scholars are misquoting data which then gets repeated to other scholars without anyone having read the original source.[9] For instance, the authors of the original study may state clearly that their findings are not statistically significant and that their conclusions are speculative and inconclusive. But by time the study gets through the scholars' rumor mill, the findings are reported as important. Another way of misrepresenting data is to report several studies as having reached similar conclusions, when in fact they reached different conclusions. This buttresses the findings of one single study by creating the impression that there is an emerging consensus, a pattern, or a trend, when there is not.

Cherry Picking

Moreover, writers or speakers may choose to report only a few studies or only some of the findings from a particular study—a bias referred to as "cherry picking." For example, articles claiming to be reviews, summaries, or analyses of the literature may report only a small portion of the existing studies. The authors choose only the studies that support only their own point of view since the readers or audience are not aware that many other studies exist to support the opposite view. Another version of cherry picking is when researchers acknowledge the limitations of their study in a professional journal article, but never mention these weaknesses to the media or to audiences where knowledgeable researchers are not present to challenge them. In other words, researchers are far more likely to woozle their data to audiences that lack the expertise to challenge or question them. By cherry picking, only those studies or only those portions of a study that support the desired woozle are reported or presented.

Confirmation Bias

A woozle is also more likely to take root and spread quickly when it confirms beliefs that people already hold. This is known as **confirmation bias**.[10] We are overly critical and inclined to dismiss data that contradict our existing beliefs. In contrast, we are too willing to accept data that confirm what we already believe. For example, if people believe that women have a maternal instinct, then they will be more likely to accept any research study—no matter how flawed—showing that women are better parents than men. As the old adage goes, "I'll see it *when* I believe it."

Correlation versus Causality

We can also be tricked by confusing correlation with causation. **Correlation** means that two or more factors are related to each other. The correlation is "positive" if as one variable increases, so does the other —or as one variable decreases, so does the other. For example, there is a positive correlation between teenage pregnancy and father absence. As father absence increases, so does teenage pregnancy. A correlation is "negative" if as one factor increases, the other decreases. For example, there is a negative correlation between the amount of time fathers spend with their daughters and teenage drug use—as fathering time increases, drug use decreases. The problem with correlations is that they cannot prove that either variable caused the other variable to change. It is possible that other factors account for the change— factors that were not included in the study. For example, maybe girls from father absent families are growing up in neighborhoods and attending schools where the teenagers are much more sexually active—or maybe their mothers are not providing adequate supervision.

Still, this does not mean that correlational studies are worthless. In fact, most social science studies are correlational. It simply means we should not allow ourselves to be woozled into believing that correlation is the same as causality. Furthermore, as we will see in many of the studies presented in this book, the most sophisticated correlational studies include several variables in the analysis, assess them separately and see how they interact with one another. This helps strengthen the case for causality by ruling out competing factors that might account for the results. For example, a study of father absence and teenage pregnancy might also include the correlations between teenage pregnancy and how well the mother supervises the children, the family's income, and the quality of the neighborhood.

Researchers' Contributions to Woozling Their Data

Researchers themselves can also inadvertently or intentionally contribute to the woozling of their data. This is more likely to happen if the researcher has some vested interest in the outcome. For example, assume a researcher makes her living by providing counseling services for divorced parents. She might then be inclined to interpret ambiguous findings in her study as evidence that children benefit most when their parents seek help from professional therapists. Researchers might also create their own measures, use unorthodox or invalid procedures, or rely on abridged versions of standardized scales that have no established validity or reliability. Consequently, data that are uninterpretable or ambiguous are presented as if they are valid and reliable. Researchers might also minimize or ignore, rather than acknowledge and address, the ambiguous or contradictory data in their study. Or they might generalize their findings to populations that have little in common with the sample in their study. Finally, researchers might mislead people to believe that their study was based on a large sample, when in fact it was not. For example, researchers can emphasize the large numbers of people in the database from which their small sample was taken. Researchers may also try to promote their particular woozle by trying to silence or to demean their critics. One technique is to attack the character of other scholars who criticize their work. For example, a researcher who believes that children should live primarily with their mother after their parents separate might accuse scholars who disagree with her as being "fathers' rights activists" who are "biased" and "do not care about children's best interests."

The sociologist Joel Best has written extensively about the woozling of statistics and research.[5,11,12] In regard to researchers being biased, Best explains that we mistakenly assume that research data:

> simply exist, like rocks, completely independent of people; and that people gather statistics much as rock collectors pick up stones. This is wrong. All statistics are created through people's actions: people have to decide what to count and how to count it. People have to do the counting and have to interpret the results and to decide what the numbers mean. (p. 27)[11]

Given this, Best suggests we ask ourselves whether researchers have any stake in their study's findings. The stake might be financial, for example, increasing the number of people who come to them for counseling services or who pay them large speaker's fees because of their "famous" research study. The stake might also be personal—the desire to protect and promote his or her reputation as "the leading expert" on a particular topic.

Researchers or reporters may also contribute to woozling through the media. For example, they might use dramatic anecdotal stories to make their data more memorable to reporters, when in fact the findings are not particularly impressive or noteworthy. Then too, as Scott Lilienfeld, one of the most renown scholars on woozling and pseudoscience has pointed out, some of the most trustworthy university scholars are reluctant to engage with the media.[13] Academicians often frown upon drawing too much media attention to their own work. But as Lilienfeld notes, this often means that the media end up having to rely on reports from people who are not experts in the field and who are more likely to woozle the data.

Compelling Stories, Confidence, and Credentials

The way research data are presented to us can also contribute to distortions and woozles. For example, when information is presented along with compelling, personal stories, we are more likely to remember it, to repeat it, and to believe it. Assume, for example, that during a media interview, the researcher recounts three horrific stories about fathers who murdered their babies. Later in the interview the researcher explains that, according to national data, mothers are just as likely as fathers to murder their babies. Listeners are more likely to remember the three horrifying stories than they are to remember the national data. Although real life stories or dramatic case studies can be useful in highlighting data, these stories are too often exaggerated and generally not representative of the problem at hand. Having aroused people's emotions, these techniques increase the odds that the data will be more widely disseminated and, in too many cases, more widely woozled.

Simple Explanations and Neuroscience

We are also more likely to believe research findings that offer relatively simple explanations for complicated questions. Our desire for simple answers may be one of the reasons why it has become increasingly popular to cite neuroscience data to buttress the findings of social science studies. Social science studies rarely provide simple answers to complex issues. In contrast, neuroscience studies are appealing because they appear to be relatively simple. We assume they are more objective and more scientific than social science data. For example, college students were more likely to believe that the findings of a hypothetical study were true when the words "brain scans indicate" were included in the findings. Even when the interpretations of the data were illogical, and even when there was no demonstrated link between the behavior and the neurological data, the students were more willing to accept the results when they included neuroscience data.[14]

In sum, as Box 1.1 illustrates, there are many ways we can be woozled, duped, deceived, and manipulated by research data and statistics. By keeping some of these common techniques in mind, we can fine-tune our woozle alert systems and hopefully be wiser consumers of the research on father-daughter relationships.

How Our Memories and Cognitive Processing Deceive Us

In addition to being woozled, our own memories and the way our brains process information can deceive us. In exploring the research on father-daughter relationships in this book, many readers will no doubt be reflecting on the father-daughter relationships in their own families. In many of the research studies, daughters were recalling events that occurred many years before or in early childhood. For that reason, we need to be aware of several findings from the research on how we create our memories and how we process information about the events in the present and in the past. This brief overview is a reminder that memory and perception are not as reliable, as trustworthy, or as accurate as we might assume.[10,15–17]

Box 1.1 Woozlers' techniques: Are you being woozled?

- A few studies are cherry-picked to support one position.
- Two or three studies are repeatedly cited and discussed as "the research" on a topic.
- Reviews of the research, especially those making policy recommendations, are based primarily on the same few studies, ignoring the bulk of the research.
- The data are often presented in dramatic ways with anecdotal stories, case studies, or emotionally laden pictures and graphics.
- The significance of the findings is overstated while the limitations are understated.
- Data from small or non-representative samples are generalized to the general population.
- Only one theoretical perspective is used to frame the question and interpret the data.
- The data are based on measures with no established reliability or validity.
- Media reports, synopses, abstracts, or press releases overstate or misrepresent the study.
- Data that are not statistically significant or are contradictory and ambiguous are reported as important.
- The study's findings are immediately appealing because they confirm widely held beliefs.
- Findings that do not support the researchers' hypothesis are dismissed or minimized.
- Definitive statements are made based on very limited or ambiguous data.
- The authors promote their own study as a basis for a particular position without putting their data in the context of the larger body of evidence.
- Studies are presented together as if they reached the same conclusion, when they did not.
- The researchers do not publicly acknowledge the weaknesses of their study.

To begin with, we pay far less attention and are less likely to remember events that are unexpected or out of line with our stereotypes and beliefs. Our attention and our memories are shaped by what we expect will happen and how we expect people to behave. Consequently, we often fail to notice much of what is happening around us or to remember what happened in the past. Moreover, the brain's information processing is affected by whatever stereotypes we happen to hold. For example, if a daughter holds the stereotypic belief that men are less empathic and less sensitive than women, then she is less likely to notice or to remember many of the empathic, sensitive things her own father and other men do. In contrast, given her stereotyped expectations, she will be more likely to notice and to remember the empathic, sensitive things her mother or other women do. Having filtered her father's actual behavior through her pre-existing beliefs, her brain processes the data inaccurately and then stores a flawed memory.

Moreover, what we remember and how we interpret those memories depend on how we felt at the time those particular events occurred. When a particular event occurred, were we angry, depressed, or distraught—or were we happy, upbeat, and content? We can remember and interpret the same incident in entirely different ways depending on our emotional state at the time—and depending on our emotional state in the present. The brain is constantly sorting through the incoming data, storing some in memory and ignoring the rest. We selectively enter some information and delete the rest. Our emotions play a major role in this sifting and sorting, storing and interpreting. For example, assume that a teenage daughter is feeling very angry with her father because her parents are going through a divorce. At that time, things he says or does are likely to be stored and interpreted in a much more negative way than those very same things would have been dealt with before she was angry with him. In contrast, her young sister is not angry with her father at the time of the divorce. The same events that the teenage sister sees and remembers negatively about her father, the younger sister does not remember negatively at all. Both sisters are wedded to their own truth and memories that continue to influence their relationship with their father.

We can also "remember" events that never actually happened. We can also remember events that happened to someone else and convince ourselves that the event happened to us. To complicate things further, what other people tell us about what happened to us in the past shapes our memories. Unfortunately, some of those people may be distorting the information because their own prejudices or feelings at the time are heavily influencing their interpretations of what is happening. For example, an angry, clinically depressed brother may tell his sister enough negative stories about past incidents with their father that the sister comes to believe that she herself "saw" her father do those things. In fact, the sister may not even have been present when those events occurred. The brother's anger and depression may also have colored his interpretations and his memories.

Ironically, the more confident we are that a memory is true and the more vividly we remember the details, the more likely it is that we are wrong. The most reliable memories are those where we are not quite certain exactly what happened—and where we cannot recount many details. For instance, one father is confident and adamant as he recalls in vivid detail the exact conversation where his recently engaged daughter promised she would get married in the family's church. The other father is not so confident. He remembers discussing a church wedding with his daughter, but he admits that he cannot recall exactly what they said. He's "pretty sure" she promised to get married in the church. Of the two, the second father is more likely to be correct than the first.

We also remember and interpret events in ways that cast ourselves and the people we like in the most favorable way. In contrast, we attend to and remember the worst about people we dislike. Then too, we gather and store information in ways that create a consistent, predictable "story." When memories or events are contradictory, ambivalent, and confusing, we feel unsettled. To feel more at ease, we sort through incoming data, store memories, and interpret events in ways that allow us to create a more coherent, more logical story. We do this even when the events and memories are not connected in any logical or consistent way. We want simple explanations for complicated situations, so we create them. Even when the actual explanations are complex, ambivalent, and contradictory, we want simplicity. We also want to find a specific cause for events where there is no single or identifiable cause. We want to see patterns when in fact the events are random.

We are also more likely to believe information that is consistent with what we already believe. In contrast, we doubt, question, and scrutinize information that is at odds with our existing beliefs. We also tend to forget the times that a particular behavior did *not* happen. For instance, if a daughter has mistakenly stereotyped her dad as someone who expects perfection and has a bad temper, she will remember the occasional times when he did get mad when she failed at a particular task. But she will tend to forget most of the times he did not get angry when she was "imperfect."

This abbreviated overview of the research on cognitive processing is relevant to father-daughter relationships in at least three ways. First, fathers and daughters process information and create memories in ways that are both advantageous and disadvantageous to their relationship. Second, recognizing the many ways in which our cognitive processes can trick us, we must realize that there is no single "truth" or no way to get at a single "truth" for most of the situations that create tension between fathers and daughters. There is the father's version and the daughter's version of the past—his interpretation of past and present events, and hers. Usually there is no reliable way to determine whose version is correct. To be clear, this does not mean that we can never trust our memories or our thinking processes. It does mean, however, that we should keep a more open mind in regard to making mistakes in processing and storing data—especially data that affects our relationships with other people.

Third, given the impact that our expectations and pre-existing beliefs have on our cognitive processes and our memories, society's stereotypes of fathers have a significant role in shaping the kind of relationships that most fathers and daughters create over a lifetime. Given this, we must explore those myths and misconceptions in our society that often create obstacles for father-daughter relationships—erroneous beliefs that limit or that undermine the kind of relationship that most fathers and daughters might otherwise develop and enjoy throughout their lives.

Finally, five common cognitive processing mistakes often undermine the accuracy of our memories and our conclusions about what is and is not true or factual. These mistakes and these real life examples are described in the 2018 book *Factfulness* by the Rossling research team—a father and his son and daughter.[18] We engage in too much "binary thinking," which means we tend to divide things into two distinct groups or two distinct thoughts, without recognizing the overlaps. For example, in 2006 the World Health Organization concluded in its review of the research that the pesticide DDT was only mildly harmful to humans and that its benefits in many situations outweigh the risks—for example, savings lives by killing mosquitoes with DDT in malaria infected refugee camps. We also have a hard time holding two contradictory thoughts or conflicting beliefs at the same time. We also tend to notice, to remember, and to over-react to bad, disastrous, or frightening things (news, data, and incidents). For instance, when a tsunami damaged a nuclear power plant in 2011 in Japan, 1600 people died— not from radioactivity, but from injuries sustained while trying to leave the area or from loss of medical care that the sick or elderly had been receiving before they fled. They brought about their own deaths by over-reacting to the "potential" threat of dying from something that frightened them even more—radioactivity.

Moreover, we fail to notice, or we dismiss, the large impact that very small increases in a particular factor can have over time. For example, if a father's income only increases by 2% a year, in 35 years this means his income has doubled. We also make the mistake of treating big numbers as if they always represent big problems. For instance, even though 4.2 million babies died worldwide in 2016, this number was exceptionally small compared to infant mortality rates in the past. This does not mean that the babies' deaths do not matter. It means that statistical data should be presented to us in perspective. Similarly, when data are presented to us on a list, we often mistakenly assume that all the items are of equal importance. In fact, however, the first item might account for 80% of the problem or 80% of the solution. In the same vein, the words "majority" or "minority" can easily mislead us. Majority might mean 51% or it might mean 95%. Minority might mean 49% or it might mean 2%.

In respect to "factfulness," the Rosslings offer us three pieces of advice to reduce the odds of our being woozled. First, we should try to control our feelings of urgency and drama and focus more rationally and more calmly on the data. For example, before upsetting fathers by announcing that there is an epidemic of eating disorders among girls, we should step back and realize than only 1–3% of all daughters ever develop an eating disorder. Second, instead of using data to try to blame a single person or single group for a problem, we should put more emphasis on ways to solve the problem. Using the example of eating disorders, we should focus more on the research that identifies the factors that contribute to eating disorders and make fathers aware of those factors. Third, we should look for more similarities between groups—and look for more of the differences within groups. For example, as we will see in future chapters, there are more similarities than there are differences between how men and women communicate and how mothers and fathers parent their children. In other words, there are more differences in parenting styles and communication styles among women than there are between men and women.

Since our cognitive processing is flawed, and since we can all be woozled by research data, we want to examine eight popular myths that have an impact on father-daughter relationships. These woozles will be more fully explored in later chapters. But we want to address them at the outset so that we are on the alert for how they may be influencing us as we examine the research about fathers and daughters. These eight woozles are so wide-spread and have such potential for damaging or restricting father-daughter relationships that they merit attention at the outset of this book.

Woozle #1 Women have a maternal instinct which helps explain why, even in prehistoric times, mothers have been in charge of the childrearing.

Another way to word this woozle is that women are "by nature" better parents than men because all females have an inborn instinct for relating to and raising children. Keep in mind that an **instinct** is a fixed pattern or a fixed behavior that is genetically encoded in *all* members of a species. There are no exceptions to the rule when a behavior is instinctive. Instincts are not learned. They are genetically imbedded in all members of that species. Instinctive or innate behavior is not based on having any prior experience, copying what other members of the species do, or being taught what to do. For example, all baby sea turtles have an instinct to scurry back into the ocean after being born on the beach. This is an instinct. All baby turtles do it—no exceptions. The belief that human females have a maternal instinct might help explain why 53% of Americans believe that, compared to fathers, mothers are better at taking care of babies.[19] The belief in maternal instinct often goes hand in hand with the belief that throughout human history the mother has raised the children, while the father has "left home" to hunt for food.

The problem with these beliefs about maternal instinct or how children were raised in prehistoric times is that they are not based on anthropological or physiological evidence.[20] To begin with, in prehistoric times, men and women gathered food together since most of their diet came from plants, not from meat. Children were not generally taken care of primarily or exclusively by their mother, but by many people in their communal group—for example, older children or elderly men and women. Further promoting the survival of the young, a "traditional" family often included one woman and two men, neither knowing which children were biologically his. Moreover, when men hunted for meat, they hunted cooperatively together and shared the bounty with all families. In short, mom as childcare provider and dad as "breadwinner" is not our evolutionary norm. Females have always relied on others to help raise their young. There is no universal or "instinctive" pattern of mothering or fathering for humans or for other primates.

But what about maternal instinct? Don't all women have a genetically determined instinct that ensures they will nurture, protect, and bond with their young? No, they do not.[20] It is true that all females' hormones change when they are pregnant and after they give birth. For example, levels of prolactin, cortisol, and oxytocin increase. The particular hormonal changes are linked to feeling calmer, less aggressive, and less agitated which increases the odds of being attentive to the newborn child. But these hormonal changes do not cause mothers to bond with the baby or cause her to behave in specific ways that are universal to all mothers—as would be the case if there was a maternal "instinct." Nor do hormones guide the mother in knowing how to care for the newborn child. Parenting behavior is not instinctive. Parenting is learned either by observing or by receiving instruction from other human beings. Furthermore, if there was a maternal instinct, then all mothers would bond with and take good care of their newborns. But this is not the case. There are mothers who feel very stressed and depressed in the months after their child's birth. There are mothers who kill, physically abuse, neglect, and abandon their infants. More important still, millions of women choose not to become mothers—which would not be the case if mothering was instinctive. In short, there is no instinct that drives women to want to become mothers or that bestows on women an innate knowledge of how to care for their babies.

Furthermore, hormonal changes also occur in new fathers.[20] Although the changes are more dramatic in mothers, fathers' cortisol and oxytocin levels also increase. A man who is living with a pregnant woman or with a newborn baby also has a decrease in testosterone levels, which lowers his aggressive tendencies.[21] Both parents' hormonal changes are also influenced by their interactions with their newborn. For example, when mothers or fathers are holding or playing together with their baby, their levels of oxytocin increase.[22] And as we will see in Chapter 3, when a father holds his premature baby against his bare chest in a Neonatal Intense Care unit, his testosterone level, heart rate, and blood pressure decrease. This, in turn, helps the father feel calmer—and also decreases the premature baby's physical stress.

Although we might assume that the "maternal instinct" woozle is harmless, this belief can undermine fathering in a number of ways. If the parents believe the mother has an instinctive bond or instinctive expertise with their newborn, the father is likely to be more withdrawn and more hesitant to engage with their baby. He might also be less willing to express his opinions about how to care for their child if he is held captive to the belief that the mother's "maternal instinct" will—or must—guide them both. As we will see in future chapters, the belief in maternal instinct can have a far-reaching, negative impact on father-daughter relationships.

> Woozle #2 Unlike the male brain, the female brain is "wired" to be more sensitive, responsive, and attuned to children—especially to infants.

Like the maternal instinct woozle, this "brain" woozle assumes that, compared to males, females are physiologically better equipped to take better care of children. Consider the impact this belief might have on new parents whose baby girl has just arrived. What might the long-range implications be for this father-daughter relationship if either parent believes that the mother's brain is somehow "superior" to the father's when it comes to raising their daughter?

Thanks to medical technology, researchers have confronted this woozle "head on" so to speak. Through advanced imaging, we can literally see which areas of the brain become more activated when parents interact with their babies or when they hear their babies coo or cry. Contrary to the woozle, when they hear their baby cry or look at pictures of their baby, similar areas of the brain become more activated in mothers and in fathers.[23] Interestingly, different areas of the brain are activated when fathers are interacting with their baby boys than with their baby girls.[21] In short, fathers' brains are not inferior to mothers' brains in terms of being responsive to their babies' cues.

An intriguing study with gay and heterosexual fathers further illustrates how the brain becomes more activated when parents interact with their babies.[24] When two gay fathers were raising a baby, the father who did most of the childcare had the most activation in those areas of the brain related to being attuned to and being "synchronized" with their baby. This was also true for mothers in heterosexual families who spent far more time than fathers taking care of the baby. In other words, the parent's gender does not matter in terms of whose brain becomes the most activated in those areas related to being synchronized with the baby. What matters is how much time a parent spends interacting with the baby—which is further evidence that there is no instinct that makes mothers more attuned to or more synchronized with babies.

> Woozle #3 Babies naturally form a stronger and quicker attachment to their mother than to their father, forming a "primary" bond to her that takes precedence over their later bond to their father.

This "primary attachment" woozle has many offshoots and has a far-reaching impact on many of our social and legal policies. According to the **primary attachment theory**, all babies form a primary attachment to the person who is their main caretaker who is almost always the mother. At some later point, the baby forms a secondary attachment to the other parent who is almost always the father. With this supposed hierarchy of attachments, the baby's attachment or bond to the mother is more important and more necessary than the bond to the father. The weaknesses of attachment theories will be fully explored in Chapter 5. But because this is one of the most damaging and widespread woozles, we highlight it here. A large body of research refutes four of the major components of the theory of primary attachment.[25–27]

First, babies do not form an attachment or a bond to either parent (or to any other adult) until about six months of age. At that point, babies attach to both their father and their mother at about the same time and with the same intensity. This does not mean that in the first six months babies do not respond to and do not enjoy being held, fed, played with, talked to, and soothed. They enjoy these kinds of interactions with any adult, not just with their mother or father. For example, babies will respond enthusiastically to daycare workers or grandparents who interact with them in caring, pleasurable ways. In the presence of caring, attentive adults, babies will be responsive, playful, and soothed. Some adults are clearly better than others at soothing, or amusing or calming babies. But the baby does not form an attachment or a bond with any specific adult until about six months of age.

Second, when adults other than the parents are taking care of the babies, even for as much as 35 hours a week in daycare centers, this does not interfere with or weaken the babies' eventual attachment to their parents. When they are developmentally ready to form attachments, babies can become attached or bonded to multiple caregivers. In terms of survival of the species, these multiple attachments are clearly beneficial. And even in the most advanced societies, having multiple attachments to several adults provides the baby with a broader, more reliable network of caregivers.

Third, babies do not form a primary attachment with one parent and a secondary attachment with the other. To the child, there is no hierarchy of first and second place in terms of importance or need. At certain stages in their development, babies and toddlers may have preferences for which parent (or other adult) they gravitate towards for play, or for comfort, or for other kinds of activities. At certain stages, toddlers may seek out their fathers more than their mothers or vice versa. These preferences are short-lived and are not "attachments" in the sense that the child considers one parent more important or more necessary than the other.

Fourth, there is a great deal of confusion in the general public and even among mental health professionals about what the word "**attachment**" means in the psychological literature and in research studies. When researchers are assessing and classifying a toddler as "securely" or "insecurely" attached to a parent, *they are not measuring the quality or the strength of the child's relationship or bond with that parent.* Attachment measures are assessing how a particular child behaves when afraid, confused, hungry, tired, anxious, or in any other way stressed. The word "attachment" is misleading because so many people assume the word is synonymous with bond or relationship. More accurately, we should think of attachment tests as "stress reaction tests." How does the toddler react when under stress?

When the toddler is "**securely attached**" to a parent, in stressful situations the child will turn to the parent for reassurance and safety. For example, when a stranger enters the room and the toddler's stress increases, if the toddler turns to the parent for comfort, this is a sign of "**secure attachment.**" Once comforted, the toddler should become less stressed and venture forth to interact with the stranger. In contrast, if toddlers do not seek comfort from the parent, they are classified as "**insecurely attached.**" They will become increasingly stressed and respond by being agitated, confused, withdrawn, and so on. Neither response is a measure of whether the child feels loved by the parent, or whether the person is a "good" parent, or whether the child loves the parent. Indeed, when stressed, some children are classified as "securely attached" even to the parent who is negligent or abusive. Likewise, when stressed, some toddlers react in insecurely attached ways to a parent who is loving and attentive. Attachment is not a measure of connectedness, or love, or the quality of the parent-child bond.

Unfortunately, the term attachment is widely misunderstood and has resulted in policies that are harmful to children. For example, based on their misunderstandings about attachment studies, some people oppose allowing children under the age of three to spend overnight time in their father's care after the parents separate because it will weaken their "secure attachment" to their mothers. These attachment myths will be explored more fully in Chapter 5. Suffice it to say here that the attachment woozle is unfounded.

> Woozle #4 Compared to mothers, fathers have far less impact on infants' and toddlers' development which is why fathers are less "necessary" in these early years than later in children's lives.

This woozle encompasses the "primary attachment", "maternal instinct," and "mothers have better brains" myths. The consensus of these woozles is that mothers are better at parenting and are more necessary than fathers, especially in the first few years of a child's life. Fathers may be beneficial to children, but less so early in the child's life. Based on these beliefs, it is only "natural" and rational that mothers spend far more time with children than fathers do until the children reach school age.

Chapter 3 dismantles this woozle by showing the significant and long-lasting contributions that fathers make to their children's development in the first months and years of their lives. Moreover, the father's contributions are separate and independent from the mother's. That is, the father makes unique contributions over and above the mother's contributions. Three studies from the large body of research discussed in Chapter 3 are mentioned here to refute the woozle that mothers matter more than fathers in the first years of a child's life.

According to an analysis of 26 studies, babies whose fathers engage in challenging and stimulating play with them are less aggressive, more socially competent, and better able to regulate their emotions than babies whose fathers are more disengaged.[28] Likewise, in a study with almost 200 two-year-olds, those whose fathers had been highly involved when they were only three months old had more advanced cognitive development than toddlers whose father had been less engaged two years earlier.[29] This held true regardless of the mother's sensitivity to the infant or whether she had been depressed two years earlier. In an even larger longitudinal study, babies whose fathers were highly involved with them at one year of age had fewer behavioral and emotional problems when they were seven years old and when they were nine years old.[30] This was especially true if the mother had shown signs of clinical depression when the child was young. In short, the father's involvement in the first months or years of his child's life does matter. Putting too little emphasis on early fathering is a disservice to children.

> Woozle #5 Compared to fathers, mothers have more effective and more suitable parenting styles in terms of meeting children's developmental needs.

Much like the myth of maternal instinct, this woozle assumes that mothers and fathers parent differently and that the mother's style is generally better. Parenting styles fall into four basic categories based on their impact on children.[31] The most beneficial parenting style for children is **authoritative parenting**. These parents have high expectations for achievement and maturity, but are also warm, loving, and responsive. Authoritative parents set rules and consistently enforce them, while openly discussing the rationale behind the rules with the children. In contrast, children have worse outcomes with **authoritarian** parents where the expectations are exceedingly high, but parental warmth, nurturance, and responsiveness are low. These parents discipline in overly harsh ways and seldom explain the rationale for the rules. At the other extreme is **permissive parenting.** These parents are too lax in setting rules or enforcing discipline, even though they are warm and nurturing. Then there is neglectful or **negligent parenting** where parents are uninvolved and indifferent towards their children.

The woozle assumes that fathers are less likely than mothers to be authoritative parents. Fathers are supposedly more likely to make one of two mistakes in terms of their parenting style. The first is to be an overly lenient "pal" or playmate to his children who fails to set and enforce rules and fails to provide adequate supervision (permissive parenting). The second is to be an overly harsh, dictatorial disciplinarian who gives his children too little love and nurturance as an authoritarian parent.

This assumption about fathers is not correct for one simple reason: mothers and fathers have remarkably similar parenting styles.[32] A recent meta-analysis of 126 studies, involving 15,034 families, compared mothers' and fathers' parenting styles with sons versus daughters in children ages 0 to 18. The differences between mothers' and fathers' use of control with boys or with girls were not significant. There were slightly more differences in the parenting styles in older studies from the 1970s, at a time when men spent considerably less time than they do today with their children. But even in the 1970s, the differences were small.

Contrary to the belief that fathers are generally the disciplinarians, in a 2016 study, the mothers were far more likely than the fathers to discipline their very young children.[33] In these married families with one- to three-year-old children, mothers were more likely than fathers to spank or to use other methods of disciplining the children. As the researchers explained, this is understandable since mothers spent far more time with children at this early age. In other words, if fathers had been the ones staying home with the children, they would likely have been the disciplinarians. In short, an adult's parenting style is not linked to gender. Indeed there are more differences in parenting styles among mothers as a group than there are differences between mothers and fathers.[32]

> Woozle #6 Females are more empathic, more communicative, more nurturing, and more concerned about relationships than males.

How likely is it that a daughter who believes this woozle will seek advice or comfort from her father—especially about personal or awkward topics that require an empathic, careful listener? How comfortable will she be trying to talk to her dad about emotional, controversial, or sensitive things if she already believes that males cannot communicate as well as females?

This belief gained widespread appeal back in 1982 when the sociologist Carol Gilligan wrote a book called *In a different voice*.[34] Her claim is that women, unlike men, are guided by doing what is in the best interests of others and are more concerned about maintaining close relationships. Supposedly females are guided by "ethics of care" for others. In contrast, males are supposedly guided by the abstract principle of justice and are focused on autonomy and separation rather than on relationships. Gilligan's conclusions came from her two studies. In the one, she interviewed 29 women who had recently terminated an unwanted pregnancy. In the other, she observed the ways that boys and girls play with their same-sex peers. It should be noted that Gilligan was never willing to share her raw data with other scholars who questioned the validity, reliability, and conclusions of her two small studies.[35]

While Gilligan's book was still receiving widespread publicity, two other bestselling books echoed many of her claims. In 1990 Deborah Tannen, a linguistics professor, wrote *You just don't understand: Men and women in conversation*.[36] Echoing Gilligan's ideas, Tannen purported that women seek to connect and cooperate with people in their conversations, while men approach conversation as a one-up or one-down competition. As a result, women often feel silenced and dominated by men in conversation. Scholars criticized Tannen's book for ignoring the empirical studies and for perpetuating unfounded gender stereotypes. Moreover, Tannen based her conclusions on anecdotes from selected works of literature and from her personal observations of friends and family members. One scholar echoed the beliefs of many others in saying about Tannen's book: "Its popularity and overwhelming acclaim are both astonishing and troubling."[37] Despite the scholars' criticisms, Tannen's book remained on the *New York Times* bestseller list for almost four years.

At about that same time, in 1992 John Gray, who refers to himself as a "relationship counselor," wrote *Men are from Mars, Women are from Venus*.[38] Among the many claims in his book, Gray asserts that when men are stressed they "withdraw into their cave" while women share their feelings and discuss their problems openly. When problems arise, Gray claims that men focus only on finding a solution and ignore the other person's feelings—in contrast to women. Like Tannen's and Gilligan's books, Gray's book has been widely criticized by scholars for promoting unfounded gender stereotypes and ignoring the large body of research showing that men and women are not significantly different in regard to communicating, solving problems, being empathic, or expressing feelings.[39,40] One *Time* magazine journalist went so far as to described Gray's book as a "tower of psychobabble" written by a "huckster."[41] It is worth noting that Gray's PhD "degree" was awarded by an online, unaccredited school that was forced to close by the California Supreme Court because it lacked credentials.[42] Nevertheless, Gray's book clearly appeals to many women, as evidenced by the fact that it sold more than 15 million copies and was on the bestseller list for 121 weeks and was published in a revised version in 2012.[43]

Despite the widespread popularity of the books by Tannen, Gray, and Gilligan, the empirical research available at the time did not support the claims of these books. As the sociologist Janet Hyde amusingly mocked Gray's claims back in 2005, according to the large body of published research: "Women are from South Dakota and men are from North Dakota."[44] Likewise, in a 1983 review of the research, scholars found no significant differences in male and female empathy.[45] Indeed, in 1974 well before Gilligan, Gray, and Tannen wrote their books, Stanford University researchers who had reviewed the literature had already concluded that gender differences are miniscule on almost every trait that has ever been measured, with the exception of physical aggression.[46] More recent research reviews continue show that the differences between male and female social behavior, empathy, communication styles, connectedness, and moral reasoning are insignificant.[47–49]

Yet even in 2019 theses woozles about men being less empathic and less communicative than women live on. For example, in 2012 a revised version of Gray's 1992 book was published and in 2018 on Amazon rankings was still selling well.[43] This is not to say that in any particular family the father might be less sensitive, empathic, and communicative than the mother. And the reverse is also true: some mothers are less empathic, sensitive, and communicative than the fathers. But it is a grave injustice to children and to their fathers to embrace the woozle that men are less caring, less sensitive, less empathic, and less communicative than women.

In a similar vein, some people might believe that mothers have a unique influence and a far greater impact on children than do fathers. But four of the most highly regarded scholars in child development have refuted this belief.[50] There is not sufficient evidence to suggest that mothering and fathering are unique or that one parent has a greater impact on children than the other. Fathers' parenting affects children's outcomes in similar ways to mothers' parenting. Especially since fathers and mothers have assumed increasingly similar roles in respect to the amount of time they spend at work and with the children, mothering and fathering are not conceptually different. Good parenting—which means authoritative parenting—has a positive impact on children, regardless of the parent's gender. In contrast, permissive, authoritarian, or neglectful/negligent parenting has a negative impact.

Woozle #7 Most mothers do an unfair "second shift" of childcare and housework while many fathers shirk their duties.

This woozle might be dubbed "second shifts and shiftless dads" because it arose from a 1965 book called *The Second Shift* by the sociologist Arlie Hochschild.[51] A revised version of her book echoing the same themes was published in 2012.[52] She asserted that when mothers came home from their shift at work, many of them were burdened by a second shift of work at home. In contrast, many fathers supposedly did little to nothing to help with childcare or chores after getting home from work. Hochschild claimed that most fathers spent only 17 minutes a day on chores and 12 minutes with their children, compared to three hours of chores and one hour with children for mothers. Her initial conclusions were based on her interviews with 50 couples who worked at a manufacturing plant. Despite the study's small, non-representative sample, the book was and still is promoted as representing how "dual career families" in America place an unfair burden on employed mothers.

This is troubling because nationally representative data from multiple studies do not support Hoschschild's claims. For example, in a 2006 study with 1,200 parents, most couples had *mutually agreed* that the father would take on the burden of earning most of the money while the mother would do most of the childcare—which amounted to his earning 67% of the money and her doing 64% of the childcare.[53] They divided the workload equally, but differently. These researchers concluded that both parents do a second shift when they get home from work. Mothers spent an average of 90 minutes a day with the children, while fathers spent 60. As for chores, fathers spent an average of ten hours and mothers spent 15. Overall then, both parents invested 64–65 hours a week in their assigned "work", leaving each with about 33 hours of free time. And when the mother worked only part-time, her total hours of all combined kinds of work were *less* than the father's.

In a more recent 2012 study with 6,572 fathers and 7,376 mothers (from different families) with children under the age of 13, mothers spent more time (49 hours) than fathers (31 hours) with the children.[54] But again, the difference was largely explained by the father working more hours outside the home than the mother. Only 60% of the mothers were employed, working an average of 22 hours a week, compared to 44 hours for the fathers. Moreover, when the mother worked, especially when she was contributing considerably to the family's income, the father spent even more time with the children. Interestingly, mothers with higher wages spent more time with their children than mothers with lower wages. This suggests that, even though higher income mothers have more options to "buy" their way out of time with their children, they *choose* to be with their children because it is pleasurable.

Compared to household chores or yardwork, spending time with children is more pleasurable and should not necessarily be construed as a burden that is unfairly hoisted on mothers. As we will see in future chapters, most fathers wish they could spend more time with their children and are unhappy that the demands of their work deprive them of this pleasure. Moreover, the amount of time each parent spends with the children or doing chores largely depends on how much time each spends at work.

Furthermore, American work and childcare policies make it more difficult for fathers to spend time with their children than the policies of 22 of the most advanced countries in the world.[55] American fathers are among the most disadvantaged in terms of having no paid paternity leaves or paid days off work to take care of their sick children. By way of contrast, Swedish parents are granted 480 days of paid leave after a baby is born or adopted.[56] For 390 of those days, they are entitled to 80% of their normal pay. Each parent is entitled to half of those 480 days. If a parent decides not to use his or her half of the allotted childcare days, the remaining days cannot be transferred to the other parent. Today in Sweden fathers take nearly 25% of all parental leave allotted to them—a figure the government wants to increase. These 480 days of parental leave can be used until a child turns eight. Parents also have the legal right to reduce their normal working hours by up to 25% until the child turns eight, with a commensurate reduction in pay. Not surprisingly, Swedish fathers are more highly involved with their children than American fathers given these father friendly policies.

Given America's family-work policies and the gendered choices that fathers and mothers make about how to divide the parenting time and income earning, it hardly appears that most fathers are exploiting mothers with a "second shift" of work. This is not to say that some fathers are not shirking their childcare and their housework duties. But the "second shift" is more a woozle than a fact.

Woozle #8 Compared to mothers, fathers are more physically abusive to their children and are more likely to kill them.

We end this chapter with an especially frightening woozle: Children are much more likely to be physically abused or killed by their fathers than by their mothers. This belief is easier to embrace if we believe that fathers are less nurturing, less sensitive, and less empathic and that mothers have a maternal instinct and a brain hard-wired to be sensitive to their children. But the belief that fathers abuse and kill their children more often than mothers do is more woozle than fact.

First and foremost, mothers are more likely than fathers to physically abuse or physically neglect children under the age of five.[57,58] Each year in the U.S. nearly 900,000 incidents of child abuse and physical neglect are reported to authorities. Of these, 65% are for physical neglect (not feeding the child, leaving a young child alone for hours, not taking the child to doctors for medical care) and 25% are for physical abuse. Nearly 1,500 children die each year as a result of physical abuse or neglect. Nearly 80% of them are under the age of four. Most of this abuse is at the hands of their mothers, not their fathers. This is not surprising since young children spend far more time with their mothers. Moreover, many neglected and abused children are being raised by single mothers who often live in poverty, have no help with childcare, and suffer from emotional or mental disorders. Mothers are also more likely than fathers to suffer from postpartum depression, which can contribute to child abuse and neglect.

Several other facts about child abuse also undermine the woozle that fathers pose far greater dangers than mothers to their children.[57] The vast majority of abused, neglected, or murdered children are from low income, single mother families. Even so, only 1.5% of children under the age of five and 18% between the ages of 14 and 17 have ever been physically abused by a parent or by any adult caregiver. Furthermore, the rates of child abuse in the U.S. have steadily declined in recent years.

As for murder, several negative beliefs about fathers are not supported by facts.[59,60] Most murdered children are killed by their own parents. For children under the age of five who are murdered, 30% are killed by their mothers and 31% by their fathers. Because juries are loath to send mothers to prison for murdering their children, almost two-thirds of these mothers are declared mentally ill and hospitalized. In stark contrast, when fathers kill their children, two-thirds of them are either sentenced to life in prison or executed. Most fathers who kill their children are either mentally ill or are in the grips of a temporary fit of rage where they are seeking revenge against the mother. Not surprisingly then, immediately after killing their children, most of these enraged or mentally ill fathers also kill themselves.

Conclusion

In ending this discussion of woozles, it is important to understand that these woozles can have a very real and negative impact on fathers' relationships with their children. For example, in a 2017 survey with 619 family court judges, those who held traditional gender role beliefs about mothers and fathers awarded significantly more parenting time to mothers in custody decisions.[61] Among these beliefs is the woozle that mothers are superior to fathers in raising children, especially young children. Likewise, in a 2013 survey of 227 people who had been summoned for jury duty, most agreed that judges were prejudiced against fathers when it came to awarding parenting time in custody cases.[62] In future chapters, we will see many examples of how the eight woozles in this chapter often restrict or damage father-daughter relationships.

Having explored the specific ways that research studies and statistics can be manipulated or woozled to deceive us, we can be wiser consumers of data. Being less gullible, we can more easily discount and more confidently question those beliefs that lead us to see father-daughter relationships in distorted ways. We will explore the eight woozles presented in this chapter in more detail throughout this book. And we will subject many other woozles to scrutiny—woozles that damage, undermine, or restrict father-daughter relationships.

As we explore the research, we also want to keep in mind that our memories about our own families are often flawed and sometimes completely incorrect. Especially when recalling highly emotional events or difficult family issues, what we remember and how we interpret those memories is colored by our emotions in the past and in the present. We want to tread cautiously in order not to dupe ourselves into believing things that may be only partially true about the past—or in some cases, not true at all.

Review Questions

1 What is a woozle and how can woozles have a negative impact on father-daughter relationships?
2 What factors contribute to the creation and promotion of a woozle?
3 What signs can alert us to the possibility that certain research is being woozled?
4 What are ten specific ways we can reduce the chances of our being woozled by particular research studies or statistics?
5 How is human memory flawed in terms of its accuracy and reliability?
6 What factors contribute to the creation of inaccurate memories?
7 What are five factors that interfere with our processing data accurately?
8 What are ten mistakes we often make that lead us to reach false or inaccurate conclusions?
9 When considering our own childhood memories, what are five research findings we should keep in mind regarding their accuracy?
10 For each of the eight woozles discussed in this chapter, explain the woozle and then present the research that refutes each woozle: maternal instinct, female brains, primary attachments, mothers' parenting styles, mothers' greater impact in early childhood, female empathy and communication, mother's second shift of childcare, physically abusive and murderous fathers.

Questions for Discussion and Debate

1 Which of the woozles surprised you most and why?
2 Which of the negative stereotypes about fathers discussed in this chapter might be limiting your relationship with your own father? How?
3 How might faulty or inaccurate memories about events in your family possibly be influencing your relationship with your father?
4 How have you been woozled with research that is cited in the media on any topic discussed in this chapter?
5 What research in this chapter did you find most disturbing or unsettling in terms of your previous beliefs?
6 What mistakes do you tend to make in terms of the common errors in cognitive reasoning discussed in this chapter?
7 When two siblings have very different perceptions and different memories about their father, what would you say to them regarding who is right?

8 Describe two commercials and two TV programs that portray fathers in negative ways and that are based on the woozles discussed in this chapter.

9 Which of the woozles in this chapter does the most damage to father-daughter relationships and which are most closely related to what you have observed in your family network?

10 What could the media, the internet, and advertisers do to refute the negative stereotypes of fathers that are refuted by the research presented in this chapter?

References

1 Gelles R. Violence in the family: A review of research in the seventies. *Journal of Marriage and Family* 1980; 42: 873–885.

2 Gelles R. The politics of research: The use and misuse of social science data. *Family Court Review* 2007; 45: 42–51.

3 Milne A. *Winnie the Pooh*. London: Metheun; 1926.

4 Park R. *Voodoo Science: The road from foolishness to fraud*. New York: Cambridge University Press; 2000.

5 Best J. *Stat Spotting: A field guide to identifying dubious data*. Los Angeles: University of California; 2008.

6 Lilienfeld S, Lynn S, Lohr J. *Science and pseudoscience in clinical psychology*. 15 ed. New York: Guilford; 2015.

7 Stanovich K. *How to think straight about psychology*. New York: Allyn & Bacon; 2012.

8 Thyer B, Pignotti M. *Science and pseudoscience in social work practice*. New York: Springer; 2015.

9 Johnston J. Introducing perspectives in family law and social science research. *Family Court Review* 2007; 45: 15–21.

10 Chabris C, Simons D. *The invisible gorilla: and other ways our intuitions deceive us*. New York: Crown; 2010.

11 Best J. *Damned lies and statistics: Untangling numbers from the media, politicians and activists*. Berkeley: University of California; 2001.

12 Best J. *More damned lies and statistics*. Berkeley: University of California; 2013.

13 Lilienfeld S. Public skepticism of psychology. *American Psychologist* 2011; 67: 111–129.

14 Weisberg D, Keil F, Goodstein J, Rawson E, Gray J. The seductive allure of neuroscience explanations. *Journal of Cognitive Neuroscience* 2008; 20: 470–477.

15 Sabbagh C. *Remembering our childhoods: How memory betrays us*. New York: Fireside; 2010.

16 Schnider A. *The confabulating mind: How the brain creates reality*. Cambridge: Oxford University Press; 2011.

17 Kahneman D. *Thinking, fast and slow*. New York: Farrar, Straus and Giroux; 2011.

18 Rosling H, Rosling O, Rosling A. *Factfulness: Ten reasons we're wrong about the world and why things are better than you think*. New York: Flatiron Books; 2018.

19 Parker K, Livingston G. *Seven facts about American dads.* New York: Pew Research Center; 2018.

20 Hrdy S. *Mothers and others: The evolutionary origins of mutual understanding.* Cambridge, MA: Belknap Press; 2009.

21 Mascaro J, Rentscher K, Hatckett P, Rilling J. Child gender influences paternal behavior, language and brain function. *Behavioral Neuroscience* 2017; 131: 262–273.

22 Gordon L, Sharon O, Leckman J, Feldman R. Oxytocin and the development of parenting in humans. *Biological Psychiatry* 2010; 68: 377–382.

23 Mascaro J, Hackett P, Gouzoules H. Behavioral and genetic correlates of the neural response to infant crying among human fathers. *Social Cognition Affect Neuroscience* 2013; 12: 166–183.

24 Abraham E. Father's brain is sensitive to childcare experiences. *Psychological and Cognitive Sciences* 2014; 111: 3792–9797.

25 Dagan O, Sagi-Schwartz A. Early attachment network with mother and father: An unsettled issue. *Child Development Perspectives* 2018; 12: 115–121.

26 Kochanska G, Kim S. Early attachment organization with both parents: Infancy to middle childhood. *Child Development* 2012; 83: 1–14.

27 Newland L, Freeman H, Coyle D. *Emerging Topics on Father Attachment.* New York: Routledge; 2011.

28 St George J, Wroe J, Cashin M. The concept and measurement of fathers' stimulating play: A review. *Attachment & Human Development* 2018; 20: 634–658.

29 Sethna V, *et al.* Father-child interactions at 3 months and 24 months: Contributions to children's cognitive development at 24 months. *Infant Mental Health Journal* 2017; 38: 378–390.

30 Boyce R, *et al.* Early father involvement and mental health problems in middle childhood. *American Journal of Child and Adolescent Psychiatry* 2006; 45: 1510–1523.

31 Baumrind D. Effects of authoritative parental control on child behavior. *Child Development* 1966; 37: 887–907.

32 Endendijk J, Groeneveld M, Bakermans M. Gender differentiated parenting revisited: Meta-analysis reveals very few differences in parental control of boys and girls. *PLOS ONE* 2016; 11.

33 Hallers-Haalboom A. Wait until your mother gets home! Mothers' and fathers' discipline strategies. *Social Development* 2016; 24: 82–98.

34 Gilligan C, Machung A. *In a different voice.* Cambridge, MA: Harvard University; 1982.

35 Sommers C. *The war against boys: How misguided feminism is harming our young men.* New York: Simon Schuster; 2000.

36 Tannen D. *You just don't understand: Men and women in conversation.* New York: Harper Collins; 1990.

37 Freed A. We understand perfectly: A critique of Tannen's view of cross-sex communication. In: Hall K, Buchholz M, Moonwomon B, editors. *Locating power: Proceedings of the second Berkeley women and language conference.* 1993. 144–152.

38 Gray J. *Men are from Mars, Women are from Venus.* New York: Harper Collins; 1992.

39 Cameron D. *The myth of Mars and Venus: do men and women really speak different languages?* New York: Oxford University Press; 2007.

40 Wood J. A critical response to John Gray's Mars and Venus portrayals of men and women. *Southern Communication Journal* 2002; 67: 201–210.

41 Gleick E. The tower of psychobabble: Is John Gray a healer or a huckster? *Time Magazine*, June 16, 1997.

42 California State Supreme Court. *California Supreme Court upholds denial of Columbia Pacific University's approval to operate, December 1, 2000.* Sacramento, CA; 2000.

43 Gray J. *Men are from Mars, Women are from Venus: The classic guide to understanding the opposite sex.* New York: Harper; 2012.

44 Hyde J. The gender similarities hypothesis. *American Psychologist* 2005; 60: 581–592.

45 Eisenberg N, Lennon R. Sex differences in empathy. *Psychological Bulletin* 1983; 94: 100–131.

46 Maccoby E, Jacklin C. *The psychology of sex differences.* Palo Alto, CA: Stanford University Press; 1974.

47 Barnett N, Rivers C. *Same difference: How gender myths hurt our relationships.* New York: Basic Books; 2004.

48 Cameron D. *The myth of Mars and Venus.* Cambridge: Oxford University Press; 2007.

49 Walker L. Gender and morality. In: Killen M, Smetana J, editors. *Handbook of moral development.* Mahway, NJ: Erlbaum; 2006. 93–115.

50 Fagan J, Day R, Lamb M, Cabrera N. Should researchers conceptualize differently the dimensions of parenting for fathers and mothers? *Journal of Family Theory & Review* 2014; 6: 390–405.

51 Hochschild A. *The second shift.* New York: Viking; 1989. First published 1965.

52 Hochschild A, Machung A. *The second shift: Working families and the revolution at home.* New York: Penguin Books; 2012.

53 Bianchi S, Robinson J, Milkie M. *Changing rhythms of the American family.* New York: Sage; 2006.

54 Raley S, Bianchi S, Wang W. When do fathers care? Mother' economic contribution and fathers' involvement in child care. *American Journal of Sociology* 2012; 117: 1422–1459.

55 Glass J, Andersson M, Simon R. Parenthood and happiness: Effects of work-family reconciliation policies in 22 OECD countries. *American Journal of Sociology* 2016; 122: 886–929.

56 Sweden. Ten things that make Sweden family friendly. 2018. Report No: https://Sweden,se/society.

57 Finkelhor D. *Childhood victimization: Violence, crime and abuse in the lives of young people.* New York: Oxford University Press; 2014.

58 Finkelhor D, Turner H, Shattuck A, Hamby S. Prevalence of childhood exposure to violence, crime and abuse: Results from the national survey of children's exposure to violence. *American Medical Association Pediatrics* 2015; 169: 746–755.

59 Oberman M, Meyer C. *When mothers kill.* New York: New York University; 2008.

60 West S, Friedman S, Resnick P. Fathers who kill their children: An analysis of the literature. *Journal of Forensic Sciences* 2009; 54: 463–468.

61 Miller A. Expertise fails to attenuate gendered biases in judicial decision making. *Social Psychological and Personality Science* 2018; (1): 8.

62 Votruba A, Braver S, Ellman I, Fabricius W. Moral intuitions about fault, parenting and child custody after divorce. *Psychology, Public Policy and Law* 2014; 20: 251–262.

Chapter 2

Fathering and Fatherhood

Figure 2.1
Source: Ethan Bullard.

Having seen how fathers are often misrepresented and maligned through woozling, we direct our attention in this chapter to those aspects of fatherhood that are particularly relevant to father-daughter relationships. We begin with how we ignore or dismiss fathers in research, policy, and practice in ways that can damage their relationships with their children. We then examine the demeaning and misleading portrayals of fathers in the media, children's literature, films, and commercials and the impact of paternity leave policies and societal attitudes towards fathers' roles. Then we explore the various components of "good" fathering and ways to assess the quality of father-daughter relationships. After examining how fatherhood changes men's lives, we end with a discussion of the impact that daughters can have on their fathers' opinions and behavior.

Does Family Income Outweigh Fathering?

Historically we have defined "good" fathering and fathers' roles largely in terms of a father's success in providing for his family financially. Defining fathers in this way restricts the non-financial contributions he makes in his children's lives. We begin then with the question: How much does the father's income matter in terms of his children's well-being? Is maximizing his income one of the most valuable contributions he can make to his children? Since maximizing his income or being the main wage earner for the family comes at the expense of less fathering time, are we over-emphasizing the importance of the father's income? If so, how much do children benefit from the tradeoff of less fathering time versus higher family income? Researchers have not addressed this specific question. Nevertheless, a large body of research has addressed the question: How closely is family income linked to various outcomes for children? This research provides us with clues regarding the importance of the father's income.

The studies presented here are merely intended to remind us of three things. First, family income has a less powerful impact on children than many of us might imagine—with the exception of children living in poverty. Second, the connection between income and children's well-being is not linear. That is, increases in family income do not go hand in hand in a stepwise fashion with improvements in children's outcomes. Third, the quality of parent-child relationships and quality of the parenting are often as closely linked as family incomes are to children's outcomes. Given these three findings, the studies that follow suggest that we may be putting too much emphasis on how much money the father earns—and on his increasing or maximizing his earnings—and putting too little emphasis on his time with his children.

First and foremost, there is no doubt that the 20% of American children who are living in poverty have more academic, emotional, behavioral,

Figure 2.2
Source: Steven Mizel.

health, cognitive, and developmental problems than the 80% who are not living in poverty.[1,2] The vast majority of these impoverished children are living in single mother homes and have a weak or no relationship with their father. It is abundantly clear that living in poverty, especially combined with too little or no fathering, takes a serious, long-lasting toll on children—a situation that will be discussed in Chapter 8.

The question addressed here is not about the 20% of children living in poverty. The question here is: How strongly is family income linked to children's outcomes in the 80% of families who are not living in poverty? If there is a strong, clear connection between family income and children's outcomes, then one of the most beneficial contributions a father can make is to maximize his income. Since fathers are the main wage earners in most American families, this burden falls mainly on him, not on the mother. Even though maximizing his income means spending less time with his children throughout their childhood, the trade-off would be worth it if the links between family income and children's outcomes were consistent and strong.

Unfortunately, the vast majority of studies on income and children's well-being have merely compared children living in poverty to children not living in poverty. Rarely have researchers compared children's outcomes in families in various income brackets above the poverty level. Consequently, we know relatively little about whether children from upper income families have significantly better emotional, social, or behavioral outcomes (i.e. depression, anxiety, relationships with parents and peers, self-esteem, drug and alcohol use) than children from middle class or working class families.[3-5] Nevertheless, several findings from this large body of research do address the question: As long as the children are not living in poverty, how much does family income matter for children's well-being?

To begin, we know that family income is more closely related to children's academic performance than it is to their behavioral, emotional, or social well-being. For example, when 12 different groups of researchers used ten different longitudinal data sets, family income was more strongly linked to children's academic outcomes than to their behavior, mental health, or physical health.[2] Even so, as long as the children were not living in poverty, there was not a linear relationship between family income and school performance. That is, as family income increased, children's academic performance did not necessarily increase. Similarly, from 1998–2010, the gap in "readiness" for kindergarten grew smaller between children living in poverty and other children. School readiness included children's cognitive skills, attention spans, and social behavior.[6] But during that 12-year span, the income gap between rich and poor families grew much larger. If income was the pivotal factor, then the gap for school readiness should have increased, not decreased. As these researchers pointed out, factors other than income accounted for the improvements for the poorest children.

A closer look at one nationally representative sample of 21,255 kindergarten children might help explain why income is not always linked to children's outcomes.[4] The researchers categorized the families into five different income brackets. Income was only weakly connected to positive parenting behavior (warmth, supervision, consistent rules) or to the parents' levels of stress. As expected, richer parents provided more stimulating activities and materials at home, for example more books. But higher incomes were only weakly linked to children having better cognitive skills or better social or emotional adjustment. As the researchers concluded:

> It is not enough to say that income matters for children. How it matters depends on the extent to which income influences the parenting behavior … Our model challenges the well-established finding of a direct association of increased income and decreased stress [for parents]. (p. 89)[4]

These American findings mirror research from other countries. For example, in an Australian study with more than 9,000 children, there was no link between family income and children's social or emotional problems. This study is important because, even though children from richer families initially appeared to have better cognitive skills, this advantage disappeared when the parenting time and the parents' mental and physical health were factored in.[7] Likewise, in a review of 34 Canadian studies, family income had little to no connection to children's behavioral or emotional problems.[8]

As for adolescent and young adult children, there are a number of surprising findings related to family income—all of which come from studies using nationally representative, large samples. Adolescents and young adults from higher income families engaged in more binge drinking and used cocaine and marijuana more often than those from less affluent families.[9] Considering all types of drug use and drinking for high school seniors in 2016, the link to family income was weak.[10] The seniors from richer families were, however, the least likely to smoke. In yet another study, teenagers and young adults from families with incomes from $110,000–$150,000 were more likely than their peers from less wealthy families to use drugs and cocaine, to be depressed and anxious, and to cut or burn themselves on purpose.[5] In short, coming from a rich family was not beneficial for the young people in these studies.

Several other studies are worth noting given the unique ways they investigated the impact of income. When comparing adopted and biological children in almost 800 families in a longitudinal study, the links between income and children's cognitive and non-cognitive measures were "modest" for the biological children; but were very weak for adopted children.[11] Concluding that genetic factors largely account for children's cognitive outcomes, these researchers stated, "These findings do not support the hypothesis that highly educated, upper income parents are more effective in fostering skill development in their children" (p. 79). Similarly, in a study with more than 600 sixth graders, those in the schools serving low-income students were more anxious and depressed than those in affluent schools.[12] Nevertheless, the poor children reported being just as close to their parents as the wealthier children and they were no more likely to use drugs or be delinquent. Similarly, in another study with a much larger sample, children's reports of the quality of their relationships with their parents was largely the same in the highest and lowest income families.[13]

So we return to the questions. How much does the father's income matter? Does a high quality relationship with his children matter as much or more than his income? Would children benefit more if their fathers worked less but spent more time with them? Although the research does not specifically answer these questions, it does leave us with three clear messages. First, with the exception of children living in poverty, family income is not consistently or strongly linked to significantly better outcomes for children in terms of their emotional or psychological well-being, behavioral problems, or the quality of their relationships with their parents. This was established in the research over two decades ago.[14] Second, factors other than income matter as much or more for children's well-being—especially the quality of parent-child relationships. Third, there is no compelling evidence that if fathers spent more time with their children, but did so at the cost of earning less money than they might otherwise have earned, their children would have worse outcomes.

Ignoring, Dismissing or Demeaning Fathers in Research and Practice

Although our society places a high value on children growing up in two-parent families, in many ways we simultaneously ignore or dismiss fathers. When it comes to the importance given to parents in the research and in societal practices and beliefs, we have generally relegated fathers to second place. But why? In large part, it is because we have embraced the damaging belief that family income is the factor that trumps all others in terms of positive outcomes for children. That is, we believe the father provides the greatest benefits for his children by earning the highest income possible given his education and experience. Even if his higher income comes at the expense of less fathering time or lower quality fathering due to the stress and demands of his work, we believe the tradeoff is worth it. As we have just seen, however, the evidence does not support this belief. With the exception of keeping his children out of poverty, it is not at all clear that a father's income is closely linked to children's well-being.

The lack of attention to fathers, especially to father-daughter relation-ships, stems from other beliefs as well. Historically there was a fear that if fathers were not involved enough with their sons, boys would become "sissies."[15,16] In part the Boy Scouts was founded in 1910 because Americans were worried that boys were becoming too weak and effeminate. By the 1950s, many believed that too many boys were being raised by overly protective mothers and that this was weakening the next generation of men. Given these fears, the father-son relationship was in the forefront of public discussions and social science research. Unfortunately, it has remained there ever since.

In the social science research fathers still receive less attention than mothers. For instance, 1,115 articles published from 1977 to 2009 in five leading journals in child development and family studies devoted far less attention to fathers than to mothers.[17] And in a 2007 review of the literature about parents who were trained to help their children with attention deficit disorders, only 13% of the studies included fathers.[18] Even in 2018, the parenting research still devoted far more attention to children's relationships with their mothers.[19] To my knowledge, my Fathers and Daughters course is still the only college course in the country devoted exclusively to father-daughter relationships. In contrast, there are literally dozens of college courses devoted exclusively to mother-daughter relationships. Yet back in 2005 I wrote a chapter urging family studies professors to create more courses on this topic in order to provide this research to students whose future careers would involve working with families.[20]

Authors of fiction and non-fiction literature also generally devote less attention to fathers' relationships with their children—especially with their daughters. For example, a small group of English professors noted that scholars had written very little about father-daughter relationships as portrayed in various works of literature, compared to many scholars' analyses of mother-daughter relationships.[21] Consequently, these professors wrote a book analyzing father-daughter relationships in many well-known pieces of literature. A survey of feminist novels also shows that most authors present father-daughter relationships as negative, emotionally abusive, or cruel.[22]

Likewise, children's books generally portray fathers as less important, less competent, and less loving than mothers, or fail to mention them at all.[23,24] Surprisingly, in 300 children's picture books published from 1902–2000 there was very little improvement in regard to gender stereotyping for mothers or for fathers.[25] For example, compared to mothers, fathers were almost five times as likely to be employed and more likely to be nothing more than playmates for the children, regardless of how recently the books had been published. Similarly, in a 2011 analysis of 160 of the most popular children's picture books, fathers were still portrayed as less involved and more "invisible" than mothers.[26]

Films and television do not fare much better than literature in these regards. In 26 animated Disney films for children, fathers were more controlling, aggressive, uncaring, and incompetent than mothers.[27] And in several analyses of feature length movies, Broadway plays, and television shows that were specifically focused on father-daughter relationships, fathers were generally portrayed as laughable, incompetent, uncaring, or unkind.[28–30] Moreover, working class fathers came off looking worse than middle or upper income fathers in ten popular TV sitcoms from 2000–2014.[31]

Commercials and internet advertising often use humor to portray fathers as incompetent, insensitive parents. Especially when taking care of very young children, fathers are made to look laughable, foolish, and stupid.[32] In their analyses of the media, ten researchers agreed that the popular media in 2015 still generally presented fathers as ignorant, helpless, hapless, laughable, and child-like.[33] Our gift-giving choices on Father's Day and Mother's Day may also partly reflect our belief that mothers are more important and deserve more attention than fathers. In 2018, Americans spent 23.6 billion dollars on Mother's Day gifts and sent 113 million cards. By contrast we spent only 15.5 billion spent on Father's Day gifts and sent only 72 million cards.[34]

More serious still, most physicians and mental health professionals tend to marginalize or ignore fathers. Pediatricians are far less likely to talk to fathers about their children's health or to include them in appointments.[35]

This is especially true for low income, poorly educated, inner city fathers whose children have chronic illnesses such as asthma.[36] In 2016 a national committee on child and family health acknowledged that pediatricians have done a poor job of including fathers in their children's care.[37] Likewise, social service agencies and mental health professionals have also generally excluded fathers from the treatment of their children's emotional and psychological problems.[38]

Mental health and medical professionals also tend to overlook fathers' emotional needs in upsetting family situations involving their children. For example, in 29 research studies about mothers who had miscarriages, fathers often felt completely overlooked by the professionals who were committed to helping the mother deal with "her" grief over "her" loss.[39] And when fathers were raising their young children on their own because their wives had recently died from cancer, there were no support groups available for widowed fathers.[40] Frustrated and surprised by this lack of help for grieving fathers, a psychiatrist and psychologist at the University of North Carolina cancer center created a group for seven of these recently widowed fathers—a group that later gained notoriety in a bestselling book about their experiences in supporting one another through their ordeal.[40]

Programs and books designed for "parents" also typically ignore or marginalize fathers. Fathers are usually not included in parenting programs offered by schools or social service agencies.[41] For example, young Asian American fathers felt they were excluded from parenting classes before and after their first baby was born.[42] This is especially troubling since reviews of the literature show that when fathers are invited to participate in early childhood parent training, the children generally benefit in terms of better behavior and better language skills.[43] For example, when low income men participated in a program where they read stories with their four- to five-year-old child at Head Start pre-schools, they reported using more positive approaches in disciplining the children at home.[44] It is worth noting too that most of these fathers were Spanish-speaking immigrants. As for parenting books, in a 2005 survey of the 25 most popular books, the authors treated fathers as secondary helpmates to mothers.[45]

This is not to say advertisers have made no progress in these regards. For example, a 2016 series of Pantene shampoo commercials showing Super Bowl champions doing their young daughters' hair in "Dad Do's" was an international hit.[46] These commercials aired during Super Bowl week and attracted worldwide praise for their positive, unique presentations of fathers enjoying and succeeding at a traditionally motherly task—styling their daughter's hair. A year later, Mattel toys produced an award winning advertising campaign called "Dads Play Barbie" (see Box 3.1 in Chapter 3). In these 2017 commercials, fathers played Barbie dolls with their young daughters, engaging in imaginative conversations with the dad using his Barbie doll "voice" for his doll.

Box 2.1 Dad Do's: Super Bowl stars style their daughters' hair[46]

Figure 2.3 Super Bowl dads styling daughter's hair
Source: Copyright Proctor & Gamble.

In the week leading up to the 2016 Super Bowl, Proctor and Gamble released a series of commercials where several players were styling their young daughter's hair. As the company's spokesperson stated in the press release: "We hope our new series of how-to videos shows Dads how easy and fun it can be to spend quality time with their daughters by doing their hair. The quality time spent with their daughters now will foster the next generation of strong and beautiful women."[47]

Constraints on Fathering Time: Work

Part of the reason we ignore or marginalize fathers is that we continue to define their roles as largely financial. We still expect fathers to be the primary wage earner and protector. By protector we mean not so much physically protecting his family from physical harm, but protecting them from financial harm. For example, he protects them by earning as much money as possible to buy a house in the safest neighborhood, to send children to the highest quality schools, or to buy a safer car. Not surprisingly then, the most formidable obstacle to more fathering time is the father's job. Despite women's advances in employment and income, most fathers still shoulder most, or all, of the financial burden for the family. Although there is more pressure on fathers to spend time with their children, there is no less pressure on men to be the main wage earners.

Compared to men, women continue to have more freedom to choose jobs that pay less but are more family friendly.[48] For example, 67% of women choose jobs in education and healthcare. In contrast, the three most common jobs for men are truck drivers, engineers, or managers. The family friendly jobs that most women choose tend to pay less but have the benefit of more flexible hours, fewer late night or early morning shifts, less overnight travel, shorter workweeks, and less weekend work. As would be expected then, women earn about 83% of what mean earn.[49,50] Because younger women are choosing jobs more similar to men's, women under the age of 34 now earn 90% of what men earn.

Several examples illustrate the differences between the vocational choices that men and women make—choices that grant women more free time to spend more time with the children. Two-thirds of the people who have jobs that require them to be at work before 8 AM are men.[51] People who earn the top 20% of salaries typically have jobs that require them to work more than 60 hours a week—and men hold most of these demanding jobs. Women under the age of 40 are now more educated than men their age, with 33% of women having a college degree versus only 23% of men. Women now earn 65% of bachelor's, 63% of master's, and 54% of doctoral degrees.[48] Still, women are less likely than men are to choose fields that pay more but are also more demanding. For example, consider the college bachelors' degrees awarded in 2016: in computer science, 12,072 women and 52,333 men; in engineering 24,381 women and 99,624 men; in education 69,790 women and 17,427 men, and in psychology 91,161 women and 26,279 men.[48] Women also choose jobs that are physically safer, which explains why 92% of the people who die from work-related injuries are men.[52] In 2016 alone, 387 women and 4,803 men died from an occupational injury.

This is not to say that fathers' and mothers' financial and parenting roles are not changing. As discussed in Chapter 1, fathers are spending more time with their children and mothers are spending more time at work. And the larger the mother's income and more hours she works, the more equally the parents share the childcare.[53] Still, 41% of Americans continue to believe that fathers should earn most of the family's money and mothers should do most of the childcare.[54] As long as the emphasis on fathers' incomes prevails, most children will spend far less time with their fathers than with their mothers throughout childhood. This belief is troubling since, as discussed in Chapter 1, there was not a significant connection between family income and most measures of children's well-being—with the exception of children who are living in poverty. It is also troubling because most fathers say their greatest regret is not being able to spend more time with their children because of the demands of their jobs.[55,56,57] For example, in studies with college-educated fathers, their gender role beliefs did not matter when it came to predicting how much time they spent with their children.[57,58] What mattered was the demanding nature of the father's work.

Studies with large nationally representative samples show us why fathers are more stressed than mothers trying to balance family and work.[59] Men's jobs are generally more demanding in terms of time and stress than women's jobs. The greatest stress is for fathers who work more than 50 hours a week, have inflexible work schedules, and have to take work home with them or respond to coworkers' messages even when they are at home. Compared to 30 years ago, men are also under more pressure to work harder and work faster and are more worried about losing their jobs if they do not "over" perform. The average father works 48 hours a week, compared to 42 hours for mothers. Nearly equal numbers of men (29%) and women (25%) are "work-centric," meaning they prioritize work over their family and personal lives. But even if they are not work-centric, 42% of fathers work more than 50 hours a week, even though most of them (58%) wish they could work less. Similarly, in a study with 3,165 low income, working class fathers, fathers who had the least flexible work hours and worked night shifts were the most stressed over not having enough time with their children.[60]

Multiple studies from the Pew Research Center further delineate the differences between mothers' and fathers' feelings about parenting and work stress.[54] Fathers are just as likely as mothers to say that being a parent is extremely important to their identity. In fact, fathers are somewhat more likely (54%) than mothers (52%) to say that parenting is rewarding "all" of the time and are more likely (46%) than mothers (41%) to say it is enjoyable "all" of the time. In 2016, fathers spent an average of eight hours a week on childcare and ten hours on household chores, almost three times as much as they spent back in 1965. Not surprisingly since they worked fewer or no hours outside the home, in 2016 mothers spent 14 hours on childcare and 18 hours on housework. Fathers are far more likely (63%) than mothers (35%) to feel they spend too little time with their kids. This helps explain why only 39% of fathers feel they are doing a "very good" job raising the children, compared to 51% of mothers. In nearly one-third (27%) of families, the father is the only wage earner in contrast to nearly half of all families back in 1970.

In sum, most fathers wish they could spend more time with their children. But given the greater demands and longer hours at work, and society's expectations, fathers' parenting time is far more restricted than mothers'.

Paternity Leave Policies

Men's jobs, however, are not the only factors working against their spending more time with their children. Paternity leaves and paid days to care for sick children also play a role. American paternity leave policies do not promote fathers' involvement in their babies' lives. By way of contrast, Sweden takes fathering very seriously.[61] Sweden was the first country to introduce paid paternity leaves in 1974 and to pass a law in 1995 stating that a family would lose one month's worth of childcare subsidies if the father did not take paternity leave. Swedish parents are allotted 480 days of paid leave for each child until the age of eight. Each parent is entitled to half of those days. If a parent does not use his or her allotted days, the days cannot be transferred to the other parent. Swedish fathers now take 25% of the parental leave allotted to them—a figure the government wants to increase.

Since most American companies do not offer paid paternity leaves, fathers generally only take one week off work after their baby is born, while half of the mothers take more than three months of maternity leave.[50] After their children are born, nearly 40% of mothers quit work and another 42% reduce their works hours for several years in contrast to only 5% of fathers.[36] This is unfortunate since fathers who take paternity leave are more involved in their children's lives even three years later.[62] It is also troubling because parents are less stressed, less depressed, and less unhappy about having had children in those countries that provide paid paternity leaves and other supportive work-family services.[63] In an analysis of 22 countries, the U.S. had the worst family-work policies and had the largest gap in happiness between parents and non-parents. That is, American parents are not as happy or as satisfied with their lives as adults who choose not to have children, as explained later in this chapter and in Chapter 5. In large part, their unhappiness is due to the financial strains of parenthood.

What Is Good Fathering?

What is "good" fathering? Regardless of how much time fathers get to spend with their children, what fathering behaviors are most likely to make children feel loved, supported, and nurtured? Specifically how do fathers promote their children's physical and mental health, school achievement, future career success, and overall well-being?

Before exploring these questions, remember that good fathering is not different from good mothering. As discussed in Chapter 1, the kinds of behaviors and attitudes that promote children's well-being are generally the same for mothers and for fathers.[64] Especially since American mothers and fathers have assumed more equal roles in childcare and in working outside the home, their parenting is more similar than different. There is no evidence to date suggesting that the father's parenting has a different impact on children than the mother's. In short, good parenting is good parenting and bad parenting is bad parenting, regardless of whether that parent is male or female.

Looking specifically at research on the fathers' impact on children, researchers have identified four basic categories of fathering behaviors that are beneficial for children.[65] First, a father must be actively engaged in a wide range of activities with his children, not just recreational or athletic activities. These activities include routine tasks such as doing homework and household chores together. Second, he must be warm and responsive, while simultaneously monitoring and supervising them in an authoritative way. He does not relate to his child as a peer, but as an adult who maintains authority and control and who disciplines when needed. Third, good fathering also means assuming responsibility for meeting the children's needs and ensuring that those needs are met, which does not necessarily involve hands-on care. For example, the father might spend considerable time planning ahead and making arrangements for his children's physical safety (a safer car, smoke detectors in the home), medical needs (a better health insurance policy), or their future financial needs (investments, a college fund). The mother's contributions to children are typically more "obvious" to everyone in the family (cooking, cleaning, taking children to appointments) than the father's contributions (doing the family's financial paperwork, meeting with insurance agents, studying the literature on various brands of computer equipment). We should never measure a parent's love, commitment, or devotion to their children by which one does the most hands-on childcare and the most "obvious" work in the home. Moreover, spending time with the children is not a punishment or a burden that is inflicted on parents. Unlike doing chores or doing the family's tax returns, most employed parents want to spend more time with their children and less time at work. It is unfair, therefore, to assume that whichever parent is spending the most time with the children is being mistreated or somehow exploited compared to the parent who has to spend the most time away from home earning most or all of the family's income.

Fourth, good fathering means providing social capital. **Social capital** is any activity that strengthens the children's connections to the community, school, or the workforce in ways that promote their well-being. For example, the father might use his connections with friends, coworkers, or acquaintances to help the children get summer jobs. Or he might do volunteer work to improve the schools or make the community safer. He also provides social capital by teaching his children work-related skills that help them at school or in a future job—for example, teaching them how to resolve problems with teachers or employers, or teaching them how to interact in social settings with adults.

Fathering Scales: Assessing the Quality of Fathering and Father-Child Relationships

Researchers have developed a number of scales to assess the quality of the father's relationship with his children and to assess the quality of his fathering. The four scales in the boxed inserts serve as representatives of these assessments.

The Paternal Involvement with Infants Scale (PIWIS) in Box 2.2 measures the frequency with which fathers participate in each of 35 activities with their babies.[66] Fathers rate themselves as to how often they perform these activities, ranging from more than once a day to as little as once or twice a month. This scale assesses fathering in five domains: positive direct engagement, indirect care, frustration, warmth and attunement, and control and process responsibility. The "frustration" subscale is especially useful because highly frustrated fathers are more likely to become depressed. So if a new father scores high on the frustration subscale, he might benefit from services that can reduce his parenting stress and lower his risks of becoming depressed. The PIWIS is important because, as we will see in the next two chapters, the quality of fathering in the first few years of a baby's life is closely linked to the child's cognitive, social, physical, and behavioral outcomes later in childhood.

As children age, the "Father Hunger Scale" (Box 2.3) assess the quality of their relationship with their father in terms of how well he meets their emotional needs, regardless of how much time they spend together.[67] **Father hunger** is defined as the emotional longing that a child has for a father who has been physically or emotionally distant and unavailable. The feeling of father "hunger" is not necessarily related to how much time the father spends with his children. For example, a father who spends three hours with his children can be much more emotionally present and more fully engaged and attentive than a father who spends six hours while preoccupied with texting or emailing, or passively watching his children at play. The attentive, attuned father interacts directly in ways that make his children feel listened to and important. "Father hunger" is linked to a number of poor outcomes for children, among them: depression, loneliness, delinquency, and problems with anger management.

Box 2.2 Paternal Involvement with Infants Scale[66]

1 Talking to your baby
2 Hugging your baby
3 Feeling that your involvement with your baby is important
4 Missing your baby when you are not with her/him
5 Soothing your baby when s/he is crying
6 Interactive playing with your baby (e.g., using stuffed animals or other toys)
7 Kissing your baby
8 Responding to your baby's facial expressions so that s/he can see your response
9 Feeling close to your baby
10 Laughing with your baby
11 Smiling at your baby
12 Choosing play activities for your baby
13 Determining when to feed your baby
14 Determining what media (TV, DVDs, music) is appropriate for your baby
15 Setting your baby's general schedule/activities
16 Knowing what foods (milk, formula, soft food) to give your baby and how much s/he eats
17 Determining which toys/play objects are appropriate for baby
18 Anticipating specific ways (monitoring health, availability of clothes, have proper amount/type of food, etc.) to assure that your baby's needs will be taken care of
19 Discuss the division of parenting responsibilities with your partner
20 Making decisions regarding your baby's well-being
21 Feeling jealous of your partner's connection with your baby
22 Giving your baby to your partner or other caregiver when your baby is crying
23 Feeling resentful of your baby due to increased responsibilities
24 Feeling frustrated when caring for your baby
25 Taking your baby to/picking up from childcare
26 Taking your baby to medical appointments
27 Arranging for childcare (e.g., babysitter, daycare)
28 Bathing your baby
29 Changing your baby's diaper
30 Reading to/with your baby
31 Swaddling your baby
32 Burping your baby
33 Putting your baby down for nap/sleep
34 Waking up during the night to take care of your baby
35 Feeding your baby

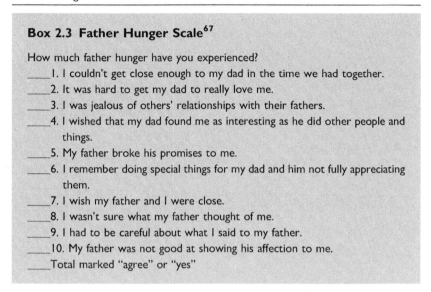

Box 2.3 Father Hunger Scale[67]

How much father hunger have you experienced?

_____1. I couldn't get close enough to my dad in the time we had together.

_____2. It was hard to get my dad to really love me.

_____3. I was jealous of others' relationships with their fathers.

_____4. I wished that my dad found me as interesting as he did other people and things.

_____5. My father broke his promises to me.

_____6. I remember doing special things for my dad and him not fully appreciating them.

_____7. I wish my father and I were close.

_____8. I wasn't sure what my father thought of me.

_____9. I had to be careful about what I said to my father.

_____10. My father was not good at showing his affection to me.

_____Total marked "agree" or "yes"

Young adults can also assess the quality of their relationship with their fathers while they were growing up with the "Father Involvement Scale" in Box 2.4.[68] This scale measures the degree to which young adults feel their father was involved in their lives throughout childhood. An especially interesting aspect of this scale is that it compares the father's actual level of involvement with the level of involvement each child wanted from him. The closer the "desired involvement" score is to the "actual involvement" score, the more the child felt the father met his or her needs.

The "Father Presence Questionnaire" (Box 2.5) is a more comprehensive instrument that asks adult children to assess ten different domains that have an impact on the kind of relationship they have with their fathers.[69] Rather than merely asking young adults to assess the quality of their relationship with their father, this questionnaire also assesses factors that influenced their relationship. For example, how supportive was their mother of their relationship with their father? How happy was the parents' marriage? What kind of relationship did each parent have with their parents as they were growing up? As we will see in later chapters, all of these factors have a bearing on the quality of a daughter's relationship with her father.

Of course, there are many other scales and questionnaires that assess the quality of fathering and quality of father-child relationships. The four presented here, however, capture the major components of good fathering—components that we will be exploring throughout the remainder of this book.

Box 2.4 Father Involvement Scale[68]

How involved was your father in your life and development? What did you want his level of involvement to be? Rate each statement on a scale from 1 to 5. The higher your score on "level of involvement", the more engaged your father was in your life. The more 3's you have on the "desired involvement" scale, the better he was at meeting your particular needs.

5. always involved		5. much more involved
4. often involved		4. little more involved
3. sometimes involved		3. just right
4. rarely involved		2. A little less involved
1. never involved		1. Much less involved
Level of involvement		**Level you desired**
_____	Intellectual development	_____
_____	Emotional development	_____
_____	Social development	_____
_____	Ethical/moral development	_____
_____	Spiritual development	_____
_____	Physical development	_____
_____	Career development	_____
_____	Developing responsibility	_____
_____	Developing independence	_____
_____	Developing competence	_____
_____	Leisure, fun, play	_____
_____	Providing income	_____
_____	Sharing activities/interests	_____
_____	Mentoring/teaching	_____
_____	Caregiving	_____
_____	Being protective	_____
_____	Advising	_____
_____	Discipline	_____
_____	School/homework	_____
_____	Companionship	_____

_____Total score of 100 possible _____number rated "3" – 20 possible

Box 2.5 Father Presence Questionnaire[69]

The higher your score on these two scales, the more emotionally and psychologically present your father was in your childhood life.

___ I could/can talk with my father about anything
___ As a child, I felt warm and safe when I was with my father
___ I felt/feel close to my father
___ I felt my father was behind me and supported my choices or activities
___ I looked up to my father
___ I felt/feel inspired by my father
___ My father has a special place in my life and no one can replace him
___ I need my father
___ My father and I enjoyed/enjoy being together
___ I want to be like my father
___ When I remember past experiences with my father, I do not feel angry
___ I do not feel disappointed with my father
___ Total marked yes (12 possible)

___ My father helped with schoolwork when I asked him
___ My father helped me learn new things
___ My father attended my school functions
___ My father and I participated in activities or hobbies together
___ My father attended my sporting event or other activities
___ I could go to my father for advice or help with a problem
___ My father helped me think about my future
___ My father was concerned about my safety
___ My father taught me right from wrong
___ My father listened to me when I talked with him
___ My father told me that he loved me
___ My father understood me
___ My father encouraged me
___ When I was a child, my father did not ignore me
___ Total marked yes (14 possible)

How Fatherhood Changes Men

While most fathering research focuses on the impact that fathers have on their children, there is an equally interesting question that has received far less attention: What impact do children have on their fathers—negatively and positively? Put differently, how does fatherhood change men's lives?

Financial Stress

As we might predict, fatherhood usually increases a man's financial burdens and his stress. In most families, this stress is greatest for the father since he is the main wage earner or the sole earner for periods of time. In families where the mother drops out of the workforce during the children's youngest years, the father's financial burden increases because the financial losses are cumulative and long lasting. Even after the mother goes back to work, the family does not fully recover financially. For example, assume that a 26-year-old mother has worked for four years and is earning $44,000 in a job with retirement benefits. After the children are born, she quits work for five years and then returns to work full time. In this scenario, by time she retires, she will have lost roughly $706,778 due to the compounding interest lost in her retirement benefits and the five years of lost income.[70] So when mothers drop out of the workforce for several years, fathers end up shouldering more financial responsibility over a much longer period to compensate for the mother's lost wages.

As for childrearing expenses, the average cost for raising one child in a middle income family is approximately $223,000 which does not include the cost of a college education and does not take inflation into account.[71] If we consider inflation, the cost of raising a child who was born in 2015 is $212,300 in the lowest income families (family income under $60,000), $284,570 in middle income families ($60,000–$107,000), and $454,770 in the highest income families (above $107,000). Put differently, the yearly cost for one child is $10,000 for the lowest income families, $13,000 for the middle-income families, and $19,000–$23,000 for the highest income families. Housing accounts for about a third of the total cost, followed by childcare as Box 2.6 indicates. Housing costs, of course, can vary considerably depending on where in the U.S. the family lives. Childcare costs can also range from virtually zero, if friends or relatives are providing free care, to thousands of dollars for daycare centers. It bears repeating that these childrearing expenses do not include the cost of a college education.

Box 2.6 The cost of raising a child[71]

$233,000 per child, excluding college
  Housing 29%
  Childcare & education (not college) 16%
  Food 18%
  Transportation 15%
  Miscellenous 7%
  Health care 9%
  Clothing 6%

To put the costs of raising a child in perspective, consider the incomes of most American families in 2016.[72] Half of all Asian American families had a total family income above $80,720 compared to $61,349 for white, $46,882 for Hispanic, and $38,555 for black families. Clearly then, the financial stress of raising children is far greater for certain groups of fathers than for others.

The financial stress of childrearing may even extend late into the father's life. For example, the number of American parents older than 65 who are forced to file for bankruptcy tripled from 1991 to 2018.[73] Although health care costs accounted for most bankruptcies, one-third of these parents reported that helping their adult children financially had contributed to their going bankrupt—for example, co-signing college and car loans or loaning them money for a down payment on a house that the children never repaid. Further, there are fathers who feel that when they refuse to continue giving money to their adult children, their relationship suddenly becomes strained.[74] Likewise, fathers and mothers whose adult children continue to make excessive financial demands on them are more dissatisfied with their lives than those whose children are financially self-reliant.[75] Historically before the U.S. became urbanized, most children were economic assets to their parents, for example helping to run the farm or family business. But that is no longer the case. As one researcher amusingly put it, "children are economically worthless, but emotionally priceless."[76]

Box 2.7 Dad, the banking machine: Are you contributing to your father's stress?

How strongly do you feel about whether your father should provide for you financially in the following ways?

> 0= absolutely not/completely disagree
> 1= maybe/somewhat agree
> 2= yes/definitely

____1. pay all of my undergraduate college costs even if he has to take out loans

____2. pay for my undergraduate college at an expensive private school even if he has to put less money in his retirement fund

____3. pay for part, or all, of my graduate education

____4. pay for most, or all, of my wedding

____5. provide some money for a down payment on my first home

____6. continue to pay my health insurance to age 26 if I am still in school or not fully employed

____7. pay for most, or all, of my first car

____8. put money aside for me or for my future children for an inheritance

____9. let me live at home for free until I pay off my debts as a young adult

____10. loan me money without charging me interest

If they were to consider and more fully comprehend the financial strains of fatherhood, older adolescent and adult sons and daughters might pause to ask themselves: How much am I contributing to unnecessary financial strain on my father? Am I placing such high financial expectations on him that I might be increasing his stress in ways that might damage his physical or emotional health? Taking the quiz in Box 2.7 might help some daughters realize that their self-centered focus or their beliefs about what they are "entitled" to are putting their father under undue stress—or, worse yet, are making him feel more like a banking machine than a beloved parent.

Stress on Parents' Relationship

In addition to more financial stress, becoming a father also increases stress and conflict in the parents' relationship with one another. While most parents say they do not regret having children, marital happiness and emotional intimacy generally decline after they become parents—especially for the first born child and during the first year of each child's life.[77] Parenting stress is discussed in more detail in Chapter 5. Suffice it to say here that the financial, emotional, and physical demands of raising children lead to more conflict and more stress between parents. For example, in an analysis of 97 studies, marital satisfaction went down after having children.[78] Surprisingly, the unhappiest parents were those with the most money who had waited later in life to have children. The researchers speculated that higher income couples who have enjoyed a number of relatively carefree years together have a harder time adapting to the dramatic change of lifestyle after becoming parents.

Although most parents say that having children was a meaningful, rewarding experience, they also say it was stressful and often boring and unenjoyable.[79] For example, for 100 married couples with two or three children, 40% of their arguments were about the children while only 20% were about money.[80] As we would predict, parents who had planned the pregnancy were less stressed and less dissatisfied with their relationship after the baby was born than parents who had not planned to have a child at this point in their lives.[81]

Understandably, the degree to which parenthood stresses the parents' relationship also depends on the personality and temperament of each child. Their relationships are more strained when their baby is temperamentally difficult or has physical, developmental, or mental problems.[82] Divorce rates are also higher when one of the children has behavioral or cognitive disorders such as hyperactivity or attention deficit disorders.[83]

Emotional Stress: Anxiety and Depression

Fatherhood is especially stressful for men when they first become parents—and during the first year of each child's life.[77] This is the time when the parents' relationship typically becomes the most strained and when both parents are at highest risk of becoming depressed. It should come as no surprise that a physically exhausted father or mother of a newborn is more likely to become depressed than those who are more well-rested.[84] For example, in a study with 150 couples with three-month-old babies, the less sleep the parents got at night, the more likely one or both of them were to become depressed and the more conflict they had with one another.[85]

What is clear is that fathers as well as mothers can become clinically depressed after their babies are born.[86] In one review of the research, 10% of fathers and 14% of the mothers became clinically depressed in the first six months of their newborn's life.[87] Most of the mother's depression was related to hormonal changes occurring after the baby's birth. In contrast, most of the father's depression was related to worrying about money, taking on a more stressful, higher paying job, losing intimacy with his wife, and helping his wife deal with her own adjustment to parenthood. In another study, an almost equal number of fathers (4.4%) and mothers (5%) were clinically depressed when their baby was 15 months old.[88] In another 18 studies, fathers often became stressed, anxious, and depressed before their babies were born.[89] These fathers were already worrying about how well they would adapt to fatherhood and how competent they would be in caring for their newborns. Then too, new parents who work night shifts are more likely to become depressed than parents who work only during the day.[90] Since fathers are more likely than mothers to work night shifts, this may also contribute to a father's depression after the baby is born.

There is also evidence that the father's testosterone levels drop during his partner's pregnancy.[91] The researchers speculated that less testosterone might somehow help new fathers feel calmer and bond more easily with their newborns. Men with low testosterone, however, are also more likely to be clinically depressed. This suggests there might be a hormonal component to the father's post-partum depression, just as there is for mothers. Unfortunately, fathers are less likely than mothers are to seek help for their depression, which leaves men especially vulnerable when dealing with parenting stress.[92]

Quality of the Parent-Child Relationship

An additional source of stress or depression is the quality of parents' relationships with their children. Not all parents' relationships with their children turn out well, no matter how well the parents get along or how dedicated they are as parents. There are fathers and mothers who are left feeling deeply hurt, rejected, disappointed, exploited, manipulated, and unloved after giving decades of their lives to their children.[93] Then too, parents whose adult children continue to have problems such as clinical depression, trouble with the police, or drug abuse are much more ambivalent about whether they should have had children than those whose adult children are well-adjusted.[94] In this nationally representative study of 1,510 parents, fathers and mothers were more likely to be clinically depressed if their child had these kinds of emotional, behavioral, or mental health problems as an adolescent or young adult. In short, the children's well-being affects the parents' mental health.

Perhaps the stressful realities of fatherhood help explain why many parents say that raising children was not as fulfilling as they expected it to be. For example, in a large national survey, 60% of the people said that having children was not necessary for a happy marriage—twice as many as in the 1990's. In fact they ranked raising children below having a fulfilling sex life together and sharing mutual interests as measures of marital happiness and success.[95]

Daughters' Impact on Their Fathers

Very few research studies have explored the specific question: How do daughters influence their fathers' opinions or behavior? According to the scant research that does exist, daughters can have a significant impact on their fathers' opinions and, in some cases, on their behavior. For example, in 1997 and in 2004, male members of Congress who had daughters were more likely than those without daughters to have voted for bills that promoted women's interests.[96] And in a British study, fathers with daughters voted more often for liberal candidates than did fathers with no daughters.[97] Earlier in U.S. history, some presidents sought their daughters' advice or heavily relied on them for care as they aged.[98,99] For example, President John Adams' daughter, Nabby, became one of his closest political advisors and served as a sounding board for him during his troubled political times. Likewise, Thomas Jefferson's daughter, Martha, was her father's political advisor and lived near him with her husband and 12 children until his death. Franklin D. Roosevelt's only daughter, Anna, served for two years as his personal assistant. She even conspired with her father to arrange for his mistress to visit him at the White House.

Male authors have occasionally written about the impact their daughters have had on them. One such collection by well-known writers was inspired by their desire to present a view of fathers other than as "embodiments of patriarchy who are portrayed as abusive, tyrannical, overpowering, predatory, absent, distant, shadowy, irresponsible, and victims themselves of traditions that denied women full human potential" (p. xi).[100] In another collection of essays fathers describe how their travel adventures with their daughters enriched their relationship and enriched his life.[101] As mentioned earlier in this chapter, however, father-daughter relationships do not receive nearly the attention that mother-daughter relationships do in fiction or non-fiction literature.

Conclusion

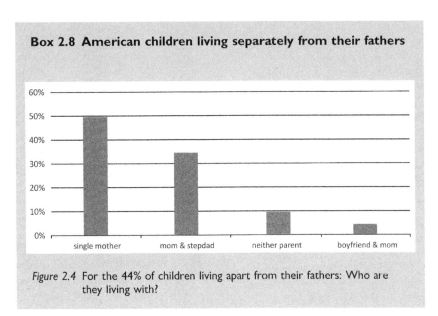

Box 2.8 American children living separately from their fathers

Figure 2.4 For the 44% of children living apart from their fathers: Who are they living with?

Although American society claims to value fathers and urges men to be more involved with their children, in many ways we continue to ignore, marginalize, or disparage men as parents. Social science research, children's and adult literature, films, commercials, paternity leave policies, and medical and mental health services continue to treat fathers unfairly in comparison to mothers. As in the past, the major obstacle to fathering is the societal expectation that men should be the primary wage earners for the family and women should provide most of the childcare. Although changes are slowly occurring, by creating more father friendly attitudes, policies, and practices, we can strengthen men's relationships with their children.

In the meantime, too many daughters and sons are experiencing "father hunger" and longing for more meaningful, more emotionally intimate relationship with their fathers. As Box 2.8 indicates, many American children are living apart from their fathers as they are growing up. This is troubling since, as we will see in the remaining chapters of this book, a daughter's cognitive, social, behavioral, and emotional outcomes are closely tied to the quality of her relationship with her father. Researchers have identified the kinds of fathering behaviors that promote closer relationships and enhance their children's well-being. The question is: How and when will our society do more to make it possible for fathers to offer more to and build stronger relationships with their children—especially to their daughters, who as we will see in future chapters, pay a greater price in many ways than sons for too little fathering.

Review Questions

1 What are the financial costs of raising a child in low, middle, and high income families?
2 What is social capital and how does it benefit children?
3 In what specific ways does fatherhood change men's lives?
4 In what ways have our definitions of "good" fathering changed and in what ways have they remained the same?
5 Specifically how have fathers been ignored, marginalized, or demeaned by researchers, authors, medical and mental health practitioners, advertisers, and filmmakers?
6 Why do father-daughter relationships receive less attention than father-son relationships?
7 How do men's and women's job choices differ and what impact does this have on fathers' relationships with their children?
8 As described and measured by researchers, what are the components of "good" fathering?
9 What is "father hunger" and how is it described on the Father Hunger Scale?
10 What is an "involved" father as described on the two Finley-Swartz scales?
11 What are the major components of the "Father Presence" scale?
12 In what ways do daughters influence their fathers?
13 How are each of these an obstacle to better fathering: societal attitudes about family roles, family leave policies, postpartum depression, night shift work, bias in the college curriculum?
14 How do Sweden's family policies differ from those in the U.S.?
15 In what specific ways does fatherhood affect men financially?

Questions for Discussion and Debate

1 How do you feel about two lesbian mothers or a single heterosexual mother raising children on their own? Do you feel the same way about widowed or divorced mothers raising daughters by themselves? Why?
2 What would you like most and least about being a father based on the research in this chapter?
3 How much financial support should a father continue to give his children after they graduate from high school in terms of: undergraduate or graduate education, car, health insurance, co-signing loads, down payment on a house, and inheritance?
4 Should a father use part of his retirement money to help his daughter with her college education or other expenses? If so, how much? At what point should a daughter be on her own completely and go to a bank instead of to her father for financial aid?

5 With the goal of increasing the time that fathers can spend with their children, what is the ideal arrangement for each parent in terms of childcare and earning money outside the home? What percent of the family income do you feel each parent should earn?

6 How do you feel about fathers staying home to raise the children while their wives earn all of the family's income? How appealing is this idea for your own life?

7 How do you feel about paternity leave? How soon should a mother return to work full time after their child is born?

8 Since most women are still choosing family friendly jobs where they have more time to spend with their children, what could fathers do to increase their parenting time?

9 How did you rate your father on the various scales in this chapter? Based on these scales, what insights did you gain about your relationship with him?

10 Leaving aside what the research says, how do you personally define a "good" father? Does your definition differ for a "good" mother? If so, how and why?

11 How have you influenced your father in his personal or his professional life both positively and negatively?

12 What negative and what positive impact do you think fatherhood has had on your father?

13 What changes would you most like to see occur in fathers' roles in the family and in the workforce?

14 After completing the fatherhood questionnaires in this chapter, what insights have you gained about your father or other aspects of your family?

15 If you had a choice, would you rather be a mother or a father based on what you have read in this chapter? Why?

References

1 Duncan G, Ziol-Guest K, Kalil A. Early childhood poverty and adult attainment, behavior and health. *Child Development* 2010; 81: 306–325.

2 Brooks-Gunn J, Duncan G. *Consequences of growing up poor.* New York: Russel Sage Foundation; 1997.

3 Cooper K, Stewart K. *Does money affect children's outcomes? A systematic review.* Cambridge: Joseph Rountree Foundation; 2013.

4 Gershoff E, Aber L, Raver C, Lennon M. Income is not enough: Incorporating material hardship into models of income associations with parenting and child development. *Child Development* 2007; 78: 70–95.

5 Luthar S, Barkin S, Crossman E. I can, therefore I must: Fragility in the upper middle classes. *Development and Psychopathology* 2013; 25: 1529–1549.

6 Reardon S, Portilla X. Recent trends in income, racial and ethnic school readiness gaps at kindergarten entry. *American Education Research Journal* 2016; 2: 1–18.

7 Khanam R, Nghiem S. Family income and child cognitive and noncognitive development in Australia: Does money matter? *Demography* 2016; 53: 597–621.

8 McEwen A, Stewart J. The relationship between income and children's outcomes: A synthesis of Canadian evidence. *Canadian Public Policy* 2014; 40: 99–109.

9 Humensky J. Are adolescents with high socioeconomic status more like to engage in alcohol and illicit drug use in early adulthood? *Substance Abuse: Treatment Prevention and Policy* 2010; 5: 12–20.

10 Johnston L, et al. *Key findings on adolescent drug use.* Ann Arbor: Institute for Social Research, University of Michigan; 2017.

11 McGue M, Rustichini A, Iacono W. Cognitive, noncognitive and family background contributions to college attainment: A behavioral genetic perspective. *Journal of Personality* 2015; 85: 65–78.

12 Luthar S, Latendresse S. Comparable risks at the socioeconomic status extremes: Preadolescents' perceptions of parenting. *Development and Psychopathology* 2005; 17: 207–230.

13 Lareau A. *Unequal childhoods: Class, race and family life.* Berkeley: University of California Press; 2003.

14 Mayer S. *What money can't buy: Family income and children's life chances.* Cambridge, MA: Harvard University Press; 1997.

15 Griswold R. *Fatherhood in America.* New York: Basic Books; 1993.

16 Bederman G. *Manliness and civilization.* Chicago: University of Chicago; 1995.

17 Goldberg W, Tan E, Thorsen K. Trends in academic attention to fathers. *Fathering* 2009; 14: 159–179.

18 Fabiano G. Father participation in parent training for ADHD. *Journal of Family Psychology* 2007; 21(4): 683–693.

19 Cabrera N, Volling B, Barr R. Fathers are parents, too! Widening the lens on parenting for children's development. *Child Development Perspectives* 2018; 12: 152–157.

20 Nielsen L. Fathers & daughters: A needed course in family studies. In: Berke L, Wisensale S, editors. *The craft of teaching about families.* New York: Haworth; 2005.

21 Boose L, Flowers B. *Daughters and fathers.* Baltimore, MD: Johns Hopkins University Press; 1989.

22 Sheldon B. *Daughters and fathers in feminist novels.* Berlin: Peter Lang; 1997.

23 Anderson D, Hamilton M. Gender role stereotyping of parents in children's picture books: The invisible father. *Sex Roles* 2005; 52: 145–151.

24 Flannery S. Fatherhood in American children's literature. *Fathering* 2006; 4: 71–95.

25 DeWitt A, Cready C, Seward R. Parental role portrayals in twentieth century children's picture books: More egalitarian or ongoing stereotyping? *Sex Roles* 2013; 69: 89–106.

26 Adams J, Walker C, O'Connell P. Invisible or involved fathers? A content analysis of representations of parenting in young children's picture books. *Sex Roles* 2011; 65: 259–270.

27 Tanner L. Images of families in Disney animated films. *American Journal of Family Therapy* 2003; 31: 355–373.

28 Devlin R. *Relative intimacy: Fathers, adolescent daughters and modern culture.* Chapel Hill: University of North Carolina; 2005.

29 Nash I. *American sweethearts:teenage girls in twentieth century popular culture.* New York: New York University Press; 2005.

30 Bruzzi S. *Bringing up Daddy: Fatherhood and masculinity in postwar Hollywood.* London: British Film Institute; 2008.

31 Troilo, J. Stay tuned: portrayals of fatherhood to come. *Psychology of Religion and Spirituality* 2017; 6: 82–94.

32 Poniewozik J. Daddy issues: What's so funny about men taking care of babies? *Time* [June 18]. 2012.

33 Podnieks E. *Pops in pop culture: Fatherhood, masculinity and the new man.* New York: Palgrave MacMillan; 2016.

34 N.R.F. Why dads get short shrift on fathers day. *National Retail Federation* 2018.

35 Allport B, *et al.* Promoting father involvement for child and family health. *Academic Pediatrics* 2018; 18: 746–753.

36 Kobylianskii A, *et al.* Experiences of inner city fathers of children with chronic illness. *Clinical Pediatrics* 2018; 57: 792–801.

37 Yogman M, Garfield C. Fathers' roles in the care and development of their children: The role of pediatricians. *Pediatrics* 2016; 138: 115–125.

38 Oren C, Oren D. Counseling fathers. In: Carlson M, Evans M, Duffey T, editors. *A counselor's guide to working with men.* New York: Wiley; 2015. 233–252.

39 Due C, Chiarolli S, Riggs D. The impact of pregnancy loss on mean's health and wellbeing: a systematic review. *BMC Pregnancy and Childbirth* 2017; 17: 315–329.

40 Rosenstein D, Yopp J. *The group: Seven widowed fathers reimagine life.* New York: Oxford University Press; 2018.

41 Ramchandani P, Iles J. Getting fathers into parenting programs. *Journal of Child Psychology and Psychiatry* 2014; 55: 1213–1214.

42 Shorey A, Ang L, Goh E. Lived experiences of Asian fathers during the early postpartum period. *Midwifery* 2018; 60: 30–35.

43 Chacko A. Engagement in behavioral parent training: Review of the literature and implicatons for practice. *Clinical Child & Family Psychology Review* 2016; 19: 204–215.

44 Chacko A, Fabiano G, Doctoroff G, Fortson B. Engaging fathers in effective parenting for preschool children using shared book reading: A randomized controlled trial. *Journal of Clinical Child & Adolescent Psychology* 2018; 47: 1537–4416.

45 Fleming L, Tobin D. Popular child-rearing books: Where is daddy? *Psychology of Men and Masculinity* 2005; 5: 18–24.

46 Rodriquez D. *Pantene celebrates the next generation of strong, beautiful women.* Cincinnati, OH: Proctor & Gamble; 2016. Report No.: February 3, 2016.

47 Beck M. *Mattel focuses on dad with new Barbie campaign.* El Secundo, CA: Mattel Toys; 2017.

48 N.C.E.S. *Degrees conferred by race and sex: 2016.* Washington, DC: National Center for Education Statistics; 2018.

49 B.L.S. *Highlights of women's earnings in 2017.* Washington, DC: Bureau of Labor Statistics: U.S. Dept. of Labor; 2018.

50 Graf N, Brown A, Patten E. *The narrowing, but persistent, gender gap in pay.* New York: Pew Research Center; 2018.

51 Mulligan C. *Gender segregation by the clock.* Chicago: University of Chicago; 2010.

52 B.L.S. *National census of fatal occupational injuries in 2016.* Washington, DC: Bureau of Labor Statistics; 2018. Report No.: December 19, 2017.

53 Raley S, Bianchi S, Wang W. When do fathers care? Mother' economic contribution and fathers' involvement in child care. *American Journal of Sociology* 2012; 117: 1422–1459.

54 Parker K, Livingston G. *Seven facts about American dads*. New York: Pew Research Center; 2018.

55 Roopnarine J, Yildirim E. *Fathering in cultural contexts*. New York: Routledge; 2019.

56 Cabrera N, LeMonda C. *Handbook of father involvement*. New York: Routledge; 2013.

57 Harrington B, Fraone J, Lee J, Levey L. *The new millennial dad: Understanding the paradox of today's fathers*. Boston, MA: Boston College Center for Work & Family; 2016.

58 Kuo P, Volling B, Gonzalez R. Gender role beliefs, work-family conflict and father involvement after the birth of a second child. *Journal of Men & Masculinities* 2018; 19: 243–256.

59 Aumann K, Galinsky E, Mator K. *The new male mystique*. New York: Families and Work Institute; 2011.

60 Nomaguchi K, Johnson W. Parenting stress among low income and working class fathers: The role of employment. *Journal of Family Issues* 2016; 37: 1535–1557.

61 Sweden. Ten things that make Sweden family friendly. 2018. Report No.: https://Sweden,se/society.

62 Petts R, Knoester C. Paternity leave taking and father engagement. *Journal of Marriage and Family* 2018; 80: 1144–1162.

63 Glass J, Andersson M, Simon R. Parenthood and happiness: Effects of work-family reconciliation policies in 22 OECD countries. *American Journal of Sociology* 2016; 122: 886–929.

64 Fagan J, Day R, Lamb M, Cabrera N. Should researchers conceptualize differently the dimensions of parenting for fathers and mothers? *Journal of Family Theory & Review* 2014; 6: 390–405.

65 Pleck J. Paternal involvement: Revised conceptualization. In: Lamb M, editor. *The role of the father in child development*. New York: Wiley; 2010. 58–94.

66 Singley D, *et al.* Development and psychometric evaluation of the paternal involvement with infants scale. *Psychology of Men & Masculinity* 2018; 19: 167–183.

67 Perrin P, Baker J, Romelus F, Jones K, Heesacker M. Development and validation of the father hunger scale. *Psychology of Men and Masculinity* 2009; 10(4): 314–327.

68 Finley G, Swartz S. The father involvement scale. *Educational and Psychological Measurement* 2004; 64: 143–164.

69 Krampe E, Newton R. Father presence questionnaire. *Fathering* 2006; 4: 159–189.

70 Madowitz M. *Calculating the hidden cost of interrupting a career for child care*. Washington, DC: Center for American Progress; 2016.

71 Lino M, *et al*. *Expenditures on children by families, 2015*. Washington, DC: U.S. Department of Agriculture; 2017.

72 Guzman G. *Household income in the U.S.: 2016*. Washington, DC: U.S. Census Bureau; 2017.

73 Thorne D, Lawless R, Foohey P. *Bankruptcy booms for older Americans*. Los Angeles: University of California: Consumer Bankruptcy Project; 2018.

74 Descartes L. Put your money where your love is. *Journal of Adult Development* 2006; 13(137): 147.

75 Fingerman K, *et al.* Helicopter parents and landing pad kids: Intense parental support of grown children. *Journal of Marriage and Family* 2012; 74: 880–896.

76 Zelizer V. *Pricing the priceless child: The changing social value of children.* Princeton, NJ: Princeton University Press; 1994.

77 Gottman J, Levenson R. Marital happiness and childrearing. *Marriage and Family* 2008; 62: 737–745.

78 Twenge J, Campbell W, Foster C. Parenthood and marital satisfaction: A meta analytic review. *Journal of Marriage and Family* 2003; 65: 574–583.

79 White M, Dolan P. Accounting for the richness of daily activities. *Psychological Science* 2009; 20: 1000–1008.

80 Papp L, Cummings M, Goeke-Morey M. For richer, for poorer: Money as a topic of marital conflict in the home. *Family Relations* 2009; 58: 91–103.

81 Rothman R. Marital satisfaction across the transition to parenthood. *Journal of Family Psychology* 2008; 22(1): 41–50.

82 Burney R, Leerkes E. Links between mothers' and fathers' perceptions of infant temperament and coparenting. *Infant Behavior & Development* 2010; 33(2): 125–135.

83 Kerns S, Prinz R. Coparenting children with attention deficit disorders and disruptive behavior disorders. In: Drozd L, Saini M, Olesen N, editors. *Parenting plan evaluations: applied research for the family court.* New York: Oxford University Press; 2016. 243–279.

84 Loutzenhiser L, McAuslan P, Sharpe D. The trajectory of maternal and paternal fatigue across the transition to parenthood. *Clinical Psychologist* 2015; 19: 15–27.

85 McDaniel B, Teti D. Coparenting quality during the first three months after birth: The role of infant sleep quality. *Journal of Family Psychology* 2018; 26: 886–895.

86 Singley D, Edwards L. Men's perinatal mental health in the transition to fatherhood. *Professional Psychology: Research and Practice* 2015; 46: 309–316.

87 Paulson J, Bazemore S. Prenatal and postpartum depression in fathers. *Journal of the American Medical Association* 2010; 19: 54–63.

88 Cheng E, Downs S, Carroll A. Prevalence of depression among fathers at the pediatric well-child care visit. *Journal of American Medical Association Pediatrics* 2018; 172: 882–883.

89 Philpott L, *et al.* Stress in fathers in the perinatal period: A systematic review. *Midwifery* 2017; 55: 113–127.

90 Jenkins M, Goldberg A, Pierce C, Sayer A. Shift work, role overload and the transition to parenthood. *Journal of Marriage and Family* 2007; 69: 123–138.

91 Ramchandani P. Postpartum depression in fathers. *Lancet* 2005; 44: 144–155.

92 McWayne C, *et al.* An examination of fathers' mental health help seeking. *American Journal of Men's Health* 2016; 10: 33–38.

93 Birditt K, Miller L, Fingerman K, Lefkowitz E. Tensions in the parent and adult child relationship: Links to solidarity and ambivalence. *Psychology and Aging* 2009; 24: 287–295.

94 Kiecolt J, Blieszner R, Savla J. Long term influences of intergenerational ambivalence on midlife parents' psychological well-being. *Journal of Marriage and Family* 2011; 73: 369–382.

95 Whitehead B, Popenoe D. *Life without children.* Piscataway, NJ: Rutgers University; 2008.

96 Washington E. How daughters affect their legislator fathers' voting on women's issues. *American Economic Review* 2008; 98: 311–332.

97 Oswald A, Powdthavee N. Daughters and left wing voting. *Review of Economics and Statistics* 2010; 92: 213–227.

98 Wead D. *All the presidents' children.* New York: Atria Books; 2003.

99 Gawalt G, Gawalt A. *First daughters: Letters between U.S. presidents and their daughters.* New York: Black Dog and Leventhal Press; 2004.

100 Henry D, McPherson J. *Fathering daughters: Reflections by men.* Boston: Beacon; 1998.

101 Knight W. *Far from home: Father-daughter travel adventures.* Minneapolis: Seal Press; 2004.

Chapter 3

The Father's Impact

Cognitive, Academic, Vocational, Social, and Emotional

Having explored the various aspects of good fathering, we turn our attention now to the specific ways in which fathers influence various aspects of their daughters' lives. We begin with his influence on her cognitive development during infancy. As she ages, her father continues to influence her grades, attitudes towards achievement, college attendance, and eventually her career choice and financial status. Then we attend to his impact on her social development which encompasses her ability to control and regulate her emotions, to interact well with peers by not being withdrawn or aggressive, and to become socially self-confident and increasingly self-reliant as she ages. Her social development also affects her ability to establish emotionally intimate, meaningful, stable relationships with her boyfriends and future husband. Finally we examine his influence on her emotional and psychological well-being which includes the likelihood of her becoming clinically depressed or suicidal.

In order to underscore how the father's impact can differ based on the family's race, studies that were conducted exclusively with African, Asian or Hispanic daughters are presented in Chapter 7. The studies in the present chapter were either conducted with exclusively non-Hispanic white samples or with samples that included daughters from more than one racial group.

Cognitive Development

Infancy to Pre-school

Beginning in her infancy, fathers influence their daughters' cognitive development in multiple ways. In the first few years of life, children whose fathers are actively involved in their care sleep better and sleep longer throughout the night.[1,2,3] While this might seem insignificant, sleep is closely linked to children's cognitive development. Children between the ages of one and three who sleep well throughout the night have fewer cognitive and behavioral problems.[4,5] Well-rested babies and toddlers have longer attention spans, are more mentally alert, are less hyperactive, and are less lethargic—all of which contribute to their acquisition of cognitive skills such as language development.

Babies and toddlers with highly involved fathers are also more cognitively active and explore the objects around them with greater attention and purpose.[6] When both parents work outside the home and the fathers are highly involved with their baby in the first nine months, two years later the children have better attention spans and are more persistent in tackling a challenging task than those whose fathers are not highly involved at the outset.[7] Moreover, the father's sensitivity to their baby is more strongly linked than the mother's sensitivity to their baby's cognitive development at 18 months and at 36 months of age.[8] Similarly, children whose fathers interact with them sensitively at three months of age have better cognitive development as two-year-olds.[9] This held true regardless of the parents' educational levels, parents' age, or the mother's sensitivity to the baby. Toddlers whose fathers only have a high school education but are actively engaged with them also have larger vocabularies, even after controlling for the mother's engagement with the child.[10] And two year-olds whose fathers are sensitive and engaged, without being overly controlling or intrusive, have better language skills and are more attentive and able to stay on task when they are three years old.[11]

These same benefits accrue in lower income and single parent families. In low income, single mother families, two- to four-year-olds whose fathers are warm and playful have better reading and math skills years later in elementary school.[12] More impressive still, in a study with 8,400 two-year-olds from intact and separated families, toddlers whose fathers engage them in cognitively stimulating ways have better vocabularies, counting skills, and reasoning abilities than those with less involved fathers.[13] Interestingly, the fathering link was stronger for the toddlers living with their single mother than toddlers living with both parents. Likewise, for 1,292 babies from intact families in rural North Carolina and Pennsylvania, half of whom were living in poverty, children whose fathers read to them at six months of age had better language skills at age three.[14] This held true regardless of the mother's educational level or whether she read to the babies. In low income families, three-year-old girls whose fathers were very stressed by the demands of parenting a year earlier had lower cognitive development and more limited vocabularies than girls whose fathers were less stressed a year earlier.[15] Interestingly though, the mother's stress was not linked to the children's cognitive skills and the father's stress was not linked to the son's skills.

The father's impact depends in large part on how he interacts with his very young daughter when they are playing together. Compared to mothers, fathers generally play with infants and preschool children in ways that are more intellectually stimulating, more challenging, and more demanding.[16,17,18] He challenges the children, even as infants, to be bolder in exploring their world, to overcome their fear of new experiences and new people, and to attempt physical and intellectual tasks that are initially intimidating. He is teaching his young child how to open up to and explore the outside world, how to cope with "threatening" situations, and how to take calculated risks. This process is referred to as the **"activation relationship"** between father and child.[19]

"Pretend" play that calls for creativity, spontaneity, and imagination is especially beneficial. In "pretend" play the father and daughter interact one on one and engage in spontaneous dialogue with each other. Two-year-olds whose fathers engage in pretend play have better language development and are better at regulating their emotions in kindergarden.[20] Not only is the father promoting her language development as a toddler, he is teaching her to regulate negative emotions (i.e. outbursts of anger). This, in turn, is likely to enhance her later achievement in school. As Box 3.1 illustrates, Mattel Toys' "Dads who play Barbie" campaign is predicated on the understanding that imaginative, pretend play can have far-reaching benefits for daughters.[21] As part of its international campaign to promote young girls' potential, Mattel highlighted the importance of fathers with its slogan: "Time spent in her imaginary world is an investment in her real world."

Box 3.1 Dads play Barbie[21]

Figure 3.1
Source: Copyright Mattel.

"Time spent in her imaginary world is an investment in her real world." Part of Mattel's "you can be anything" worldwide campaign to promote girls' potential is to feature the importance of father-daughter relationships. In the ads Mattel is acknowledging that fathers promote their young daughters' cognitive development, self-confidence, and future career success by engaging with her in imaginary play. In the Dads Play Barbie commercials, fathers are helping their daughters imagine a future as anthropologists, astronauts, mathematicians, firefighters, doctors—and promoting the idea that fathers matter.

Endeavor Excitement

The father also contributes by encouraging an attitude referred to as **endeavor excitement**.[22] This is the pleasure toddlers feel when exploring their surroundings, discovering something new or mastering new skills. When fathers encourage this excitement, toddlers become more autonomous and more confident about interacting with new, "strange" things and attempting challenging tasks. As she ages, her father should continue to encourage her endeavor excitement by encouraging her to take pleasure in her own achievements. In contrast, an uninvolved or overly protective father encourages her to be passive, timid, withdrawn, or indifferent to what is going on around her—none of which will serve her well in school or in a future career.

Toddlers' parents should also be encouraging them to develop a sense of agency. **Agency** means the young child takes an active role in interacting with her environment, instead of passively waiting for things to happen to her. Rather than being a passive, helpless observer, she is becoming an active participant in her own life. At this young age, she is learning to assume the initiative and to be self-directed—traits which are linked later in her life to school and job success. Children can acquire this sense of agency from either parent. More often than not, however, it is the father who instills this "take charge, can do" attitude, beginning in the first few years of his daughter's life.[16]

Childhood Through Early Adulthood

When the daughter ages and enters school, her father continues to influence her cognitive development as reflected in her grades, school anxiety, and college attendance. Based on an innovative, sophisticated research design, researchers have been able to establish a causal effect between father absence and many negative outcomes for children.[23] Based on this advanced analysis of 47 studies, father absence has the strongest impact on children's high school graduation rates and the second strongest impact on their aggressive behavior and teenage delinquency. These findings are extremely important because the sample size is so large and because the analysis ruled out factors (i.e. divorce, family income) other than father absence that might account for the children's outcomes.

Fathers also have an impact on their daughter's **locus of control attitudes,** which in turn affect her school achievement. **Locus of control** refers to our beliefs about how much control we have over what is happening or what will happen to us.[24] Children acquire these beliefs from their parents. People with **internal locus of control** attitudes generally feel that their own behavior, efforts, and decisions will influence the outcomes or the circumstances in their lives. They take responsibility for most of the consequences—good and bad—that befall them. In contrast, people with **external locus of control** attitudes generally feel powerless and helpless because they believe that external factors over which they have no control will largely determine most outcomes. External locus of control beliefs are reflected in beliefs such as: it doesn't pay to try hard, or when you do something wrong there is very little you can do to make it right, or most people are just born good at sports. Hence, external locus of control attitudes are referred to as **learned helplessness**.

Children learn their locus of control attitudes largely from their parents.[19] Interestingly, the fathers and mothers seem to have a different impact on their daughters' attitudes. For example, 9- to 11-year-old daughters' locus of control attitudes were closely linked to their father's attitudes, but not to their mother's.[25] Similarly, women aged 26–58 who had close relationships with their fathers in childhood had higher (better) internal locus of control scores and were less depressed when confronted with bad events in their adult lives.[26] These well-fathered daughters felt less helpless and more in control when faced with stressful situations.

Daughters benefit academically when their fathers encourage them to work hard, push themselves, and strive to improve. For example, sixth grade girls from low income families who had a warm relationships with their father were more optimistic about and more committed to their school work, regardless of the quality of their relationship with their mother.[27] Likewise, when fathers helped their children with their homework, the daughters were less anxious about school.[28] The mother's help with homework, however, had no significant impact on the daughter's anxiety. Then too, in college, daughters with higher grade point averages had closer relationships with their fathers than those with poor father-daughter relationships.[29]

There can be a downside, however, if a daughter feels her father expects her to be perfect in terms of her academic achievements. If she believes she has to be perfect in order to earn or maintain his love, she becomes a perfectionist who puts herself under constant, excessive pressure to achieve.[30,31] This kind of perfectionism increases her risk for clinical depression, anxiety and eating disorders, and stress related physical illnesses. In striving for unattainable perfection, these daughters never feel "good enough" in the eyes of their father. Good fathering means finding a balance between strongly encouraging or gently pushing his daughter to improve her academic, athletic, or vocational skills and not making her feel that she must be perfect in order to be loved by him.

Vocational Development

Cognitive development, locus of control attitudes, and school achievement matter because the daughter's future career success and her future income are tied to these factors. In short, her father's influence extends far beyond her years in school.

Women who have reached the highest levels in their chosen career often credit their success largely to their fathers. As far back as the 1970s, 25 female corporate presidents attributed their achievements to their fathers, as did female students in Harvard's almost exclusively male M.B.A. program in 1964.[32] The fathers' influence may also help to explain why first-born daughters and daughters with no brothers are over-represented among the world's political leaders.[33]

Fathers also influence their daughters' academic interests and future career plans. Young teenage girls whose fathers hoped they would someday enter a profession typically dominated by males (science, technology, engineering, math) are much more likely to be working in those professions by the age of 28 than daughters whose fathers had more gender stereotyped views.[34] Daughters aged 7 to 13 whose fathers do a large part of the housework express a greater interest in working outside the home and in pursuing a less female stereotyped job when they grow up than those whose fathers do little or no housework.[35] By demonstrating to his young daughter that he believes in gender equity, the "housework" father might have an impact on her future career aspirations. And in a study that followed 203 children from the age 10 to the age of 26, daughters who spent the most time with their fathers in childhood chose less gender typed jobs than daughters who spent the least time with their fathers.[36] In contrast, the amount of time spent with their mothers had no impact on the daughters' future career choices.

It also appears that fathers may have a greater impact on their daughters' academic and vocational achievements than on their sons'. In a study with 300 tenth graders living with their single fathers and 1,900 living with their single mothers, the girls who lived with their fathers had higher grades.[37] These fathers were less inclined than the mothers were to be "friends" with their daughters or to abdicate their parental authority. The fathers also demanded more from their daughters academically. In the same vein, in a sample with 7,900 teenagers, for those whose fathering time was decreased because their parents divorced, the daughters' math, science, and reading achievement scores declined more sharply than the sons'.[38] Likewise, in a study that followed 13,000 children from birth to age 33, those who had good relationships with their fathers were more successful in school and in their careers—but the link was much stronger for daughters than for sons.[39]

In her adult years, the father continues to have an impact on his daughter's career plans. Compared to daughters who are not close to their fathers, female undergraduates with close relationships say they would be more willing to change their minds if their father strongly disapproved of their future career plans.[40] His influence might also partly explain why daughters born in the 1970s were three times more likely to work in the same field as their fathers than daughters born at the beginning of the 20th century.[41] Of course, society's less sexist attitudes account for much of this change. Still, these researchers attributed 20% of the change to fathers' mentoring their daughters much more than they did in the past. For example, fathers are much more likely to transfer the family business to their daughter nowadays.[42,43] The father's encouragement and mentoring may also help explain why young women now place as much or more importance on having a high paying job as do young men. In ongoing Pew Research national surveys, in 2011, 66% of women aged 18 to 34 said that being successful in a high paying job was one of the most important things in their lives, compared to 59% of the men.[44] By contrast, in 1997 only 25% of the women said that career success was one of their top priorities.

Overall then, fathers influence their daughters' cognitive development, academic achievements, and future careers in many ways. Positively, his relationship with her should promote her endeavor excitement, sense of agency, and internal locus of control attitudes.

Social Development

Even the most academically and vocationally successful daughters can have problems in their social and romantic relationships that are linked to the quality of their father-daughter relationships. Social relationships include children's relationships with their peers, with adults outside the family (i.e. teachers, caregivers, coaches), and with the people they date or eventually live with or marry. People who are withdrawn or excessively shy, overly dependent, aggressive or emotionally volatile (have difficulty controlling or regulating their emotions) have more troubled social and romantic relationships. In contrast, daughters who are relatively self-confident, self-reliant, friendly, and emotionally self-regulated (able to control their extreme emotions) get along better with others and have more satisfying friendships and romantic relationships. In all of these regards, fathers can have a negative or a positive impact on their daughters' social and romantic lives.

Relationships with Peers and Teachers

During the first few years of her life, fathers are teaching their daughters how to relate to others and how to cope with frustrating "social" interactions. Especially through play, the father is teaching his very young daughter how to relate to people. By indulging or tolerating her overly dependent, withdrawn, unruly, aggressive, or age inappropriate childish behavior, he is doing her a disservice in terms of her developing more mature social skills.

Infants whose fathers are highly involved in their care get along better with their peers and teachers years later in kindergarten.[45] This held true even when the mothers had been depressed and even when the parents were not living together. Likewise, in married, middle class families, at three months of age and again at 12 months of age, babies with highly involved fathers are less likely to throw tantrums or to kick and bite other children or adults than those with less involved fathers.[46] As the researchers pointed out, this matters because roughly 6% of babies who act out their emotions in these ways at the age two continue to interact poorly with people throughout childhood. And in a unique study where 120 babies were assessed at ages one, seven, and nine, children whose fathers were highly involved with them at age one had better social behavior in elementary school.[47] Even when the mothers had been depressed when the baby was young, in first and in third grades, the children whose fathers were highly involved when they were babies got along better with their peers, parents, and teachers. In an even larger study with 865 children, girls who had warm relationships with their father in first grade had more advanced social skills in third grade.[48]

Two large analyses that involved 50 studies merit special attention. In the first analysis of 26 studies, children whose fathers engaged in stimulating and challenging play with them were less aggressive, more socially competent, and more in control of their emotions that those whose fathers did not engage in this kind of play.[49] In the second analysis of 24 studies involving 22,300 children, those whose fathers were more involved with them got along better with their peers and with their teachers than those with less involved or absent fathers.[50]

Sexual Behavior, Romantic Relationships, and Marriage

As his daughter ages, the father also has a profound impact on her sexual behavior as a teenager and young adult. Because sexual behavior is closely related to physical health and physical safety, it is discussed in the next chapter. Suffice it to say here that teenage and young daughters with good relationships with their father are less likely to get pregnant, to contract sexual disease, to be date raped, or to be victims of dating violence.

Focusing on the quality of daughters' relationships with boyfriends or husbands, the daughter who has a supportive, loving relationship with her father benefits most. She is the most likely to be able to create and maintain emotionally intimate, fulfilling relationships with her boyfriends or her future husband. Through her relationship with her father, she learns how to communicate openly and honestly with men, resolve rather than ignore problems in the relationship, freely express her own needs, and express anger and disappointment in appropriate ways.

As young adults, well-fathered daughters have better relationships with their boyfriends than daughters with absent fathers or distant father-daughter relationships. They feel more satisfied, more trusting, and more secure in their relationships.[51–54] They are more likely to seek comfort from their boyfriends.[55] They are less likely to agree to have sex with their college boyfriend merely to appease or make him happy.[56] In contrast, when a father becomes emotionally overly reliant on his daughter while she is growing up—relying on her to be his confidante, helpmate, or best friend—she is

Figure 3.2
Source: Steven Mizel.

more dissatisfied and more insecure in her relationships with boyfriends in college.[57] These fathers have "reversed roles" with their daughter, treating her as if she is his parent—a damaging situation that we will examine in Chapter 5. It is also worth noting that how secure young adult daughters feel in their romantic relationships has been linked to how sensitively their father related to them as infants and toddlers.[58] In this unique study, the researchers assessed the quality of the father's parenting over the course of 16 years. Then, when the daughters were young adults, they reported on the quality of their relationships with boyfriends.

A good father-daughter relationship also bestows benefits when the daughter eventually marries. Well-fathered daughters have more emotionally intimate marriages and are more happily married even when their own parents are divorced.[39,59] Having a secure, loving relationship with their fathers, daughters are less anxious about whether their husband loves them or how committed he is to the marriage.[60] This study is especially interesting because the quality of the mother-daughter relationship was not linked, as the father's was, to how the daughter felt about her husband's love and commitment.

Given his influence, it is unfortunate that many daughters wish their fathers had spent more time talking to them about romantic relationships.[61] Others feel that the idea of being "daddy's little girl" is a barrier to more open communication with their fathers about dating and relationships.[62] In sum, as the checklist in Box 3.2 illustrates, daughters who grow up without fathers or with distant, troubled relationships with him have an assortment of problems in their romantic relationships or marriages.[63,64]

Box 3.2 Daughters' romantic relationships: The impact of father absence[63,64]

- Feeling fundamentally unlovable and unworthy of a man's love
- Choosing men who are married or otherwise can't commit to a relationship
- Feeling that you never quite measure up
- Feeling that you always have to be in control—especially in relationships with men
- Continually searching for a man to give you what dad didn't give
- Looking for love through meaningless or promiscuous sex
- Feeling an unresolved pain that resurfaces every time a relationship ends
- Comforting yourself by abusing drugs, alcohol, or food
- Being unable to trust men enough to create a stable relationship
- Feeling extremely angry and resentful towards men in general
- Suffering from clinical depression
- Acting like a super woman who can handle everything without anyone's help
- Feeling that most men—especially fathers—are no good
- Having a baby at an early age in an attempt to feel loved
- Choosing men who aren't good to you or good for you
- Being extremely needy or overly dependent on men
- Feeling that you have to be nearly perfect before a man can love you
- Leaving a decent relationship instead of working through the problems because you assume he's going to leave you anyway
- Feeling that you have to change things about yourself because you're not lovable

Depression and Suicide

Given the benefits of good fathering for daughters' social and romantic relationships, and academic and career achievements, it is not surprising that these daughters are also less likely than poorly fathered daughters to ever become clinically depressed or suicidal.

It appears that fathers have a greater impact on their daughters than on their sons with respect to depression. When children's fathers died early in their lives, they were more likely to become clinically depressed than when their fathers died later in their lives. The daughters, however, were more likely than the sons to become clinically depressed when their father had died while they were young.[65] Then too, when the father was clinically depressed, daughters were more likely than sons to be depressed.[66] Similarly, when their fathers put excessive pressure on them to conform, female undergraduates were more depressed and suicidal than male undergraduates.[67]

Several studies merit special attention because their samples sizes are so large. In a study with 7,100 teenagers from intact families, girls were much more dissatisfied than boys with their relationship with their fathers—and more girls than boys were clinically depressed.[68] Over the course of three years, however, girls who felt their relationships with their fathers had improved became less depressed, while the other girls' depression remained unchanged. In a study that followed 13,000 children from birth to age 33, those who had good relationships with their fathers were less likely to have ever been clinically depressed, regardless of the family's income or whether the parents had divorced.[39] The connection, though, was much stronger for daughters than for sons. More noteworthy still, in an analysis of 24 studies involving 22,300 children, father involvement was more closely linked to daughters' than to sons' depression, anxiety and mood disorders.[50] And in an even larger meta-analysis of 220 studies from 23 nations, teenage and young adult daughters' psychological adjustment was more closely linked to how accepted or rejected she felt by her father than by her mother.[69] In other words, feeling rejected by her father was more likely to lead to depression and anxiety disorders than feeling rejected by her mother.

Other studies confirm the impact fathers have on the daughter's mental health. Clinically depressed teenage girls felt more rejected by their fathers and had more trouble communicating with him than non-depressed girls.[70] Likewise, female undergraduates who had poor relationships with their fathers were more likely to be depressed than daughters who were close to their fathers.[71] Even much later in their lives, women aged 26 to 58 who had close relationships with their father as children were less likely to get depressed when faced with difficult, stressful events.[26] A large body of research on eating disorders also confirms that clinically depressed daughters are less likely to become anorexic or bulimic if they have close, communicative relationships with their fathers—a topic that will be discussed in the next chapter.[72]

Two other studies are worth noting with respect to their possible connection to a daughter's depression. Young adult daughters who felt their fathers favored or were closer to one of the other children had more stressed, conflicted relationships with the favored sibling.[73] This was not true, though, when the daughter felt her mother favored one of the other children. The mother's favoritism had no impact on the siblings' relationship with each other. Similarly, undergraduate women who felt rejected by their fathers were more aggressive socially and had less control over their angry impulses than women who felt accepted by their fathers.[74] As the researchers pointed out, people who cannot control their feelings of anger, frustration, or unhappiness are the most likely to lash out against others.

In sum then, a strong father-daughter relationship offers considerable protection against depression, anxiety and poor regulation of one's emotions.

Identity and Individuation

Daughters who are doing well in those aspects of their lives discussed in this chapter are forming an identity of their own—an identity that is separate from their father.[75] Psychologists refer to this process as becoming **individuated** from our parents. **Individuation** is part of the process of ego development where children should separate enough from both parents to form an autonomous, strong identity of their own. In contrast, children who fail to become individuated or to develop a strong ego remain dependent on one or both parents in ways that interfere with their social, intellectual, and vocational development. Even as an adult, a daughter who has not become individuated from her father may remain overly dependent on him to make decisions for her or to take care of her financially and emotionally. She seeks and abides by his wishes because she does not have a strong enough identity of her own.

> ## Box 3.3 Fathers and daughters in plays and mythology[76]
>
> In Greek mythology Athena was a motherless goddess whose great intellect and power came from her father, the god Zeus. Athena was not born or raised by a mother. Nor did she need one. Instead she "sprang from her father's head" as a fully grown, armed woman. As the female embodiment of and companion to her father Zeus, the devoted and adoring Athena never married. She chose instead to rule alongside her father as the dutiful daughter. Likewise, the youngest daughter in Shakespeare's play about King Oedipus also gave up her identity to serve her father. Unlike her sisters, Antigone remains unmarried and becomes her father's lifelong caretaker after he goes blind and loses all his power as King. Psychologists sometimes refer to daughters who fail to individuate from their fathers as having an "**Antigone Complex**."

Box 3.4 Sigmund and Anna Freud: A father-daughter story[77]

Sigmund Freud and his daughter Anna Freud on holiday in the Italian Dolomites. [Public domain via Wikimedia Commons]

Figure 3.3
Source: Copyright Mattel.

Perhaps the most famous relationship illustrating the "Antigone Complex" is Sigmund Freud and his youngest daughter, Anna, whom he nicknamed Antigone. The youngest of six children (three sons and three daughters), Anna Freud devoted her life to her father. Even though he had three sons, Freud referred to Anna as his "true son." She never married and, even while her mother was still alive, she was her father's caretaker, helpmate, and colleague for the last 20 years of his life. After Freud's death, Anna carried on his work for the remaining 43 years of her life.

A good father enhances his daughter's individuation and ego development from the earliest years of her life. By helping her develop a sense of agency, endeavor excitement, internal locus of control, and self-reliance, he promotes her forming an identity separate from his. As she ages, he allows and encourages her to have and to express opinions that differ from his, to become increasingly self-reliant, and to make her own decisions, even when it might not be the path he would have chosen for her. He makes her feel loved and respected for being herself, rather than being a mere reflection of himself.

Daughters with famous, wealthy, powerful fathers may have a more difficult time becoming individuated.[76,77] As Box 3.3 illustrates, this theme is echoed in Greek mythology and in Shakespeare's plays. And as Box 3.4 illustrates, Anna Freud, daughter of the internationally famous psychoanalyst, Sigmund Freud, can serve an example of a daughter who may never have become individuated from her father.

Box 3.5 Fathers' influence on prominent daughters' careers

Susan B Anthony (1820–1906) Leader of Women's Suffrage Movement[78]

Very few girls received a formal education in the early 1800's. But Susan B. Anthony's father, Daniel, believed in equal education for boys and girls and so she was educated. Her father was a political activist who opposed slavery and often had famous reformers, such as the African American abolitionist Frederick Douglas, to their home. Not surprisingly, Susan became a prominent leader along with her best friend, Elizabeth Caty Stanton, in the movement that won American women the right to vote.

Marie Curie (1867–1934) Nobel Prize Winner in Physics and Chemistry[79]

The fifth and youngest child, Marie's passion for science developed early on from her father, Władysław Skłodowski, a highly respected math and physics teacher in Poland. He not only inspired her intellectually, he raised all five children after her mother died from tuberculosis when Marie was only 12. Her achievements included the development of the theory of radioactivity, a term that she coined, and the discovery of two elements, polonium and radium. She was the only person ever to win a Nobel Prize twice and to win in both physics and chemistry. Sadly, she died at the age of 66 from anemia caused by her exposure to radioactive materials in her work.

Hillary Clinton, Senator, Presidential Candidate, Secretary of State[80]

"During my high school and college years, our relationship increasingly was defined either by silence, as I searched for something to say to him, or by arguments, which I often provoked because I knew he always engaged with me over politics and cultures – Vietnam, hippies, bra burning feminists, Nixon. I also understood that, even when he erupted at me, he admired my independence and accomplishments and loved me with all his heart."

If a daughter feels that she must please her father by following in his footsteps or must not stray too far from his values, beliefs, or plans for her life, she is more likely to fail to create an identity of her own. On the other hand, if she feels she is his favorite and favored child, she may forego her own identify in order to fulfill his expectations. If he is wealthy, famous, or powerful, she may be on constant display as a tribute to his accomplishments, much like an adoring princess to her father the king. Although he may support her becoming well educated and accomplished, he never allows her to outshine him. He may enjoy showing her off at social functions and having her impress people with her intellect. In order to retain her favored position, however, she must remain devoted, loyal, and admiring without a strong identity of her own. The famous, yet narcissistic, father treats his daughter as an extension and a reflection of himself. He loves her not for being herself in ways that differ from him, but for enhancing his public image and devoting herself to him.

Conclusion

From her infancy onward, fathers can have a positive influence on their daughters' cognitive development in multiple ways. He helps her succeed by promoting her endeavor excitement, sense of agency, and internal locus of control. Without making her feel that she must be perfect in order to win his approval, he encourages her to persist at challenging tasks and to pursue academic interests and careers that only males have traditionally pursued. By not being overly protective or not disapproving as she creates an identity of her own, he helps her develop the self-reliance, confidence, and initiative she needs to excel in school and in her future career.

Fathers also help their daughters develop the skills and attitudes that lead to more satisfying relationships with peers, teachers, romantic partners, and future husbands. By making her feel that she is loved and lovable, her father gives her the confidence to choose boyfriends or a husband who is good *to* her and good *for* her. Further, a strong father-daughter relationship reduces the odds that daughters will become clinically depressed or develop anxiety or eating disorders at some point in their lives. While no father can ensure his daughter's happiness or success in any area of her life, his love, encouragement, and guidance gives her the best chance for creating a fulfilling, successful future for herself.

Review Questions

1   What does a father do to contribute to each of these attitudes and how does each affect the daughter's cognitive or social development: endeavor excitement, agency, locus of control attitudes?

2 When she is an infant, toddler, or preschooler, how and why is the father and daughter playing together important for her development?

3 Specifically how is the father's impact different from the mother's in regard to the daughter's cognitive, social, sexual, or identity development?

4 In what ways and in what domains does the father's impact seem to be greater on his daughter than on his son?

5 In what specific ways does a father influence his daughter's cognitive and social development in the first five years of her life?

6 What are individuation and ego development and what should fathers do to enhance their daughters' lives in those respects?

7 What kinds of problems do poorly individuated daughters have?

8 Using findings from specific research studies to support your answer, in what specific ways do daughters benefit from having good relationships with their fathers?

9 What is "good" fathering in terms of the specific behaviors that result in the best outcomes for daughters?

10 When daughters have absent fathers or troubled father-daughter relationships, what attitudes or behaviors do they exhibit in their romantic relationships?

Questions for Discussion and Debate

1 How has your father affected these aspects of your life: academic, career, social, psychological, social, sexual, and identity?

2 In what areas of your life has your father's influence been greater or lesser than your mother's influence?

3 How can a father encourage his daughter to do her best without making her feel she has to be perfect or that she is always under pressure to please him?

4 What was the most upsetting or most surprising research presented in this chapter? Why did it upset or surprise you?

5 What mistakes have you noticed fathers making with their teenage or young adult daughters in respect to the issues discussed in this chapter?

6 What kinds of play did you and your father engage in together when you were a very young child and how did it influence you?

7 What could teachers, physicians and family counselors do to promote more father involvement and to be less sexist in their own treatment of fathers?

8 What are the best and worst situations you have witnessed in terms of fathers having an impact on their daughters' romantic relationships or marriages?

9 What are some examples of famous, wealthy or powerful fathers whose relationships with their daughters remind you of Zeus and Athena, Anna and Sigmund Freud, or Antigone and King Lear?

10 As a father, what would you worry most about while your daughter was in high school or in college—and what would you do about it?

References

1 Tikotzky L, Sadeh A, Volkovich E, Manber R, Meiri G, Shahar G. Infant sleep development from 3 to 6 months: Links with maternal sleep and paternal involvement. *Monographs of the Society for Research in Child Development* 2015; 36: 107–123.

2 Ayalon M. The role of the father in child sleep disturbance. *Infant Mental Health Journal* 2015; 36: 114–127.

3 Bordeleau S, Bernier A, Carrier J. Children's sleep patterns. *Journal of Family Psychology* 2012; 26: 254–262.

4 Licis A. Sleep disorders assessment and treatment in preschool aged children. *Child and Adolescent Psychiatric Clinics of North America* 2017; 26: 587–594.

5 Hoyniak C. Less efficient neural processing related to irregular sleep and less sustained attention in toddlers. *Developmental Neuropsychology* 2015; 40: 155–166.

6 Bronte J, Carrano J, Horowitz A. Involvement among resident fathers and links to infant cognitive outcomes. *Journal of Family Issues* 2008; 29: 1211–1244.

7 Lang S, *et al.* Relations between fathers' and mothers' infant engagement patterns in dual earner families and toddler competence. *Journal of Family Issues* 2014; 45: 1–21.

8 Malmberg L. The influence of mothers' and fathers' sensitivity in the first year of life on children's cognitive outcomes at 18 and 36 months. *Child Care Health & Development* 2016; 42: 1–7.

9 Sethna V, *et al.* Father child interactions at 3 months and 24 months: Contributions to children's cognitive development at 24 months. *Infant Mental Health Journal* 2017; 38: 378–390.

10 LeMonda C, Baumwell L, Cabrera N. Fathers' role in children's language development. In: Cabrera N, LeMonda C, editors. *Handbook of father involvement.* New York: Routledge; 2013. 135–151.

11 Cabrera N, Shannon J, Tamis-LeMonda C. Fathers' influence on children's cognitive and emotional development from toddlers to pre-K. *Applied Development Science* 2007; 11: 208–213.

12 Coley R, Bjarnason T, Carrano J. Does early paternal parenting promote low income children's long term cognitive skills? *Journal of Family Issues* 2011; 32: 1522–1542.

13 Fagan J, Lee Y. Effects of fathers' and mothers' cognitive stimulation and income on toddlers' cognition. *Fathering* 2014; 10: 140–158.

14 Pancsofar N, Feagans L. Fathers' early contributions to children's language development in families from low income rural communities. *Early Childhood Research Quarterly* 2010; 25: 450–463.

15 Harewood T, Vallotton C, Herb H. More than just the breadwinner: The effects of fathers' parenting stress on children's language and cognitive development. *Infant and Child Development* 2016; 25: 235–242.

16 Lamb M. *The role of the father in child development.* New York: Wiley; 2010.

17 Newland L, Freeman H, Coyle D. *Emerging topics on father attachment.* New York: Routledge; 2011.

18 Cabrera N, LeMonda C. *Handbook of father involvement.* New York: Routledge; 2013.

19 Paquette D, Bigras M. The risky situation. In: Newland L, Freeman H, Coyl D, editors. *Emerging topics in father attachment.* New York: Routledge; 2011. 32–50.

20 Cabrera N, Karberg E, Malin J, Aldoney D. The magic of play: low income mothers' and fathers' playfulness and children's emotional regulation and vocabulary skills. *Infant Mental Health Journal* 2017; 38: 1–14.

21 McGrath K, Neal K. Ads for dads: Wake Forest University professor advises on new Barbie campaign. *Wake Forest University Press Release* 2017.

22 Tessman L. Father's contributions to the daughter's ways of loving and working. In: Cath S, editor. *Father and child*. Boston: Little Brown; 1994.

23 McLanahan S, Tach L, Schneider D. The causal effects of father absence. *Annual Review of Sociology* 2013; 22: 399–427.

24 Nowicki, S. *Choice or chance: Understanding your locus of control and why it matters*. New York: Prometheus Books; 2016.

25 Tully E. Family correlates of daughters' and son's locus of control expectancies during childhood. *Early Child Development and Care* 2016; 186: 1939–1951.

26 Forest R, Moen P, McLain D. Effects of childhood family stress on women's depressive symptoms. *Psychology of Women Quarterly* 1996; 20: 81–100.

27 Suizzo S. The unique effects of fathers' warmth on adolescents' positive beliefs and behaviors: Pathways to resilience in low income families. *Sex Roles* 2017; 77: 46–58.

28 Tan E, Golberg W. Parental school involvement in relation to children's grades and adaptation to school. *Journal of Applied Developmental Psychology* 2012; 30: 442–453.

29 Waterman E, Lefkowitz E. Are mothers' and fathers' parenting characteristics associated with emerging adults' academic engagement? *Journal of Family Issues* 2017; 38: 1239–1261.

30 Smith M. The intergenerational transmission of perfectionism. *Personality and Individual Differences* 2017; December: 242–248.

31 Prewitt T, Fisher L, Odenheimer E, Buchanan R. He just wanted everything to be perfect, me to be perfect: NCAA daughter athletes' experiences of the father-daughter relationship. *Sport Exercise and Performance Psychology* 2016; 5: 144–160.

32 Hennig M, Jardim A. *The managerial woman*. New York: Doubleday; 1977.

33 Steinberg B. The making of female presidents and prime ministers. *Political Psychology*, 2001; 22(1): 89–114.

34 Chhin C, Blecker M, Jacobs J. Gender typed occupational choices: The long term impact of parents' beliefs and expectations. *Gender and occupational outcomes*. Washington, DC: American Psychological Association; 2008: 215–234.

35 Croft A. The second shift reflected in the second generation. *Psychological Science* 2014; 25: 1418–1428.

36 Lawson K, Crouter A, McHale S. Links between family gender socialization in childhood and gendered occupational attainment in young adulthood. *Journal of Vocational Behavior* 2015; 90: 26–35.

37 Lee S, Kushner J, Cho S. Effects of parents' gender on children's achievements in single parent families. *Sex Roles* 2007; 56: 149–157.

38 Sun Y, Li Y. Post divorce family stability and adolescents' academic progress. *Journal of Family Issues* 2009; 30: 1527–1539.

39 Flouri E. *Fathering and child outcomes*. Hoboken, NJ: John Wiley; 2005.

40 Li C, Kerpelman J. Parental influences on young women's career aspirations. *Sex Roles* 2007; 56(1–2): 105–115.

41 Morrill M, Hellerstein J. Dads and daughters: The changing face of women's occupational choices. *Journal of Human Resources* 2009; 46: 333–372.

42 Haberman H, Danes S. Father-daughter and father-son family business management transfer. *Family Business Review* 2007; 20(2): 163–184.

43 Overbeke K, Bilimoira D, Somers T. Shared vision between fathers and daughters in family businesses: the determining factor that transform daughters into successors. *Frontiers in Psychology* 2018; 6: 625–630.

44 Patten S, Parker K. *Gender reversal on career aspirations.* New York: Pew Foundation; 2012.

45 Mezulis A, Hyde J, Blark R. Father involvement moderates effects of maternal depression during child's infancy on child behavior problems in kindergarten. *Journal of Family Psychology* 2004; 18: 575–588.

46 Ramchandani P. Do early father infant interactions predict the onset of externalizing behaviors in young children? *Journal of Child Psychology and Psychiatry* 2013; 54: 56–64.

47 Boyce R, *et al.* Early father involvement and mental health problems in middle childhood. *American Journal of Child and Adolescent Psychiatry* 2006; 45: 1510–1523.

48 Webster L, Low J, Siller C, Hackett R. Understanding the contribution of a father's warmth on his child's social skills. *Fathering* 2013; 11: 90–113.

49 St George J, Wroe J, Cashin M. The concept and measurement of fathers' stimulating play: A review. *Attachment & Human Development* 2018; 20: 634–658.

50 Sarkadi A, Kirstiansson R, Oberklai F, Bremberg S. Fathers' involvement and children's developmental outcomes. *Acta Paediatrica* 2008; 97: 153–158.

51 Bartell D. Influence of parental divorce on romantic relationships in young adulthood. In: Fine M, Harvey J, editors. *Handbook of divorce.* New York: Routledge; 2006. 339–361.

52 Last R. Parental attachment styles of late adolescents. *Journal of Counseling Psychology* 2009; 47: 316–329.

53 Schaick K, Stolberg A. Paternal involvement and young adults' intimate relationships. *Journal of Divorce and Remarriage* 2001; 36: 99–121.

54 Scharf M, Mayseless O. Late adolescent girls' relationships with parents and romantic partners. *Journal o f Adolescence* 2008; 31(6): 837–855.

55 Black K, Schutte E. Recollections of being loved. *Journal of Family Issues* 2006; 27(10): 1459–1480.

56 Katz J. Father emotional responsiveness and college women's sexual refusal behaviors. *American Journal of Family Therapy* 2010; 38(4): 344–356.

57 Baggett D, Shaffer A, Muetzelfeld H. Father daughter parentification and young adult romantic relationships among college women. *Journal of Family Issues* 2015; 36: 760–783.

58 Grossman L, Grossman L, Kindler H, Zimmerman P. Attachment and exploration: The influences of parents on psychological security from infancy to adulthood. In: Cassidy J, Shaver P, editors. *Handbook of attachment.* New York: Guilford Press; 2008. 857–879.

59 Haaz D, Kneavel M, Browning S. The father-daughter relationship and intimacy in the marriages of daughters of divorce. *Journal of Divorce & Remarriage* 2014; 55: 164–177.

60 Shaver P, Belsky J, Brennan K. The adult attachment interview and self-reports of romantic attachment. *Personal Relationships* 2000; 7: 25–43.

61 Nielsen L. College daughters' relationships with their fathers: A fifteen year study. *College Student Journal* 2006; 54: 16–30.

62 Hutchinson K, Cederbaum J. Talking to daddy's little girl about sex. *Journal of Family Issues* 2010; 38: 1–14.

63 Barras J. *Bridges: Reuniting daughters and daddies*. Baltimore: Bancroft; 2005.

64 Barras J. *Whatever happened to daddy's little girl*. New York: Ballantine; 2000.

65 Beyer A, Van Doorn C, Kasl S, Levy B. Paternal attachment as risk factor for depression in older women. *Journal of Mental Health and Aging* 2003; 9: 157–169.

66 Landman K, Ormel J, VanSonderen E. Risk of emotional disorder in offspring of depressed parents. *Depression and Anxiety* 2008; 25: 653–660.

67 Miller M, Day E. Family communication and college students' suicidality. *Journal of Family Communication* 2002; 2: 167–184.

68 Videon T. Parent child relationships and adolescents' psychological wellbeing. *Journal of Family Issues* 2005; 26: 55–78.

69 Ali S, Khaleque A, Rohner R. Pancultural gender differences in the relation between perceived parenting acceptance and psychological adjustment of children and adult offspring: A meta-analytic review of worldwide research. *Journal of Cross-Cultural Psychology* 2015; 46: 1059–1080.

70 Demidenko N, Manion I, Lee C. Father-daughter attachment and communication in depressed and nondepressed adolescent girls. *Journal of Child & Family Studies* 2015; 24: 1727–1734.

71 Rostad W, Silverman P, McDonald M. Daddy's little girl goes to college. *Journal of American College Health* 2014; 62: 213–220.

72 Agras S. Fathers' influence on daughters' eating disorders. *Journal of the American Academy of Child and Adolescent Psychiatry* 2007; 56: 110–119.

73 Gilligan M, Suitor J, Kim S, Pillemer K. Differential effects of perceptions of mothers' and fathers' favoritism on sibling tension in adulthood. *Journal of Gerontology, Psychological Sciences and Social Sciences* 2013; 68: 593–598.

74 McKenzie M, Casselman R. Perceived father rejection and young adult aggression. *Journal of Family Issues* 2017; 38: 1089–1108.

75 Arnett J, Tanner J. *Emerging adults in America*. Washington, DC: American Psychological Association; 2006.

76 Young E. On famous fathers and their youngest daughters. *Psychoanalytic Inquiry* 2008; 28(1): 27–38.

77 Britton R. Forever father's daughter. In: Trowell J, Etchegoyen A, editors. *The importance of fathers: Psychoanalytic perspectives*. New York: Routledge; 2002. 107–119.

78 Cooper I. *Susan Anthony*. New York: Franklin Watts; 1984.

79 Pflaum R. *Great obsession: Madam Curie and her world*. New York: Doubleday; 1989.

80 Frist K. *Love you, Daddy boy*. New York: Taylor; 2006.

Chapter 4

Fathers' Impact on Their Daughters' Physical Well-being

In addition to the impact that a father has on his daughter's cognitive, social, and psychological well-being, he influences her physical well-being. His impact on her physical health begins when she is born and extends into her adult years. Indeed the father's influence on her physical health continues even after his death in terms of the long-range implications for her health late in her own life.

In order to underscore how the father influences his daughter's health and physical well-being in various racial groups, studies that were conducted exclusively with African, Asian, or Hispanic daughters are presented in Chapter 7. The studies in the present chapter were either conducted with exclusively white non-Hispanic samples or with samples that included daughters from more than one racial group.

This chapter begins with the father's influence on his daughter's health during infancy and the preschool years. Even at this young age, her stress reactivation and immune systems, recovery from being born prematurely, and sleep patterns are linked to the kind of relationship her father has with her. As she ages, her father continues to influence her health in terms of her weight, physical fitness, eating disorders, and safety in sports. During her adolescence and young adult years, his influence extends to her drinking, using drugs, smoking, vaping, having safe sex, and behaving responsibly on dates. Safe sex and responsible dating reduce her odds of contracting a sexually transmitted diseases (STD), getting pregnant, and being physically attacked or raped. In short, a close, communicative father-daughter relationship is one of the best preventatives against a host of health problems throughout her life.

Premature Baby Care

The father's impact begins when his daughter is born in regard to three important aspects of her well-being: improving her health if she is born prematurely, establishing healthy sleep patterns, and creating a healthy response to stress in her endocrine system.

American babies who are born prematurely spend the first weeks or months of their lives in incubators in a Neonatal Intensive Care Unit (NICU) where machines regulate their breathing and nutritional intake until the child can survive on its own. Traditional medical practice has kept these fragile infants apart from their parents, except for an occasional touch through the openings in the incubator. But a more recent approach, referred to as "kangaroo care" (Box 4.1) takes the opposite tact. In **kangaroo care**, the premature infant is removed from the incubator and placed on the parent's bare chest for an hour or so. Of course, the baby remains attached to the equipment that regulates breathing and monitors vital signs under the supervision of medical staff. Premature infants who receive this "skin to skin" contact become healthier faster and have better overall health six months later than other premature babies. The mother's body also becomes less physically stressed, with lowered blood pressure and lowered cortisol levels. Moreover, ten years later the "kangaroo care" children have better physical health, are less anxious, sleep better, and have better cognitive development than premature babies who did not receive the "skin to skin" care.[1]

Box 4.1 Kangaroo care: Fathers and their premature babies

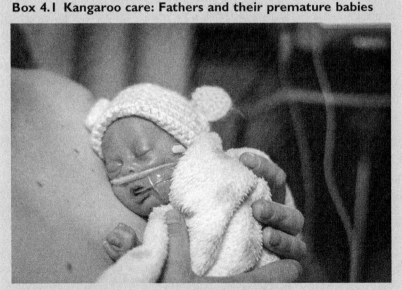

Figure 4.1 Fathers who provide skin to skin "kangaroo care" for their premature babies reduce their own levels of stress and contribute to their infant's physical and mental well-being
Source: Creative Images/shutterstock.com.

Babies do not just benefit, however, from kangaroo care from their mothers. They benefit equally from kangaroo care from their fathers. In 12 studies, the father's bare chested kangaroo care resulted in better health for the babies.[2] Like the mothers, the fathers benefitted physically as well. After just 75 minutes of holding his baby against his bare chest, the father's blood pressure and cortisol levels decreased. While cuddling his baby, he became less physically stressed.[3] And as discussed in Chapter 1, when parents are less stressed, they provide higher quality parenting.

Adequate Sleep

Even when babies are born in good health, their father's attentive care in the first few months of their lives is beneficial to their physical health. The first few months of a newborn's life are the most stressful for parents, largely because conflict and physical exhaustion increase.[4] As discussed in an earlier chapter, both fathers and mothers are more likely to become clinically depressed during this stressful period of their newborn's life.[5] In large part the increased conflicts, stress, and depression are due to a lack of sleep at night. For example, regardless of income or education, parents whose three-month-old babies frequently wake them up at night are more depressed and have worse coparenting relationships than parents whose babies wake them up less often.[6] Since most babies sleep longer at three months than at one month, the parents' depression also decreases as they become more well-rested. In short, if fathers can help their babies sleep longer through the night, both parents benefit.

Babies, toddlers, and preschoolers benefit in multiple ways when they are able to sleep for longer periods during the night. Sleep deprived babies and toddlers have more behavioral problems and have a harder time paying attention and staying on task.[7,8] They are more fretful, uncooperative, agitated, and aggressive. More surprisingly, in 42 studies, from infancy through adolescence, children who did not get enough sleep were more obese—a major health problem that affects more daughters than sons.[9]

Fortunately, fathers can play a major role in helping their young daughters get adequate sleep. One- to three-year-olds with sensitive, highly involved fathers sleep better than those with less involved, less attentive fathers.[10] And regardless of family income, three- and four-year-olds whose fathers interact with them positively and attentively when they are a year old sleep better than those whose fathers interact poorly with them as one-year-olds.[11] In short, adequate sleep should not be under-rated as a significant health issue for very young children.

The Daughter's Physical Reactions to Stress: Cortisol and the HPA Axis

The father-daughter relationship is also linked to how the daughter's **hypothalamus-pituitary-adrenal (HPA axis)** glands react to stressful, challenging, or unfamiliar situations.[12] **Cortisol** is a hormone released by the adrenal gland in response to stress. Sustained, chronic stress leads to high cortisol levels which are linked to more mood disorders, anxiety, depression, and a weaker immune system. Cortisol levels also appear to be permanently altered in negative ways during childhood if there is ongoing, high stress. Long after the childhood stress has ended, cortisol levels and the HPA axis may be altered in ways that make it more difficult for these individuals to deal with stress—and more likely that they will develop stress-related illnesses and diseases. Moreover, compared to sons, daughters have a stronger cortisol response to socially stressful situations.[12]

When fathers are actively involved in positive ways with their infants and toddlers in rough and tumble play and challenging tasks, children are learning to deal with stressful situations without over-reacting and without becoming overly stressed physically. In these strange or somewhat frightening situations, by providing comfort and supervision, fathers are helping children learn how to cope with stress without becoming physically overwhelmed. It now appears that fathers are temporarily destabilizing their children's cortisol levels while teaching them to bring those levels back to normal by becoming comfortable in these risky or new situations.[13] In contrast, infants and toddlers who have negative, unsupportive relationships with their fathers have elevated cortisol levels when they are confronted with challenging tasks or new situations.[14]

The link between children's cortisol levels and family stress are becoming increasingly clear. When young children are exposed to high family conflict, their cortisol levels become elevated and stay elevated for several days afterwards.[15] Other stressful disruptions, such as the father's absence if the parents separate, can also raise children's cortisol levels, causing them to become more withdrawn with their peers.[16] Children whose parents are unhappily married or in high conflict have abnormal cortisol levels, as do adults aged 18–37 whose parents divorced before the children were 18.[17]

Father absence is also linked to children's health by way of their telomeres.[18] A **telomere** is the region at the end of each chromosome that protects the chromosome from deteriorating or from fusing with other chromosomes. People with shorter telomeres have less robust immune systems and higher rates of cancer and other age related diseases. In a study with 2,420 nine-year-olds, children growing up in father absent families had shorter telomeres than children in two parent families. Researchers speculate that father absence may increase children's stress in ways that shorten their telomeres, though we need further research to confirm these results.

What is clear is that a daughter's cortisol levels are linked to the quality of her relationship with her father. Daughters who have distant or conflicted relationships with their fathers or who come from high conflict families have abnormal cortisol levels.[17] In contrast, daughters with warm father-daughter relationships from low conflict families have normal cortisol levels. Similarly, when they first entered college (a stressful situation), students who had elevated cortisol levels were more anxious and became even more anxious by the end of the spring semester than students who had normal cortisol levels at the outset.[19] The students who started college with normal cortisol levels were even less anxious at the end of the year than they were at the beginning. But the more intriguing finding is that a father's cortisol level in a stressful family situation arranged by the researchers was linked to his daughter's cortisol level.[20] Fathers whose cortisol levels were high in the stressful situation had daughters with higher cortisol levels and greater anxiety than fathers with more normal cortisol levels under stress.

College daughters' cortisol levels are also linked to the quality of their relationships with their fathers.[20] These female undergraduates' relationships with their fathers fell into one of two categories. In the positive relationships, the daughter reported that she and her father did special things together, that his expectations for her were consistent and clear, and that he supported her autonomy by expecting her to be honest with him about her thoughts and feelings. In the negative relationships, the daughter reported that her father did not find her likable, that he often changed the rules and expectations for her, and that they often got into coercive, manipulative power struggles. The daughters with the positive relationships had normal cortisol levels. When the researchers had these daughters talk to a close friend about their lives, they discussed fewer relationship problems than those daughters who had the negative relationships with their fathers. Those with the bad father-daughter relationships also had elevated cortisol levels. The researchers speculated that good father-daughter relationships contribute to normal cortisol levels, which in turn helps daughters deal better with stress and explains why they spent less time talking about their problems when talking with a friend. In yet another college study with daughters from divorced families, those who had maintained close relationships with their fathers had fewer stress-related health problems (i.e. insomnia, headaches, stomach problems) than those with poor father-daughter relationships.[21]

In sum, daughters with normal cortisol levels have fewer health problems, including sleep disturbances, obesity, alcoholism, autoimmune disorders (i.e. chronic fatigue syndrome, fibromyalgia, and rheumatoid arthritis), high blood pressure, and heart disease. From infancy on, good fathering is a protective factor for daughters' maintaining healthy cortisol levels.

The Obesity Epidemic

Fathers also have an impact on one of the most serious and lifelong health conditions facing their daughters: obesity.[22] Between 1970 and 2000 American obesity rates tripled for children and doubled for adults. The average

American female adult is 5'4" tall. At this height she should weigh less than 145 pounds. Unfortunately the average 5'4" female adult weighs 170 pounds. As Box 4.2 illustrates, far too many American children and adults are obese—daughters more so than sons. In 2018, roughly 40% of adults were obese, rising to 57% for black women, 46% for Hispanic women, and 38% for white women. For children ages 2 to 19, 17% are overweight and an additional 6% are obese. By time they are teenagers, 31% are overweight. For daughters aged 12–19, 25% of African American, 23% of Hispanic American, and 20% whites are so overweight they are obese. Despite the increased public awareness of the dangers of obesity, rates have continued to increase for males and females in all age groups.

Box 4.2 The obesity epidemic[22]

Children and Adolescents (Youth)

Estimated Percentage of US Youth with Obesity*, Ages 2–19, 2013–2014 NHANES Data

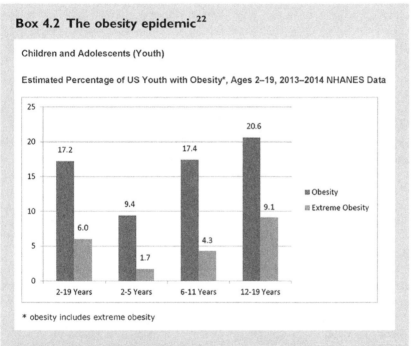

* obesity includes extreme obesity

Figure 4.2 Estimated percentage of US youth with obesity, broken out by age: 2–19 years, 2–5 years, 6–11 years, and 12–19 years
Source: Centers for Disease Control.

The more overweight the individual, the greater the risk of heart attacks, high blood pressure, strokes, cancer, kidney and liver failure, and damaged joints.[22] Obese people are also far more likely to develop diabetes which can eventually lead to the amputation of toes and legs and to blindness. Given the young age at which many children become overweight or obese, teenage rates of diabetes, high blood pressure, joint and muscle problems, and other weight-related problems have rapidly increased.

For daughters, being overweight carries additional risks. Their excessive fat increases their risk of being unable to get pregnant, having miscarriages, and having premature babies with multiple health problems. Their children are also two to three times more likely to become schizophrenic.[23] Overweight daughters also have higher rates of cancer as adults.[24] For example, they are 20–40% more likely to develop breast cancer and seven times more likely to develop endometrial cancer. Teenage girls who are overweight are also more likely to smoke cigarettes or vape e-cigarettes than girls of normal weight.[25]

Parents have control over many of the factors that contribute to their children being overweight, especially at a young age. Among these factors are: over-eating, exercising too little, eating junk food, not getting eight hours of sleep, and spending too much time on TV, computer, smartphones, and other such devices.[22] But the quality of the parent-child relationship and the parents' health behaviors also play a role. Given this, it is unfortunate that fathers only represent 17% of the parents who have been included in research studies on parenting and childhood obesity.[26] Since African American daughters are the most obese, it is troubling that only eight studies have considered the impact of black parents on their daughter's weight.[27]

Fathers influence their daughters' weight in multiple ways. Not surprisingly, teenage girls whose fathers encourage healthy eating are less overweight than girls whose fathers ignore this aspect of their daughters' health.[28] As would be expected, even as preschoolers, children whose fathers are physically inactive and fat are more overweight than children with active, normal weight fathers.[29]

More surprisingly, the quality of the father-daughter relationship and her weight are linked. In a sample of 3,768 teenagers, girls with high quality relationships with their father were less likely than those with low quality relationships to be overweight and to eat junk food.[30] Daughters who had warm, low conflict relationships with their fathers were also more likely to get eight hours of sleep, which is linked to better overall health and less obesity. In another study with 917 teenagers, daughters who had good relationships with their fathers were less overweight and had lower blood pressure and lower resting heart rates than daughters with hostile, high conflict relationships.[31] All of these factors predict cardiovascular health later in life. Moreover, the father-daughter relationship had a stronger impact than the mother-daughter relationship. This study is especially important because the parents reported the quality of their relationships with their children at various points from infancy until adolescence.

As explained in the last chapter, daughters are less depressed and have higher self-esteem when their fathers help them feel good about their

Figure 4.3
Source: shutterstock.

appearance. Still, daughters do not benefit when their fathers ignore the fact that they are gaining far too much weight, especially during childhood when eating and exercise habits lay the groundwork for lifelong health.

Physical Activity and Sports

One ways fathers can help their daughters maintain a healthy weight and improve their overall fitness is to encourage them to be physically active or to play sports. Not only does this benefit her physical health, it can benefit the father-daughter relationship.

Not surprisingly, fathers with traditional gender role beliefs are somewhat less supportive of their daughters playing sports, especially traditionally masculine sports. But the good news is that teenage girls (50%) are now almost as likely as boys (60%) to play on a sports team.[32] Young adult daughters and their fathers often say that their relationship became closer when they participated in an athletic activity together, for example playing golf or jogging.[33,34] Many teenage daughters feel closer to their fathers when he encourages or challenges her to participate in a sport, even if she is initially reluctant.[35,36] Fathers often build their daughter's confidence in her physical abilities by allowing or encouraging her to take certain calculated physical risks as a young child. For example, fathers were more likely than mothers to allow their three- and four-year-old daughters to play on a five foot high catwalk or walk across a three foot high beam.[37]

Box 4.3 Famous female athletes and their fathers

Serena Williams, International Tennis Champion[39]

Internationally famous tennis champion Serena Williams has had a close relationship with her father since early childhood. In an African American family with five daughters, Serena's dad Richard started her playing tennis at the age of five. He also coached and home schooled her and her award winning tennis star sister, Venus. At the age of 33, Serena was playing a match to become the first player in 27 years to sweep all four Grand Slams in the same season. But her father was unable to attend due to poor health. As Serena has said: "He's been the most important person in my career."

Chloe Kim, Olympic Gold Medalist, and Her Korean Immigrant Father[40]

At the 2018 Winter Olympics 17-year-old Chloe Kim, an Asian American whose parents emigrated from South Korea in 1982, achieved international fame by winning the Gold Medal in snowboarding. But her father, Jong Jin Kim, also won international applause by being widely heralded as a stellar father who had committed himself wholeheartedly to his daughter's athletic career. As an immigrant in Southern California, he worked minimum wage jobs until he saved enough money to attend college where he eventually earned a degree in engineering. Having introduced Chloe to snowboarding when she was only four, Jong Jin Kim eventually gave up his job as an engineer to help her pursue her Olympic dreams.

Lindsey Vonn, Gold Medal Olympic Skier[43]

Lindsey Vonn was pushed hard by her father, a former ski champion, who taught her to ski when she was three. As her coach, he wholeheartedly supported her athletic endeavors even after her parents divorced. At the age of 17 she raced in her first Olympics. But she and her father became estranged when at age 22 she married a fellow Olympic skier nine years her senior whom she had met when she was 17. Her husband became her coach and manager. Four years later when she and her husband divorced, she reached out to her father and they eventually reconciled.

Nowadays most Americans expect fathers to encourage their daughters to be physically active or to play a sport.[34,38] Not surprisingly then, internationally famous female athletes often attribute their success largely to their fathers, as the stories in Box 4.3 illustrate.[39,40] Especially for these elite athletes, and as daughters have become more involved in sports, their injuries have increased.[41] For example, 13% of daughters incur at least one concussion as a result of a sports injury.[32] This means fathers are having to be more attentive and play a more active role in helping their daughters reduce their risks of injury.[41] Then too, fathers must be more vigilant when their daughters are participating in sports, such as gymnastics or long distance running, where eating disorders are far more prevalent.[42]

There is, however, a downside to a father being overly involved in his daughter's athletic endeavors—especially if he is her coach or if she becomes a collegiate or professional athlete. Daughters whose fathers are their coaches often feel that this stresses their relationship. While most female athletes appreciate their father's interest and support, they resent his being too critical and overly involved. For example, female college athletes, when the father was overly controlling and expected her to conform to his beliefs and ideas about her athletic performance, felt less confident in setting her own goals and meeting them.[44] By expecting her to conform to his beliefs and to have a strong allegiance to him, the father was undermining her autonomy and confidence. Some fathers also put far too much pressure on their athletic daughters. As one female athlete put it: "He just wanted everything to be perfect, me to be perfect" (p. 153).[45] Most female athletes wish their fathers were less focused on her athletic performance and more focused on other areas of her life. Sadly, some daughters feel that they would have no relationship at all with their father if they were not athletes.[45,46,47]

But even when her father is not overly involved in her athletic life, female athletes and their fathers face situations that are challenging and sometimes damaging to their relationship. A review of the literature on athletes' relationships with their parents identifies five areas of conflict, along with specific recommendations for fathers.[48] First, fathers should encourage their young children to participate in several types of sports instead of focusing on excelling in only one sport. Second, fathers must keep their focus and the daughter's focus on the pleasure of playing more than on winning. Third, he must control his emotions and teach his daughter to control hers when the competition is fierce or when she or her team are losing. Fourth, he should not give her specific advice on how to improve her performance. Coaching should be the job of the coach, not the father. Fifth, certain sports put a far greater financial strain on parents and demand far more of the parents' time than others, especially if their daughter is competing at an elite level. These demands can strain the parents' marriage, increase sibling rivalry, and intensify father-daughter conflicts. Sixth, if his daughter becomes an elite athlete whose coach inevitably becomes a central figure in her life, her father must learn to step back and take second place. Conflict or jealousy between fathers and coaches further strains the father-daughter relationship.

Being a female athlete can either strengthen or weaken father-daughter relationships. Wise fathers promote their daughters' physical health by encouraging them to be physically active or to become athletes. Unwise fathers fail to recognize the hazards that can damage their relationship with their athletic daughter.

Eating Disorders: Anorexia and Bulimia

In contrast to the large numbers of daughters who endanger their health by being overweight or obese, roughly 3% of daughters are in danger because they are grossly underweight due to having an eating disorder.[49]**Anorexia nervosa** is a psychological disorder afflicting a small percentage of clinically depressed daughters. If she develops an eating disorder, the depressed daughter limits her food intake and often begins to exercise excessively until she becomes dangerously thin. Anorexia sometimes occurs along with **bulimia**. After going for days of eating little to nothing, the bulimic daughter binges on large amounts of food, gorging on high calorie or sweet foods. After binging, she quickly tries to eliminate the food from her body before any calories can be absorbed. After binging, she purges the food from her body either by forcing herself to vomit or by taking laxatives.

Although males can develop eating disorders, nearly 90% of anorexics are adolescent or young adult females.[48] Anorexia is largely a disorder confined to non-Hispanic white daughters from middle and upper income families. The average age of onset is fifteen and the condition usually runs its course in eighteen months. Even though fewer than 80 females die from anorexia each year in the U.S., the disorder can pose a life-threatening situation and create tremendous emotional upheaval for their families. The physical damage includes ceasing or never starting to menstruate, loss of muscle, weakened bones, swollen joints, distended abdomen, and swollen cheeks due to enlarged salivary glands from vomiting.

While older theories blamed eating disorders largely on society's pressures for women to be excessively thin, more current research shows that genetic factors and family dynamics play a much larger role—especially the father-daughter relationship.[48–50] A daughter is more likely to develop an eating disorder if her father continually criticizes her weight or seems extremely uncomfortable with her becoming physically and sexually mature. She is also more at risk if she feels ignored, rejected, or unloved by her father. Because many anorexics' fathers are well educated and financially successful, their daughters often assume they have to be perfect in all aspects of their lives in order to live up to their father's expectations. In her obsessive quest for perfection, she pressures herself to be an outstanding student, a stellar athlete, and a grand social success. In some cases, it is true that her father is pressuring her to be perfect. But in other cases, the daughter's clinical depression skews her beliefs about her father. The pressure for perfection is coming from within herself, not from her father.

In regard to family dynamics, daughters are more likely to become clinically depressed and consequently at higher risk of developing eating disorders if their parents are unhappily married or divorced.[50] For example, female undergraduates whose mothers discussed the parents' marital problems with the daughter had more eating disorders than those whose mothers did not disclose the parents' problems.[51] When unhappily married parents are in high conflict, daughters are also more likely to have eating disorders.[52] In these high conflict families, however, if the daughter has a warm relationship with her father, she is less likely to become depressed or anorexic. Moreover, the link between eating disorders and the quality of the parent-child relationship was twice as strong for fathers as for mothers.

The families where daughters have eating disorders also have communication problems.[50] They avoid and discourage open, honest, direct communication. Rather than discussing personal or family problems, the family cloaks itself in secrecy, deception, and denial. Everyone is under pressure to maintain a public image of the ideal family, which requires hiding, denying, or lying about the conflicts and unpleasant realities. Overly stressed, anxious, depressed, and unable to discuss her feelings, a daughter is more likely to stop eating as a way to have control over some aspect of her "out of control" family life.

This does not mean, however, that a poor father-daughter relationship, an unhappy marriage, a divorce, or dysfunctional family communication cause eating disorders. Clearly this is not the case since so few daughters develop eating disorders, while so many grow up in families with these kinds of problems. These factors may each contribute to eating disorders— especially if many of them exist simultaneously. Still, catalysts are not causes. It is also a mistake to assume that society's pressure for women to be thin causes eating disorders. Almost all daughters are exposed to the same media messages about being thin, yet only 1–3% become anorexic.

In fact clinical depression and the eating disorders that sometimes ensue have a strong genetic component.[53] That is, some daughters are born with a genetic predisposition to become clinically depressed or anorexic. Both disorders run in families. For example, the parents of anorexics are much more likely than other parents to be clinically depressed and to have anxiety or obsessive compulsive disorders.[54] Estimates are that a daughter has a 55% to 85% chance of becoming clinically depressed and developing an eating disorder if any female in her immediate extended family has ever had an eating disorder.

There are several messages for fathers in this research. First, a father should find out if any women in the immediate or extended family have ever had an eating disorder or been clinically depressed. If so, he should be on alert as his daughter approaches adolescence that she is entering the time in her life when she will be at highest risk for becoming clinically depressed or anorexic. With this awareness, the father can reach out to his daughter if he notices signs of depression or disordered eating.

Overview of Teenage and Young Adult Substance Use

While it is highly unlikely that an eating disorder will endanger a daughter's health, it is likely that drinking or using drugs during her teenage or young adult years will pose a threat.[32] Fathers should be alert to the fact that almost half of the young people who die between the ages of 10 and 24 are killed in motor vehicle (22%) or other preventable accidents (20%). These preventable deaths generally involve drinking or using drugs. For example, 22% of Hispanic American teenage daughters have ridden in a car in the last month with a driver who was drinking.

Fathers should also take a more active role in talking to their daughters about two other risk factors related to preventable deaths: texting and emailing while driving and not getting enough sleep at night.[32] Almost half (46%) of non-Hispanic white teenage girls text or email while driving, compared to only 26% of black girls. Only 25% of teenagers get at least eight hours of sleep on school nights, which helps account for teenage injuries or fatalities caused by a teenage driver falling asleep at the wheel.

As Box 4.4 illustrates, teenagers and young adults are much more likely to drink than to smoke, vape, or use drugs.[55] By twelfth grade, 63% of teenagers have had a drink, 45% have been drunk, and 45% have tried marijuana. In contrast, only 13% either smoke or vape nicotine and even fewer have ever used cocaine (4%), ecstasy (5%), LSD (5%), or opioids (2%).

Box 4.4 Health risks for adolescent daughters[32]

75% sleep less than 8 hours on school nights
60% have had a drink before age 18
45% text or email while driving
40% have sex before age 18
31% are overweight or obese
31% have engaged in binge drinking
25% use marijuana
15% get no physical exercise
13% vape e-cigarettes
11% have been raped on a date
9% smoke regular cigarettes
1%-3% have an eating disorder

As for gender and race, girls are as likely as boys to smoke, vape, drink, and use marijuana and there are very few differences among racial groups.[55] Girls, however, are more likely than boys to engage in binge drinking—a fact that should alarm fathers since binge drinking increases her health risks from having unsafe or unwanted sex. Teenagers from rural areas or smaller cites are just as likely as teenagers from large cities to smoke, drink, or use drugs. And teenagers with highly educated, financially well-off parents are just as likely to drink or use recreational drugs as less well-off teenagers. Students who are college bound, however, are less likely to smoke than those who do not plan to attend college.

Teenage and Young Adult Drinking

Box 4.5 Alcohol Use Disorder: Do you or someone you know have a drinking problem?[57]

The criteria for being diagnosed with AUD are described in the Diagnostic and Statistical Manual of Mental Disorders as meeting any two of these 11 criteria during the past 12 months:

- Had times when you drank more or longer that you intended?
- More than once wanted to cut down or stop but couldn't?
- Spent a lot of time drinking or being sick afterwards?
- Experienced a craving, a strong need, or urge to drink?
- Found that drinking often interfered with taking care of your home or family, or caused job or school problems?
- Continued to drink even though it was causing trouble with your family or friends?
- Given up or cut back on activities that were interesting or pleasurable in order to drink?
- More than once gotten into situations while drinking that increased your chances of getting hurt (having unsafe sex, driving, using machinery, walking in a dangerous area)?
- Continued to drink even though it was making you feel depressed or anxious or adding to another health problem?
- Had to drink much more than you once did to get the effect you want?
- When the effects of alcohol were wearing off, had withdrawal symptoms such as trouble sleeping, shakiness, irritability, anxiety, depression, restlessness, nausea, or sweating?

Since alcohol is the substance used most often by young people, we begin by discussing female teenage and young adult drinking. To put this in context, the vast majority of parents drink.[56] Nearly 70% of Americans have had a drink in the last year and 56% in the last month. Nearly 25% either drink heavily or engage in the most dangerous form of drinking—**binge drinking**. Binge drinkers consume dangerously large amounts of alcohol over the course of a few hours. Most binge drinkers are young people who do not drink on a daily basis because, being under age, they cannot easily obtain it and because they are either living with their parents or on a college campus where drinking is not allowed.

Heavy drinking that is severe, chronic, and frequent is referred to as alcoholism or as an **alcohol use disorder.** [57] Approximately 15.1 million American adults have an alcohol disorder—9.8 million men (8.4% of all men) and 5.3 million women (4.2% of women) and 623,000 adolescents aged 12–17.[55] While not all heavy drinkers are physically addicted to alcohol, one out of every four people is born with a genetic predisposition to become addicted.[58] Using the checklist in Box 4.5, you can assess whether you or someone you know is abusing alcohol to the extent that it is considered an alcohol use disorder.

The link between a father's and daughter's drug or alcohol use is not clear. In some studies there is a link. For example, teenagers whose fathers abuse alcohol or marijuana are more likely to drink and use marijuana before the age of 15.[59] In other studies, however, there is no connection. For instance, American Indian children with an alcoholic parent were not more likely to have drinking problems between the ages of 11 and 20.[60] But they were more likely to drink if they disliked school or came from high conflict families. In yet another sample, teenagers were more likely to drink or use drugs if their father drank or used drugs when he was a teenager, but not if he only drank or used drugs as an adult.[61]

The causes of teenage drinking and alcohol addiction are complex and are beyond the scope of this chapter. But what is clear is that teenagers and young adults are far less likely than older adults to drink safely and responsibly.[55] During their teenage and young adult years, young people are the most likely to binge drink, drink heavily, and drive or engage in dangerous recreational activities (i.e. jumping into pools, boating, skiing) while drinking or drunk. Some fathers may not be aware that college students are more likely to drink (58%) than other young adults their age (48%). Nearly 20% of college students meet the criteria for having an alcohol use disorder. For those young people who have a genetic predisposition to become addicted to alcohol, their "harmless", occasional recreational drinking may develop into a lifelong alcohol addiction. In that regard, if alcoholism runs in the family, fathers should make even greater efforts to educate their daughters about the risks of drinking. The criteria listed in Box 4.5 can help fathers and daughters assess the severity of either of their drinking habits.

It is especially important that fathers be aware that their teenage and young adult daughters are just as likely as their sons to use and abuse alcohol—and are more likely than sons to incur certain types of physical harm when drinking.[62] Adult men are more likely than adult women to drink and to become addicted to alcohol. The reverse is true, however, between the ages of 12 and 20. By time they graduate from high school, 63% of girls versus 58% of boys have had a drink and girls are more likely to binge drink. Hispanic girls have higher rates (16%) of binge drinking than males or females in any other racial group.[32] Daughters also run the additional health risk of being more likely to get pregnant and to be victims of violence or sexual assault when drinking.

Fortunately, fathers can reduce the chances of their daughter using or abusing alcohol by maintaining a strong father-daughter bond. In a large, national, longitudinal study, girls who had close relationships with their father and communicated well with him were less likely to drink and less likely to regret their sexual behavior in situations where they had been drinking.[63] Likewise, sons and daughters in their 30s who had supportive relationships with their fathers drank less than those with distant or troubled relationships.[64] Similarly, in a study that included 1,800 college students from nine universities, daughters who felt loved and accepted by their fathers were less likely to engage in risky health behaviors: binge drinking, driving while drunk, having sex while drinking (especially with someone they had just met), having unprotected sex, and using drugs. Even if the parents were divorced, the close relationships with their fathers benefitted the students. Moreover, the students' risky behaviors were more closely linked to the quality of their relationships with their fathers than with their mothers.

Smoking and Vaping

In contrast to drinking, teenage daughters are less likely to smoke than they were in previous decades. Nevertheless, 26% of teenage males and 23% of females use e-cigarettes (vaping), 12% of males and 10% of females smoke regular cigarettes, and 8% of males and 7% of females vape and smoke.[25] Since 2006, for males and for females, smoking decreased for white teenagers but increased for black and Hispanic teenagers.[65] Surprisingly, young people are less likely to start smoking as teenagers (2%) than as young adults (6%) —which is a reversal of previous trends.[65] Although smoking has declined, vaping has increased. More than three million students in middle and high school have vaped in the past month.[66] In the U.S. e-cigarettes are a 2.5 billion dollar business that spends $125 million a year in advertising— most of which is directed at the young because most people begin using nicotine as teenagers.[66]

It should also be troubling to fathers that many teenagers mistakenly believe that e-cigarettes have no negative impact on their health. Vaping increases teenage asthma.[67] Long term vaping is linked to higher rates of anxiety and mood disorders and less impulse control. Because young females are now almost as likely as males to smoke and vape, they are as likely to die from lung cancer, strokes, heart disease, and chronic obstructive pulmonary disease.[62] Daughters who smoke or vape while pregnant also have more premature births and higher rates of infant sudden death syndrome.[66]

People who vape or smoke as teenagers are also exposing their brain to nicotine at a time when it is still undergoing significant development. So during adolescence nicotine use is likely to interfere with the growth of brain circuits that control attention, learning, impulse control, and lifelong susceptibility to addiction.[66] Moreover, nicotine is a highly addictive substance—at least as addictive, if not more, than alcohol or cocaine.[59]

Marijuana

Like drinking, using marijuana (cannabis) poses somewhat greater health risks for daughters than for sons.[68] By the age of 21, 56% of males and 52% of females have tried marijuana, with peak use at 16 and 18. More than 11 million young adults aged 18 to 25 have used it in the past year. Although teenagers are less likely to use it than in the past, they are more likely to believe that heavy use has no negative impact on their health. Although marijuana does not lead to using harder drugs, those who use it regularly as teenagers are four to seven times more likely to become addicted than those who wait until they are past the age of 18. Smoking marijuana regularly also damages the lungs and can lead to regular cycles of severe nausea, vomiting, and dehydration that sometimes require emergency medical care. The results are mixed about the link between marijuana and teenage depression, anxiety, or suicidal thoughts.

For daughters, using marijuana leads to more unwanted pregnancies and STDs because they are more likely to have unprotected sex. Daughters aged 18–27 who start using marijuana as young adolescents are more likely to have unsafe sex than daughters who wait until they are older to try marijuana or who never use it.[69] And if the daughter uses marijuana while pregnant, the baby is more likely to be born at low birth weight and to have more problems with attention, memory, and problem solving as a young child.[70]

The father's influence over his daughter's marijuana use is unclear. For example, young adolescent daughters were more likely to have sex, drink, and use marijuana if their father was currently a heavy marijuana user.[71] Yet in another study, the father's present marijuana use was not linked to his teenage daughter's drug use.[56] On the other hand, the quality of their relationship does appear to have an impact on her drug use. As previously mentioned, in a large study with almost 1,800 students from nine universities, daughters who had good relationships with their fathers were the least likely to use any type of illicit drug.[72]

Opioids

In contrast to marijuana, very few (5%) daughters use opioids as teenagers. Still, fathers need to be mindful that opioid use has reached epidemic proportions for people in their 20s—and that daughters are more likely than sons to become addicted to this class of drugs.[71] **Opioids** are a class of highly addictive drugs that include cocaine, codeine, hydrocodone, heroin, oxycodone, and fentanyl. Originally developed as prescription drugs to control severe pain, opioids are now widely used recreationally without a doctor's prescription. Nearly 2.5 million American adults are addicted to opioids, resulting in 42,249 deaths a year.

Several facts about opioids should alarm fathers with daughters.[73] Compared to males, females are more likely to become addicted and to start using at an earlier age.[62] The vast majority of opioid addicts (68%) who are also clinically depressed or have an anxiety or other mood disorder are female.[74] Regardless of gender, the least educated people are the most likely to use opioids. Of those who use opioids, only 10% have graduate degrees versus 65% who never attended college. Almost all (80%) users are non-Hispanic whites. West Virginia has the highest nationwide rates of opioid use and deaths, five times higher than the lowest rates in Nebraska.[75] From 1994 to 2007, opioid prescriptions from doctors doubled for teenagers and young adults.[73] It is estimated that 80% of all opioid prescriptions are written by only 20% of the doctors.[76] So during his daughter's teenage years, the father should mainly focus on her drinking and using marijuana. But once she enters her 20's, he should become increasingly concerned about the possibility of her using opioids.

Sexual Behavior and Physical Health

A teenage and young adult daughter's sexual behavior also poses significant health risks—some of which have lifelong and irrevocable consequences. These aspects of her health are closely linked to the quality of the father-daughter relationship and to father absence. Before we explore this research, take the quiz in Box 4.6 and tally your score. The perfect score should be "15" because all of these statements are true.

The good news for fathers and daughters is that teenage and young adult sexual behavior poses fewer health risks than in the past.[77,78] By time they graduate from high school, 40% of daughters have had sex. This the lowest rate since 1991, with the biggest declines for black teenagers. Fortunately, 90% of sexually active teenagers use contraceptives, most often condoms which help prevent pregnancy as well as STDs. As a result, teenage pregnancy and abortion rates are lower than they have been in 80 years. Between 2007 and 2013 alone, teen pregnancies dropped by 47% for Hispanic, 33% for white, and 38% for black daughters. If they become pregnant, 30% of teenagers terminate the pregnancy. Black daughters are four times more likely than non-Hispanic white daughters and 2.5 times more likely than Hispanic daughters to end these unwanted pregnancies.

Box 4.6 Adolescent daughters: Sexual behavior and health risks

How many of these statements do you believe are true?

____1. Nearly half of all teenagers have had sex by time they are 19.

____2. At age 15 only 13% of teens have had sex.

____3. Teenagers are waiting longer to have sex than they did in the past.

____4. More than 75% first had sex with a steady boyfriend, or fiancé.

____5. Only 10% of girls who have sex before age 20 were coerced into it against their will.

____6. About 10% of girls have engaged in oral sex but not in sexual intercourse.

____7. Almost 80% of teenagers use contraceptives the first time they had sex.

____8. Although 15–24-year-olds are only one-fourth of sexually active people, they account for nearly half of new STDs each year.

____9. There is a vaccine to prevent HPV, which if untreated can lead to cervical cancer.

____10. Nearly a third of all teen pregnancies end in abortion.

____11. Pregnancy among black teenagers decreased 40% between 1990 and 2000.

____12. Almost 85% of teen pregnancies are accidental.

____13. Most teenagers who get pregnant accidentally are 18 to 19 years old.

____14. Teen pregnancies are much higher in the U.S. than in other developed countries.

____15. Almost 60% of teenagers who have abortions do so with their parent's knowledge.

____ Number you marked true

Clearly, though, fathers need to do more to help their daughters reduce the health risks of being sexually active, as evidenced by the sobering statistics in Box 4.4.[77,78] For women of all ages, almost half (45%) of the 66.1 million pregnancies each year are accidental. The highest rates, though, are for 15 to 19 year-old girls. African and Hispanic American daughters between the ages of 18 and 24 are the most likely to become mothers. The vast majority of these young mothers are unmarried, poor, and poorly educated. Compared to older, more educated women, these young mothers also have more health problems during pregnancy. Because they often do not realize or do not admit that they are pregnant in the first trimester, most do not receive adequate prenatal health care. Many receive no care at all. Yet these first 12 weeks are the time of greatest and most long lasting damage to the fetus, especially if the mother is overweight, smokes, drinks, or uses drugs. These young women are also the most likely to develop diabetes and dangerously high blood pressure during their pregnancy, which can lead to a life-threatening complication known as pre-eclampsia.

Despite the increase in condom use, sexually active daughters still face multiple health risks from STDs. In fact, the U.S. has the highest rates of STDs in the industrialized world.[79] People aged 13–24 account for half of the 20 million new cases of STDs every year, even though they represent only 25% of sexually active Americans. And even though the human immunodeficiency virus (HIV) that causes AIDS decreased by 25% between 2010 and 2015, it is estimated that 60,300 young people between 13 and 24 carry the virus—half of whom do not know they are infected.[80]

The most common STDs are **chlamydia** and the **human papilloma virus (HPV)** which have more negative effects on daughters than on sons.[79] Although curable, if untreated, chlamydia can lead to pelvic inflammatory disease which makes it more difficult for women to get pregnant. Most (65%) cases of chlamydia are detected in 14 to 19 year-old girls. In contrast, **HPV (genital herpes)** is not curable and infects nearly 1 in 8 Americans—90% of whom do not know they are carrying this virus. For daughters, HPV can have serious long-term consequences because it is the single most important risk factor for developing cervical cancer. Once a daughter contracts the virus, there is no cure. Fortunately, there is now a vaccine to protect daughters against HPV. Within six years of its release, HPV decreased by 64% for teenagers. The only way to fully protect daughters from this virus is to administer the vaccine *before* they become sexually active. Because African American women and Latinas have the highest rates of cervical cancer, it is especially troubling that they are less likely than white women to be vaccinated against HPV.[81]

As most fathers are no doubt aware, even if their daughters have not yet had sex, they are more at risk of being physically harmed once they start dating.[82,83] Teen dating violence is broadly defined as any form of physical aggression that one partner inflicts on the other. Dating aggression can range from hitting, shoving, or slapping to being threatened or physically injured by someone with a lethal weapon. To be clear, being a victim of dating violence and aggression does not mean the person has been raped. It means they have been forced or coerced physically against their will into engaging in some kind of sexual behavior (kissing, fondling, oral sex, or intercourse).

Approximately 23% of females and 13% of males say they have experienced some kind of dating aggression by time they are 18.[80,81] For women of all ages, it is estimated that 18% have been raped, with 11% having been raped before the age of 18. Most at risk are daughters who start having sex at an early age, have multiple sexual partners, drink or use drugs, come from violent families, or grow up in fatherless homes. For example, teenagers who were the most likely to be involved in dating violence had parents who were alcoholic and did not have warm relationships with their children.[84] These risk factors may help explain why only 5% of women who are in college have been raped and why girls who are raped as teenagers are three times more likely than other females to be raped again as adults. Importantly, these risk factors are closely related to father absence and to the quality of the father-daughter relationship.

Daughters from father absent homes have the highest rates of teen pregnancy and STDs. In fact, the younger the daughter is when she is separated from her father, the more likely she is to have sex and become pregnant as a teenager.[85,86] In an especially unique study, researchers compared the sexual behavior of older and younger sisters in the same family for divorced and for intact families. In the divorced families, the younger sister had sex at a younger age than the older sister. In the intact families, however, younger sisters were not more likely than older sisters to have sex as young teenagers. Since the older sisters in the divorced families had lived with their father for a longer time than their younger sisters, it appears that more fathering time or a closer father-daughter bond were the probable causes of the older sister's safer sexual decisions.[87]

It is not just the father's physical presence, however, that matters. It is also the quality of his relationship with his daughter. In non-college samples, Latina women who had close relationships with their fathers waited longer to first have sex as teenagers and waited longer to have children.[88] In 3,300 intact families, teenage daughters whose fathers knew them well were the least likely to have had sex.[89] And in a national sample of 3,600 teenagers, daughters who felt emotionally connected to their fathers waited longer to first have sex and had sex less often.[90] Similarly, adult daughters who had grown up in very low income families waited longer to have sex and to become mothers if their fathers had been actively involved in their lives.[91]

Fathers also have an impact on their daughters' sexual decisions in college. In samples from five different colleges, daughters who felt their fathers were emotionally engaged in their lives were more likely to have boyfriends who used condoms, had sex with fewer men, and disapproved more of casual sex outside of a committed relationship.[92] In nine other university samples, daughters who felt accepted by their fathers were less likely to have unprotected sex, to have sex with someone that they had just met, or to have sex while drinking or using drugs.[72] Undergraduate women who had close relationships with their fathers were also less likely to be coerced into having sex just to please their boyfriend.[93] This is important because for 3,793 women, voluntarily having sex as a teenager was not linked to a higher divorce rate. But being coerced or forced into having sex as a teenager was linked to a higher divorce rate. The father's impact might be related to the fact that in college, compared to sons, daughters are more concerned about not disappointing their fathers by making foolish sexual decisions.[94]

Given his impact, it is unfortunate that mothers are more likely than fathers are to talk to their daughters about sex and dating. For example,

African American teenage daughters whose fathers had talked to them about sex engaged in less risky sexual behavior.[95] And in a meta-analysis of 52 studies, teenagers practice safer sex when either their fathers or their mothers have talked with them about sex.[96]

Conclusion

It is abundantly clear that fathers have an impact on their daughter's health and physical well-being from infancy onward. By caring for premature babies, helping babies sleep through the night, and influencing young children's physiological reactions to stress, fathers set the stage for their daughters' future health. As his daughter ages, the father also has an impact on her weight, her physical fitness and involvement in sports, and unhealthy eating or excessive exercise habits that might lead to eating disorders. During her teenage and young adult years, the quality of their relationship or his absence are linked to her drinking, smoking, vaping, using drugs, and risky sexual behavior that can lead to STDs, pregnancy, dating aggression, or date rape.

Hopefully fathers will strive to have an even more positive impact on their daughters' health by spending more time talking about health and safety issues and by participating with them in healthier eating and exercise habits. By not assuming that their daughter's health is primarily the mother's responsibility—especially issues related to her sexual health and safety—fathers can promote stronger father-daughter relationships as well as healthier daughters.

Review Questions

1 How does the father affect his infant or toddler daughter's physical health in respect to premature baby care, healthy sleep patterns, weight, and physical activity?
2 What is the relationship between cortisol, father-daughter relationships, and the daughter's lifelong reaction to stress?
3 What are the advantages and disadvantages of having a father who is heavily involved in his daughter's sports activities?
4 What unique problems or challenges affect female athletes' relationships with their fathers and how might each be resolved or minimized?
5 How serious a risk is obesity in terms of specific health problems and which daughters are the most likely to be overweight?
6 In what specific ways is the daughter's health affected from infancy through adolescence when she does not get enough sleep?
7 What are telomeres and how are they related to father-daughter relationships?
8 Citing specific percentages, how great a risk do each of these pose to the daughter's health relative to one another and at what ages or for

what groups of daughters are these risks the greatest: obesity, smoking, vaping, drinking, eating disorders, using drugs (compare each type of drug), texting and emailing while driving, sexually transmitted diseases.

9   What specific health risks do daughters face when they start dating and which daughters are most likely to face these risks?

10 What is kangaroo care and specifically how do parents and children benefit from it?

11 In terms of how serious an impact they can have on daughters and the numbers of daughters affected, what five health problems should most concern fathers?

12 How do daughters and sons differ in regard to drinking, drug use, smoking, opioid use, and obesity?

13 What factors contribute to eating disorders and which daughters are most likely to be develop these disorders?

14 How prevalent are each of these problems for teenage daughters: dating violence, date rape, teenage pregnancy and abortion, unprotected sex, STDs.

Questions for Discussion and Debate

1   How and when should fathers have conversations with their daughters about: safe sex, drug use, smoking, obesity, and dating violence?

2   If a daughter suspects that his daughter has an eating disorder, what should he do?

3   If the father is overweight, or a smoker or heavy drinker, how can he discuss these issues with his daughter in regard to her own health?

4   If an extremely conservative father strongly disapproves of teenagers having sex, but discovers that his daughter is sexually active, what should he do?

5   If a daughter has been raped or is being forced into engaging in sexual activities against her will, how can she discuss this with her father—or should she?

6   Without making his daughter feel bad about herself, how can a father tell her that she is gaining far too much weight and jeopardizing her health?

7   What are some of the most troubling situations you have seen regarding the impact of the father-daughter relationship on the daughter's health?

8   What research in this chapter was most surprising or most disturbing to you?

9   How has your father influenced the various aspects of your physical health discussed in this chapter?

10 If you were a father, what would you do if you strongly suspected that your teenage daughter was engaged in these unhealthy or risky

activities: smoking, vaping, using marijuana or any other drug, having unprotected sex, texting or emailing while driving, binging on food and then purging?

References

1 Feldman R, Rosenthal Z, Eidelman A. Maternal preterm skin to skin contact enhances child physiological organization and cognitive control across first ten years of life. *Journal of Biological Psychiatry* 2014; 75: 56–64.

2 Shorey S, Hong-Gu H, Morelius E. Skin to skin contact by fathers and the impact on infant and paternal outcomes: An integrative review. *Midwifery* 2016; 40: 207–217.

3 Varela N, *et al*. Cortisol and blood pressure levels decrease in fathers during the first hour of skin to skin contact with their premature babies. *Acta Paediatrica* 2018; 107: 628–632.

4 Cummings M, Davies P. *Marital conflict and children*. New York: Guilford Press; 2010.

5 Paulson J, Bazemore S. Prenatal and postpartum depression in fathers. *Journal of the American Medical Association* 2010; 19: 54–63.

6 McDaniel B, Teti D. Coparenting quality during the first three months after birth: The role of infant sleep quality. *Journal of Family Psychology* 2018; 26: 886–895.

7 Licis A. Sleep disorders assessment and treatment in preschool aged children. *Child and Adolescent Psychiatric Clinics of North America* 2017; 26: 587–594.

8 Hoyniak C. Less efficient neural processing related to irregular sleep and less sustained attention in toddlers. *Developmental Neuropsychology* 2015; 40: 155–166.

9 Miller M. Sleep duration and incidence of obesity in infants, children and adolescents: a systematic review and meta-analysis of prospective studies. *Sleep* 2018; 41: 244–253.

10 Ayalon M. The role of the father in child sleep disturbance. *Infant Mental Health Journal* 2015; 36: 114–127.

11 Bordeleau S, Bernier A, Carrier J. Children's sleep patterns. *Journal of Family Psychology* 2012; 26: 254–262.

12 Hollanders J, Van Der Voorn B, Rotteveel J, Finken M. Is HPA axis reactivity in chlidhood gender specific? A systematic review. *Biology of Sex Differences* 2017; 11: 1–11.

13 Paquette D, Bigras M. The risky situation. In: Newland L, Freeman H, Coyl D, editors. *Emerging topics in father attachment*. New York: Routledge; 2011: 32–50.

14 Mills-Koonce R, *et al*. Father contributions to cortisol responses in infancy and toddlerhood. *Developmental Psychology* 2011; 30: 388–395.

15 Flinn M. Evolution and ontogeny of stress response to social challenges in the human child. *Developmental Review* 2006; 26: 138–174.

16 Flinn M, Muehlenbein M, Ponzi D. Evolution of neuroendocrine mechanisms linking attachment and life history in middle childhood. *Behavioral and Brain Sciences* 2009; 32: 27–28.

17 Luecken L, Kraft A, Hagan M. Negative relationships in the family predict attenuated cortisol in emerging adults. *Hormones and behavior* 2009; 55: 412–417.

18 Mathur M, *et al*. Perceived stress and telomere length: A meta-analysis. *Brain, Behavior and Immunity* 2016; 54: 158–169.

19 Johnson V, Gans S. Parent cortisol and family relatedness predict anxious behavior in emerging adults. *Journal of Family Psychology* 2018; 30: 802–811.

20 Byrd J, Auer B, Grander D, Massey A. The father-daughter dance: relationship quality and daughters' stress response. *Journal of Family Psychology* 2012; 26: 87–94.

21 Fabricius W, Luecken L. Postdivorce living arrangements, parent conflict and long term correlates for children of divorce. *Journal of Family Psychology* 2007; 21: 195–205.

22 Hales C, *et al*. *Prevalence of obesity among adults and youth: 2015–2016*. Atlanta, GA: Centers for Disease Control & Prevention, report # 288; 2017.

23 Khandaker G, Dibbin C, Jones P. Does maternal body mass index during pregnancy influence risk of schizophrenia in the adult offspring? *Obesity Research* 2012; 13: 518–527.

24 N.C.I. *Obesity and cancer*. New York: National Cancer Institute; 2018.

25 Cho B, *et al*. Adolescent weight and electronic vapor use. *American Journal of Preventive Medicine* 2018; 55: 541–550.

26 Davison K. Fathers' representation in observational studies on parenting and childhood obesity: A systematic review. *American Journal of Public Health* 2016; 106: 14–21.

27 Reed M, Wilbur J, Schoeny M. Parent and African American daughter obesity prevention interventions: A review. *Journal of Health Care for the Poor and Underserved* 2015; 26: 737–760.

28 Berge J, *et al*. Parenting characteristics in the home and adolescent overweight. *Epidemiology* 2010; 18: 818–825.

29 Vollmer R, *et al*. Investigating the relationships of body mass index and physical activity level between fathers and their preschool aged children. *Journal of the Academy of Nutrition and Dietetics* 2015; 115: 919–926.

30 Haines J, *et al*. Family functioning and quality of parent-adolescent relationship: Associations with adolescent weight related behaviors and weight status. *International Journal of Behavioral Nutrition and Physical Activity* 2016; 13: 1–12.

31 Shongzhengi N, *et al*. Impact of childhood parent-children relationships on cardiovascular risks in adolescence. *Preventive Medicine* 2018; 108: 53–59.

32 Kann L, *et al*. *Youth risk behavior surveillance: 2017*. Atlanta, GA: Centers for Disease Control & Prevention; 2018.

33 Barrett E, Morman M. Turning points of closeness in the father daughter relationship. *Human Communication* 2012; 15: 241–259.

34 Lobo R. *Fathers, daughters and sports*. New York: Ballantine Books; 2010.

35 Coakley J. The good father: Parental expectations and youth sports. *Journal of Leisure Studies* 2006; 25: 153–163.

36 Daily R. Parental challenge: A measure of how parents challenge their adolescents. *Journal of Social and Personal Relationships* 2012; 25: 643–669.

37 Hagan L, Kuebli J. Mothers' and fathers' and preschoolers' physical risk taking. *Journal of Applied Developmental Psychology* 2007; 28: 2–14.

38 Kay T. *Fathering through sports and leisure*. New York: Routledge; 2010.

39 Robson D. This one's for dad. *Sportsworld com* 2015; August 31, 1–2.

40 Boren C. Chloe Kim's father wins gold as the ultimate Olympic dad. *Washington Post* 2018, February 13.

41 Sokolove M. *Warrior girls: Protecting our daughters against the injury epidemic in women's sport*. New York: Simon & Schuster, 2008.

42 Thompson A, Petrie T, Anderson C. Eating disorders and weight control behaviors change over a collegiate sport season. *Journal of Science and Medicine in Sport* 2018; 20: 808–813.

43 Minutaglio R. Who is Lindsey Vonn? *Good Housekeeping*, January 12, 2018.

44 Erdner S, Wright C. The relationship between family communication patterns and the self-efficacy of student athletes. *Communication and Sport* 2018; 6: 368–389.

45 Prewitt T, Fisher L, Odenheimer E, Buchanan R. He just wanted everything to be perfect, me to be perfect: NCAA daughter athletes' experiences of the father-daughter relationship. *Sport Exercise and Performance Psychology* 2016; 5: 144–160.

46 Schmid O. "It's not just your dad, it's not just your coach." The dual relationship in female tennis players. *Sport Psychologist* 2015; 29: 224–236.

47 Willms N. Fathers and daughters: Relationships in sport. In: Kay T, editor. *Fathering through sport and leisure.* New York: Routledge; 2009. 122–145.

48 Holt N, Knight C. *Parenting in youth sport: From research to practice.* New York: Routledge; 2014.

49 Agras S. *Oxford handbook on eating disorders.* New York: Oxford University Press; 2010.

50 Lock J. *Treatment manual for anorexia nervosa.* New York: Guilford Press; 2015.

51 Ketisch T, *et al.* Boundary disturbances and eating disorder symptoms. *American Journal of Family Therapy* 2014; 42: 438–451.

52 Salafia E, Schaefer M, Haugen C. Connection between marital conflict and adolescent girls' disordered eating: Parent-adolescent relationship quality as a mediator. *Journal of Child and Family Studies* 2014; 23: 1128–1138.

53 Zucker N. Anorexia nervosa and autism spectrum disorders. *Psychological Bulletin* 2007; 133: 43–49.

54 Ravi S, Forsberg S, Fitzpatrick K. Parental psychopathology and adolescents with anorexia nervosa. *Eating Disorders* 2009; 17(63): 71–83.

55 Johnston L, *et al. Key findings on adolescent drug use.* Ann Arbor: Institute for Social Research, University of Michigan; 2017.

56 N.I.A.A. *Alcohol facts and statistics.* Washington, DC: National Institute on Alcohol Abuse and Alcoholism; 2018.

57 A.P.A. *Diagnostic and Statistical Manual of Mental Disorders.* Washington, DC: American Psychiatric Association; 2013.

58 Erickson C. *The science of addiction.* New York: W.W. Norton; 2018.

59 Henry K. Fathers' alcohol and cannabis use disorder and early onset of drug use by their children. *Journal of Studies on Alcohol and Drugs* 2017; 78: 458–462.

60 Stanley L. Predicting an alcohol use disorder in urban American Indian youths. *Journal of Child & Adolescent Substance Abuse* 2014; 23: 101–108.

61 Nadel E, Thornberry T. Intergenerational consequences of adolescent substance use. *Psychology of Addictive Behaviors* 2017; 31: 200–211.

62 N.I.H. *Substance use in women.* Washington, DC: National Institutes of Health; 2018.

63 Goncy E, Dulmen M. Fathers do make a difference: Parental involvement and adolescent alcohol use. *Fathering* 2010; 8: 93–108.

64 Reczek A. Relationships with parents and adult children's substance use. *Addictive Behaviors* 2017; 65: 198–206.

65 Thompson A, *et al.* Time trends in smoking onset by sex and race among adolescents and young adults: findings from the 2006–2013 national survey on drug use and health. *Nicotine & Tobacco Research* 2018; 20: 312–320.

66 C.D.C. *E-cigarette use among youth and youth adults: A report of the surgeon general.* Atlanta: Centers of Disease Control and Prevention; 2016.

67 Schweitzer R, *et al*. E cigarette use and asthma in a multiethnic sample of adolescents. *Preventive Medicine* 2017; 105: 226–231.

68 Chen X, *et al*. Current patterns of marijuana use by age among U.S. adolescents and emerging adults. *American Journal of Drug and Alcohol Abuse* 2018; 43: 261–270.

69 Agrawal A. Adolescent cannabis use and repeated voluntary unprotected sex in women. *Addiction* 2016; 111: 2012–2020.

70 N.I.H. *Drug facts: Marijuana.* Washington, DC: National Institutes of Health: Institute on Drug Abuse; 2018.

71 Cho, B. Associations of father's lifetime cannabis use disorder with child's cannabis use, alcohol use and sexual intercourse by child gender. *Substance Use & Misuse* 2018; 14: 2330–2338.

72 Schwartz S, *et al*. Perceived parental relationships and health risk behaviors in college attending adults. *Journal of Marriage and Family* 2009; 71: 727–740.

73 A.S.A.M. *Opioid addiction 2016: Facts and figures.* New York: American Society of Addiction Medicine; 2017.

74 Davis M, Lin L, Liu H, Sites B. Prescription opioid use among adults with mental health disorders in the United States. *Journal of the American Board of Family Medicine* 2017; 4: 407–416.

75 Hedegaard H, Warner M, Minino A. *Overdose deaths in the United States, 1999–2016.* Hyattsville, MD: National Center for Health Statistics; 2017.

76 Seth P, Rudd R, Noonan R, Haegerich T. Prescription opioid data. *American Journal of Public Health* 2018; 108: 4–28.

77 Kost K, Zimet I, Arpaia A. *Pregnancies, births and abortions among adolescents and young women: 2013.* New York: Alan Guttmacher Institute; 2016.

78 Witwer E, Jones R, Lindberg L. *Sexual behavior and contraceptive and condom use among U.S. high school students, 2013–2017.* New York: Allan Guttmacher Institute; 2018.

79 C.D.C. *Sexual risk behaviors: HIV, STD & teen pregnancy prevention.* Atlanta, GA: Centers for Disease Control and Prevention; 2018.

80 C.D.C. *HIV among youth: 2016.* Atlanta, GA: Centers for Disease Control; 2018.

81 Galbraith K. Parental acceptance and uptake of the HPV vaccine among African Americans and Latinos: A literature review. *Social Science & Medicine* 2016; 159: 116–126.

82 Wolfe D, Temple J. *Adolescent dating violence: Theory, research and prevention.* Cambridge, MA: Academic Press; 2018.

83 C.D.C. *Teen dating violence.* Atlanta, GA: Centers for Disease Control & Prevention; 2018.

84 Livingston J. Etiology of teen dating violence among adolescent children of alcoholics. *Journal of Youth and Adolescence* 2018; 47: 515–533.

85 Ellis B, Bates J, Dodge R. Father absence and teenage pregnancy. *Child Development* 2003; 74: 801–821.

86 Ellis B, Schlomer G, Tilley E, Butler E. Impact of fathers on risky sexual behavior in daughters. *Development and Psychopathology* 2012; 24: 317–401.

87 DelPriore D, Scholmer G, Ellis B. Impact of fathers on parental monitoring of daughters and their affiliation with sexually promiscuous peers. *Developmental Psychology* 2017; 53: 1330–1343.

88 Biggs M. Factors associated with delayed childbearing in Latinas. *Hispanic Journal of Behavioral Sciences* 2010; 33: 77–103.

89 Coley R, Drzal E, Schindler H. Mothers' and fathers' parenting and adolescent sexual risk behaviors. *Child Development* 2009; 80: 808–827.

90 Rink E, Tricker R, Harvey S. Onset of sexual intercourse among female adolescents. *Journal of Adolescent Health* 2010; 41: 398–406.

91 Vigil J, Geary D. Parenting and women's life-history development. *Journal of Family Psychology* 2006; 20(4): 597–604.

92 DelPriore D, Hill S. The effects of paternal disengagement on women's sexual decision making. *Journal of Personality and Social Psychology* 2013; 105: 234–246.

93 Katz J. Father emotional responsiveness and college women's sexual refusal behaviors. *American Journal of Family Therapy* 2010; 38(4): 344–356.

94 Miller M, Lee J. Communicating disappointment. *Journal of Family Communications* 2001; 1: 111–131.

95 Peterson S. Father-daughter relationships and sexual risk taking. *Journal of Human Behavior in the Social Environment* 2006; 13: 67–83.

96 Widman L. Parent adolescent sexual communication and adolescent safer sex behavior: A meta-analysis. *JAMA Pediatrics* 2018; 170: 52–61.

Chapter 5

The Mother's Impact on Father-Daughter Relationships

Among the many factors that can influence the quality of father-daughter relationships, one of the most powerful is the mother. From the time their daughter is born, the mother both promotes and impedes the father-daughter relationship in a multitude of ways. As we will see in the next chapter, her influence is especially powerful if the parents are no longer living together. In most families, mother-daughter relationships also differ from father-daughter relationships in many ways that we will explore in this chapter.

The mother's influence can be considered in light of three over-arching theories where mothers play a major role in the father-child relationship: Psychoanalytic Theories, Attachment Theories, and Family Systems Theories. We begin then with a brief overview of those aspects of these three theories that relate to the mother's influence on the father-daughter relationship.

Psychoanalytic Theories

According to psychoanalytic perspectives, fathers play a crucial role in their daughters' lives.[1] One of their primary roles is to help the young child become less dependent on and more separated from the mother. This lays the groundwork for becoming more autonomous and self-reliant throughout childhood. The mother is in the pivotal position because she has the power either to encourage the father's bond with their infant child or to discourage it. The mother must be willing to step back enough to encourage the very young child to begin the process of separating from her.

Between the ages of three and six, the daughter supposedly becomes more focused on her father than on her mother. She longs to be like him. She identifies with him instead of identifying with her mother. The father, traditionally being the parent who is the most engaged in the world of work, represents the power and the excitement of the world beyond the family. The daughter becomes more demanding of her father's time and attention because she is jealous of her mother's relationship with him—the **Electra complex**. The analogous experience for boys and their mothers is referred to as the **Oedipal complex**. In 1913 Sigmund Freud's colleague, Carl Jung, coined the term **Electra complex** to describe this phase of the daughter's development.[2] The term is derived from the Greek myth of Electra, the daughter who plots the murder of her mother for having murdered Electra's father. In the course of healthy psychosexual development, the daughter resolves her Electra complex by shifting her focus from her father and "identifying" with her mother. This enables the daughter to form a healthy, heterosexual female gender role identity. Resolving her Electra complex enables the daughter to have a non-competitive, satisfying relationship with her mother and to develop loving, romantic relationships with men. If her Electra complex is not resolved, the daughter remains overly attached and overly identified with her father in ways that make it difficult for her to have satisfying romantic relationships with men.

Psychoanalytic theories now hold a far less prominent role than they once did. Still, those aspects of the theory described above are in accord with at least three fundamental tenets of attachment theories and family systems theories that are popular today. First, the mother has a significant impact on the father-daughter relationship. Second, her impact begins at the daughter's birth and is especially strong in the earliest years of her life. Third, father and daughter need to bond early in her life and to develop a strong relationship. But during her teenage and young adult years, their relationship should become far less involved. This enables her to develop the attitudes and independence she needs to create fulfilling relationships with men other than her father.

Attachment Theories

Like psychoanalytic theories, attachment theories contend that mothers have a profound impact on the kind of relationship fathers and children develop. The creator of attachment theory, John Bowlby, made several claims 40 years ago that the empirical research supports.[3] Many of his claims, though, have been proven wrong by decades of research. It is beyond the scope of this chapter to discuss the decades of heated debate over attachment theories. Instead, we will focus on the basic aspects of Bowlby's original theory that are and are not supported by the empirical data now available.[4,5,6]

First and foremost, it is extremely important to understand that "attachment" classifications are *not* assessments of whether children have a secure or insecure *relationship* with their parent. The term "attachment" is not synonymous with "bond" or "love." Attachment classifications merely describe how very young children react when they feel stressed. Babies and toddlers become stressed when they are tired, hungry, sick, afraid, or uncertain in new situations and around new people. They also become stressed when a stranger is present or when they encounter something "strange" and unfamiliar. Children with a **secure attachment** style comfortably seek out their attachment figure when stressed. With the attachment figure available if needed, the child is relatively relaxed and confident in exploring or interacting with unfamiliar people and things. In contrast, when stressed, children with **insecure or avoidant** styles react to their parent with confusion or anger—or avoid going to the parent for comfort. They are more timid or anxious or agitated and less confident than children with a secure style. Again though, when under stress, a child with an insecure or an avoidant style does not necessarily have a worse relationship with a parent than a child with a secure style. When a child's behavior under stress is too inconsistent or too erratic to be categorized in either of these three ways, it is referred to as a **disorganized attachment.**

Several aspects of Bowlby's theory have been upheld by research studies.[5,6,7] First, babies and toddlers who develop a secure style are generally the most well-adjusted from there on. They get along better with peers, have more fulfilling romantic relationships, are less depressed and anxious, and are more self-confident and socially skilled than a child with an insecure, avoidant, or disorganized style. Second, parents who are sensitive and attentive, without being overly protective and without infantilizing the child, promote a secure style. In contrast, parents who are inconsistent, insensitive, inattentive, or harsh promote insecure or avoidant styles in their babies and toddlers.

Other aspects of Bowlby's theories, however, have not been upheld by decades of research on this topic.[5,6,7] Bowlby theorized that babies develop only one "primary" attachment—the attachment to their "primary caregiver" who is almost always their mother. This concept is referred to as **monotropy.** Bowlby also theorized that babies do not become attached to their fathers until a year or so after they have become attached to their mothers. Even then, however, the child's bond with the father supposedly is "secondary" in the hierarchy. Bowlby also claimed that frequent separations from the mother make it more difficult for the baby to bond to her.

A number of damaging beliefs and policies arose from Bowlby's beliefs. For example, it was widely believed that putting young children in daycare would weaken their bonds to their mothers. This meant that mothers should not work outside the home while their children were young. More damaging still, there is still a prevailing belief in custody law that very young children should live exclusively with their mothers after their parents separate. There is also the belief that spending too many nights away from their mother in their father's care will weaken the baby's bond to the mother. We will explore these beliefs more fully in the next chapter. Needless to say, beliefs such as these can weaken or undermine fathers' bonds with their babies and toddlers, especially if the parents are not living together. Indeed, the psychologist who developed one of the most widely used measures of attachment, Everett Waters, warns us not to use the term "attachment" when making custody decisions for very young children. "The less often we use the word attachment in this discussion, the better off we'll all be" (p. 474).[7]

Contrary to Bowlby's theories, a large body of research has demonstrated that babies form an equally strong bond with each parent at roughly six months of age.[5,6] To the baby, neither parent is more "primary" than the other. There is no hierarchy of attachments. Babies are somewhat more likely to turn to their mothers for comfort and to their fathers for more intellectually stimulating, physical, challenging interactions. As discussed in Chapter 2, these differences are shrinking as mothers and fathers are more equally sharing childcare and work outside the home. More importantly, these differences do not mean babies bond more closely to one parent than to the other. Moreover, babies can have a different attachment style with each parent. Researchers have not yet determined whether being securely attached to the mother is linked to better long-term outcomes than being securely attached to the father. What is clear is that very young children have better social, emotional, and behavioral outcomes in future years when they are securely attached to at least one of their parents.

As for Bowlby's claims about the dangers of being separated from their mother, the impact of infants spending up to 30 hours a week in daycare centers has been studied for more than 25 years and published in 249 scientific papers.[8] At the age of 12, the children who had been in daycare or cared for by their fathers or their grandparents as infants were compared to those who had been cared for only by their mothers. There were no significant differences in their emotional or behavioral well-being or in their attachment styles.

A few representative studies illustrate the flaws in Bowlby's original theories. At the age of six and again at the age of eight, children who had secure attachment styles when they were babies had fewer emotional and behavioral problems than children who had been categorized as insecure.[9] They were less likely to be bullies, to lie, to be overly shy and anxious, and to be defiant. This is what Bowlby would have predicted. But, in contrast to Bowlby's theories, being securely attached to their mothers as infants had no greater impact than being securely attached to their fathers. In other words, mothers were not "primary" and fathers were not "secondary" in importance or influence. Likewise, in contrast to Bowlby's theory, young adults who felt secure in their romantic relationships had more secure attachment styles with their fathers when they were babies than the young adults with insecure romantic relationships.[10] In other words, their early childhood attachment to their fathers predicted the later quality of their romantic relationships.

In sum, contrary to Bowlby's theories, attachment research studies have shown us that fathers and mothers are equally important in their young child's development. Both parents can help their child develop a style for coping with stressful situations and for relating to new people.

Family Systems Theories

Attachment theories are in accord with **family systems theories** in that both emphasize the mother's influence on fathers' relationships with their children. According to **family systems theories**, every member of a family is part of an interactive, influential "system" where each person's behavior and where each of the separate relationships have an impact on each individual. This theory was developed nearly 40 years ago by Murray Bowen.[11] As a psychiatrist working mainly with schizophrenic young adults, Bowen developed an approach to therapy that was shockingly unconventional in his time: family therapy. In conventional therapy, only the client and the psychiatrist worked together. In contrast, Bowen's family therapy involved other members of the client's family in the process. According to Bowen's groundbreaking theory, each member of the family contributes and the relationships within the family contribute to the patient's problems. Unless the psychiatrist understands the dynamics of the family, the patient will be unlikely to make progress. Up until then, it was inappropriate, if not unethical, to include any member of a patient's family in therapy sessions. Initially Bowen only included the patients' mothers in the therapy sessions because he believed her relationship with the child was most strongly related to the schizophrenia. But Bowen revised his theories by realizing the importance of fathers and including them in the family therapy as well.

Bowen's family systems theory is widely used to explain family dynamics that affect each member of the family.[12] Three concepts are especially relevant to the role that mothers play in father-daughter relationships: **triangulation, enmeshment,** and **role reversals or parentification.** These damaging situations are most likely to occur when the parents' relationship with each other is unhappy or dysfunctional. Moreover, these three situations are more likely to damage the children's relationship with their father than with their mother—especially female children.

Triangulation is a situation where two people whose relationship is not going well start focusing on a third person as a way to avoid acknowledging and resolving their own relationship problems. The troubled couple draws a third person into a "triangle" when the real problem has little or nothing to do with the third person. In families where the parents' relationship is an unhappy one, parents may choose to focus intensely, or to exaggerate or to obsess over one of their child's problems—to triangulate the child. As long as the parents convince themselves that the "problem child" is the reason for the tensions in the family, everyone remains in denial about the real source of the problems affecting the family—the parents' relationship. The triangulated child may have problems that are linked to the unspoken, unresolved problems in the parents' relationship. Unless the parents resolve their own marital problems, however, the triangulated child's problems are unlikely to improve. Triangulating a child may enable a bad marriage to limp along for years, but it also damages the father's connection with the triangulated child.

Box 5.1 Role Reversal Scale[13]

1=strongly agree, 2=somewhat agree, 3=somewhat disagree, 4=strongly disagree

Rate each of your parents. When I was growing up,

_____ 1. seemed overwhelmed with taking care of the house
_____ 2. seemed overwhelmed with dealing with a family
_____ 3. relied on me to tell him/her what to do
_____ 4. relied on me for advice
_____ 5. didn't think I loved him/her enough
_____ 6. expected me to take his/her side in an argument
_____ 7. I felt bad about leaving my parent to go and play with friends
_____ 8. was jealous when I began to date
_____ 9. depended on me for emotional support
_____ 10. tried to protect my father from my mother
_____ 11. I felt responsible for how my parent feel
_____ 12. if I hurt myself, I worried more about his/her reaction than mine
_____ 13. confided in me more than he/she did in anyone else
_____ 14. kept me up at night when he/she needed someone to talk to
_____ 15. expected me to keep him/her company
_____ 16. acted more my age than his/her
_____ 17. enjoyed my friends more than his/her own
_____ 18. I was often preoccupied with understanding my parent's moods
_____ 19. expected me to know what he/she was feeling
_____ 20. I knew what my parent wanted better than he/she did
_____ 21. I seemed to be able to read my parent's mind
_____ Total score

A second damaging situation within the family system is **enmeshment**. Enmeshment occurs when any two people become so overly involved in one another's lives, thoughts, and feelings that they lose their separate identities and autonomy. Instead of functioning as two separate or "individuated" people with separate needs, thoughts, and feelings, the two people think, feel, and behave almost as if they had morphed into one person. When this happens between a parent and child, the enmeshed child cannot develop an identity that is separate and independent from the parent. In healthy families, there is a **personal boundary** that keeps the individuals separate enough from each other to develop their own thoughts, feelings, and identities. When the parents are unhappy in their relationship, one parent—typically the mother—may turn to one of the children—typically the daughter—for so much emotional support and comfort that they become enmeshed because the parent-child boundaries have collapsed.

The third damaging situation is referred to as **role reversal or parentification.** One parent—typically the mother—chooses one of the children—typically a daughter—to be her confidante, advisor, helpmate, and "friend." Since the parents are unhappily married, role reversals mean the daughter is hearing negative things about her father and is aligning with her mother against him.

In sum, attachment theories, psychoanalytic theories and family systems theories concur that the mother has a significant impact on the father-daughter relationship. Moreover, her impact begins while their daughter is still an infant. We turn our attention now away from these theories to the differences in daughters' relationships with their mothers and fathers.

Closeness, Communication, and Conflict with Mothers Versus Fathers

In most American families, daughters have closer relationships with their mothers than with their fathers. Daughters and mothers generally talk about more personal things with one another than do fathers and daughters throughout their lifetimes.[14–16] For example, male undergraduates shared more information with their fathers and females shared more with their mothers.[17] And in another college sample, sons and daughters were less likely to discuss personal issues with their father than with their mother.[18] Daughters generally turn to their mothers for advice on personal issues such as dating, problems with friends, loneliness, or depression. In contrast, daughters are more likely to turn to their fathers for advice on less personal topics such as academic problems, careers, or financial matters. Consequently, most mothers and daughters feel they know one another better than do most fathers and daughters. These recent studies reach the same conclusion as much earlier studies: Most teenagers—especially daughters—feel closer to their mother and generally confide and seek more advice from her than from their father.[19]

Since daughters share more personal information with their mothers, it is not surprising that daughters generally have more conflict and arguments with their mothers than with their fathers.[16–18] For example, in a study with 1,510 parents between the ages of 35 and 54, mothers argued and had more conflicts with their children than did fathers.[20] Nevertheless, these mothers were just as likely as the fathers to say they enjoyed their relationships with their adult children. Similarly, for 200 families with teenage children, sons and daughters had more conflicts with their mothers than with their fathers.[21] This is not surprising since these mothers knew more about what was going on in their teenage children's lives than did the fathers.

Daughters may be more reluctant than sons to talk with their father about personal issues because daughters may be more afraid of disappointing him. For example, for college undergraduates, daughters and sons were worried about disappointing their parents in terms of their grades, sex, drug use, grades, athletic achievements, and irresponsible behavior (letting the car run out of gas, bouncing checks).[22] But the daughters were more worried than sons that their father would disapprove of their sexual behavior. This was ironic since these daughters said their mothers were more critical of them than their fathers were. Other daughters in college also said they told their fathers less about their lives because they thought he would be more critical than their mother.[23] These daughters also said they felt more comfortable arguing with their mothers because it took longer to get over arguments with their fathers. Female undergraduates also said they felt more comfortable arguing with their mother than with their father over issues related to their future career choices.[24]

Figure 5.1
Source: Oleg Golovnev/shutterstock.com.

Those daughters who felt close and connected to their father, though, were just as comfortable disagreeing with him as they were with their mother.

Female undergraduates have offered a number of explanations for why they are hesitant to discuss personal or potentially controversial topic with their fathers—reasons that are probably fairly typical for non-college educated daughters as well.[25] Some are afraid their fathers will get angry, possibly angry enough to cut their daughters off financially. Others worry that their fathers might feel embarrassed, or cry, or become extremely sad if the daughter brought up certain topics. Not surprisingly, many avoid any topic that might make them look "bad" in their father's eyes. Even as young women, they want to maintain the image of "daddy's innocent, perfect little princess," even though many suspect their fathers already know this is not true. Sadly, some daughters desperately want to talk to their fathers about certain problems in the family that they both know exist. These daughters fear, however, that other members of the family—especially their mothers— will get angry if they discover that the daughter and father discussed these taboo topics. Surprisingly, even as young adults, some daughters avoid topics where they fear the information might cause them to have less admiration or less respect for their father. He might "fall off his pedestal" and no longer be the perfect "hero" dad. It is especially troubling and sad that many daughters feel their relationships with their fathers are strained, uncomfortable, or growing more distant because they are not talking about these personal, difficult issues. If fathers and daughters communicated more directly and more honestly from the time she was very young, they would no doubt have an easier time discussing personal, emotional, or controversial topics as she aged.

Unfortunately, fathers and daughters often rely on mothers to do the communicating for them. The up side is that fathers and daughters generally have less conflict than mothers and daughters, because they communicate less, especially about personal topics. The down side, though, is that neither the father nor the daughter are learning to communicate directly with one another or to resolve their problems together without the mother's assistance or intervention. Another down side is that many fathers and daughters are missing opportunities to become closer to one another. For example, when parents are willing to share personal information about themselves with their young adult children, the parents and the children feel that their relationship becomes closer.[26]

On the other hand, when a parent shares information in ways that denigrate the other parent, this is not beneficial for children regardless of their age.[27,28,29] This kind of sharing stresses children by placing them in the middle of parent conflicts, encouraging them to align with one parent against the other, or making them feel they must rescue or take care of one of their parents. Because mothers are far more likely than fathers to disclose damaging information and to disclose more to their daughters than to their sons, father-daughter relationship are at greatest risk.[24,25,26]

A series of three studies with adult children by one research team illustrates many of these differences in adult children's communication, conflict, and closeness with each parent.[30-32] In this sample of 302 fathers and 331 mothers from different families, there were 1,251 children, 75% of whom were 18 to 29 years old, though some were as old as 49. The researchers divided the adult children's problems into two categories. "Lifestyle problems" included drinking or drug problems, financial difficulties, trouble with the law, divorce, and troubled relationships with family members, romantic partners or spouses. "Emotional problems" included depression, mental health issues, or personality problems. The most common problem (26%) was having financial difficulties and still relying on their parents for money.

Both mothers and fathers felt their relationships with their adult children were more strained and less satisfying when there were problems in their relationship, but not when the children had lifestyle problems. Fathers, but not mothers, were less satisfied if children had emotional problems and were unsuccessful in their career. Sons and daughters felt they had the most conflict with their mothers, even though the parents reported equal amounts of conflict. As for how they dealt with the tensions with the children, mothers used a more avoidant style than fathers—but this avoidance style resulted in lower quality relationships with their children. Interestingly white parents were more likely to use the avoidant style than African American parents—which meant the white parents had worse relationships with their children. As the researchers concluded, the old adage is wrong: "If you can't say something nice, don't say anything at all."

Importantly, in all three studies, there were differences between sons and daughters. Daughters reported more tensions with both parents that did sons. Daughters' lifestyle and parent-child problems had a greater impact than sons' on how their parents felt about their relationships with their children. Fathers and mothers felt they had less satisfying relationships with their daughters than with their sons. Not surprisingly, certain groups of parents reported worse parent-child relationships when the children had lifestyle problems: those who were not in good health, those who had to provide a lot of financial support, and those who were more highly educated.

As the stories in Box 5.2 illustrate, daughters are generally aware that certain aspects of their relationships with their mothers are not beneficial for the father-daughter relationship. No doubt, the woozles discussed in Chapter 1 are partly responsible for the kinds of communication problems that contribute to this stress or distance between fathers and daughters.

Box 5.2 The mother's impact: Reflections by daughters

SUZANNE: Mom has always told me that women have a special intuition that men don't have. But I think what's really going on is that she'd be hurt if I was really close to dad.

DERRICA: My mom is constantly putting my dad down for small things she doesn't like about him. So I have also taken on a nagging tone with him. I know he hates the way we talk to him like he's a child. I've got to stop doing this.

SANDY: Mom tells me about their fights. This puts me in the middle. When they're fighting, she asks me to go to dinner with her. Once she actually turned the car around and drove us back home because I refused to listen to her complain about my dad.

NANCY: When I was a teenager, dad always took my brother off on fishing trips and I was so jealous. When I would complain to mom, she'd say that it wouldn't look right for my dad and me to go away together for a weekend now that I was a young woman. In retrospect, I don't think she should have had that attitude.

RHONDA: I'm not able to talk alone to dad, not even on the phone. When he and I are trying to talk, mom talks over him. If I ever did go somewhere just with him, it would reinforce her insecurities about not having a career. The entire relationship I'm trying to build with my dad is like a slap in the face to her. She has always wanted me to feel closer to her and need her more than I need him.

Love Versus Closeness and Communication

The fact that most daughters communicate and share less personal information with their fathers does not mean that fathers and daughters love one another any less or consider their relationship less important than do mothers and daughters. First, as discussed in Chapter 1, fathers generally spend as much time with their daughters as with their sons.[33–35] Second, the fact that they communicate less often reflects our society's myths and woozles more than it reflects the love that fathers and daughters feel for one another. The stereotype is that fathers are less empathic, less tolerant, less insightful, less sympathetic, and less interested in their daughter's personal lives than are mothers. If she were to go to him for advice, he would be less forgiving, less accepting, and less understanding. Since stereotypes shape our behavior and our expectations, it is little wonder that most fathers and daughters end up communicating on a less personal level. Moreover, since members of a family often share the same stereotypes, everyone is trapped in the same script. The daughter sees no need to change the way she communicates with her father. The father thinks his daughter would be uncomfortable if he tried to have more personal conversations. The mother feels fulfilled being the communications' director for the entire family. Nobody sees the harm to the father-daughter relationship in leaving everything exactly as is. A family's self-fulfilling prophecy can arise from exaggerated or unfounded stereotypes and woozles.

Even though daughters communicate less with their fathers than with their mothers, fathers are just as likely as mothers to experience the "empty nest" syndrome when their daughters leave home for college. In a comprehensive review of the literature, mothers did not feel sadder, lonelier, or more upset than fathers when children left for college.[36] It is also worth noting that, even though daughters feel closer to their mothers, in none of the studies previously discussed did daughters say they loved their father less than their mother or felt less loved by him.

Then too, there can be turning points in the daughter's or the father's life that draw them closer together. For example, in a small study with 43 daughters and fathers (who were not related to one another), they reported a number of situations that had strengthened the father-daughter relationship.[37] These turning points included the daughter's going away to college, getting married or having children, and working together in the family business. During her teenage years, they often drew closer when she started dating, when her father was involved in her athletic activities, and when they shared special vacations together.

In sum, the fact that most daughters seek more advice and share more personal information with their mother does not mean that they have a better relationship with her than with their father. Nor does it mean daughters love their mothers more than they love their fathers. Still, communicating more about personal topics would surely enrich many father-daughter relationships.

Maternal Gatekeeping

The quality of the father-daughter relationship also depends in large part on how welcoming and supportive her mother has been of their relationship since she was born. In most families, mothers are the "gatekeepers" who determine how involved the father will be in the children's lives.[38,39] As the gatekeeper, she can either open or close the metaphorical "gate" between the father and the children. The **Maternal Gatekeeping Scale** in Box 5.3 describes the kinds of controlling, or encouraging or discouraging behavior that restrict or facilitate father-child relationships.[38] For example, the mother may constantly supervise, or correct or criticize the father's interactions with his daughter. She may also complain to other people, to the daughter, and to him about his fathering. Or she can be encouraging by asking his advice on parenting issues and supporting his ways of parenting, even though they are different from hers. Gatekeeping occurs regardless of whether the parents are married, cohabiting, or separated—though as we will see in Chapter 6, gate closing is more common after the parents separate.[40]

Box 5.3 Maternal Gatekeeping Scale[38]

How often does the mother engage in these behaviors: rarely, occasionally, often, almost always? The more often mothers engage in "control" and "discouragement" behaviors, the more negative the impact of her gatekeeping.

Control

___ Make him do what you want him to do with the child
___ Monitor his time with the child
___ Impose your will on him
___ Keep him from making parenting decisions
___ Set the rules for how he parents the child
___ Supervise his interactions with the child

Encouragement

___ Say positive things about how he talks/interacts with the child
___ Compliment him about his parenting
___ Ask his opinion about parenting
___ Say positive things like "you're good with the children"
___ Support him in completing a parenting task
___ Tell the child positive things about him

Discouragement

___ Tell other people what you dislike about his parenting
___ Not cooperate with him on parenting tasks
___ Criticize him as a father
___ Roll your eyes at him when he talks/interacts with child to show your frustration
___ Tell the child what you think the father did wrong
___ Pretend to support his parenting decisions
___ Say sarcastic comments when he interacts with the child
___ Attempt to undermine his parenting decisions

Gate "closing" is not necessarily intentional. A mother may be unaware that she is closing the parenting gate in ways that have a negative impact on her children's relationship with their father. Still, her behavior and attitudes undermine the father's self-confidence and make him feel unwelcomed as an equal parent. Her behavior makes clear to the children and to the father that he is the less valued, less competent parent. The mother may jealously hoard most of the parenting for herself, especially if the child is a girl and even when the child is just an infant. For example, parents argued more and had worse co-parenting relationships when the father was actively involved in caregiving activities for their four-year-old child than when he limited his interactions with the children to play.[41] But this was more true for daughters than for sons. Similarly, with their three-month-old babies, fathers became more disengaged and interacted less with their babies when the mother was behaving in ways that were critical and disapproving.[42] And with their eight-month-old babies, when the fathers were very skilled in taking care of their babies, their wives felt worse about their own competence as mothers than if the fathers were not very skilled in taking care of their baby.[43]

It is worth noting that gay and lesbian couples also engage in gatekeeping. In the first study to examine this question, mothers in heterosexual relationships did more gate closing than fathers or mothers in same sex relationships.[44] In same sex relationships, gay fathers were more likely than lesbian mothers to be engaged in gatekeeping. In other words, children with heterosexual parents were the most likely to have their relationship with their father restricted by their mother.

In sum, even though mothers may not be aware that they are closing the gate, their behavior has a negative impact on the children by restricting their relationship with their father.

Quality of the Co-parenting Relationship

Gatekeeping is one of several important aspects of the co-parenting relationship. **Co-parenting** means how well the two parents work together as a cooperative, supportive team and how much conflict they have in raising their children. Successful co-parents affirm one another's competence, respect each other's contributions, opinions, and decisions, and work together to resolve differences with as little conflict as possible. Co-parenting has emerged as one of the most important factors influencing children's well-being. For example, in a three year study with over 500 married couples, the level of conflict in the co-parenting relationship predicted adolescents' antisocial behavior as strongly as did marital happiness.[45] The quality of the co-parenting relationship largely affects children because it has such a powerful impact on the quality of the father's relationship with the children. When the mother opens the parenting gate and encourages the father to participate fully in co-parenting, he is far more involved with their children. But when the mother sees herself as the primary parent and the father as secondary, the co-parenting is competitive, conflicted, and unsupportive and the father withdraws further from the parenting.

How well the parents co-parent can differ from sibling to sibling because the child's characteristics affect the co-parenting relationship. Some children are much easier to parent and to co-parent than others. Parents generally have worse co-parenting relationships when one of their children has a difficult temperament, behavioral or emotional problems, or an attention deficit disorder or hyperactivity.[46,47] Regardless of whether the parents are married, when one of their children has serious behavioral or emotional problems, the parents' relationship becomes more stressed and they are more likely to separate.[48]

Like gatekeeping, the quality of the co-parenting relationship begins to influence the father-daughter relationship even during the child's infancy. When the mother is overly critical of the father's parenting, the co-parenting relationship deteriorates and he tends to withdraw from their children—a pattern that often continues as the child ages.[48,49] For example, in a study with 1,630 couples who were living together during the first five years of their child's life, fathers were much more involved with their children when the parents had a cooperative co-parenting relationship.[49] The vast majority of these parents were low-income minority families who were not married. Interestingly, whether or not the parents were married, the quality of their co-parenting relationship had a similar impact on how involved the father was with the children.

Mothers who are the most likely to open the parenting gate and allow fathers to be equal co-parents generally share several things in common.[50] These mothers generally had loving, supportive relationships with their fathers while they were growing up. For example, fathers who spent a lot of time with their newborns had wives with better relationships with their fathers than fathers who spent less time with their infants.[51] The gate-opening mothers who value co-parenting also believe that men and women are equally competent in parenting. They realize that although men and women sometimes relate differently to their children, women's ways of parenting are not superior. In contrast, the gate-closers with poor co-parenting relationships more often grew up in single parent, divorced or unhappily married families. Their relationships with their fathers were distant, troubled, or virtually non-existent. In these ways, the father-daughter relationship in one generation spills over into the next generation through the mother's willingness or unwillingness to support the father-child bond.

Quality of the Parents' Relationship and Parenting Stress

Not only do gatekeeping and the quality of co-parenting have an impact on father-daughter relationships, so does the quality of the parents' relationship with each other. When parents are in a happy, satisfying relationship, fathers' relationships with their children tend to be stronger than when the parents are not happy with one another. As explained in earlier chapters, when the parents are happy in their relationship, fathers are more actively involved with their children. In contrast, for unhappy couples, fathers tend to withdraw from their children, while mothers tend to become more involved. As the father's bond with the children is growing weaker, the mother's bond is growing stronger. As described earlier in this chapter, unhappy marriages are more likely to lead to enmeshment, role reversals, and triangulation—all of which are more likely to weaken the father's bond with his daughter than with his son.

While the quality of the parents' relationship influences children's relationship with their father, the reverse is also true. Children influence the quality of the parents' relationship with one another. Neither stands alone. They are intertwined.

After their child are born, the quality of the parents' relationship with one another usually declines in terms of being less emotionally intimate and having more stress and conflict.[52,53,54] For example, in a study with 100 married couples, 40% of their conflicts were about the children while only 20% were about money.[54] This may partly explain why people who have children do not report being happier than people who choose not to have children.[55] According to an analysis of 97 studies, marital satisfaction decreases after having children, more so in higher than in lower income families.[56] The researchers speculated that because lower income parents generally marry younger and spend fewer childfree years together before having children, they might find the transition to parenthood a less dramatic and less stressful change for their relationship and lifestyle. As would be expected, parents who planned the pregnancy and were happy with their relationship before the baby was born had less decline in happiness than those whose children were unplanned.[53]

The decline in marital happiness is understandable given the increased stress, conflict, and depression that arise over child-rearing differences, co-parenting issues, and the sheer physical and emotional exhaustion of caring for children—especially caring for a first-born child. For example, fathers are almost as likely (10%) as mothers (14%) to become clinically depressed after the birth of their first baby as they adjust to first time parenthood.[57] Moreover, if the mother becomes depressed after the baby is born, the father is almost three times as likely to become depressed himself.[58] Fortunately, when mothers in intact or separated families are depressed, the more involved the father is in their baby's or toddler's childcare, the more emotionally and behaviorally well-adjusted the child is in kindergarten.[59] Although the mother's depression strains the parents' relationship with one another, at least the father's involvement with the baby can help to offset the negative impact for the child. A mother's depression and stress in the first few years of her baby's life are also the likely reasons why children under the age of three are the most likely to be killed by their mothers.[60] Stress and depression also help explain why mothers are much more likely than fathers to physically discipline their one- to three-year-old children.[61] Especially with sons, mothers are more likely to spank, yell, or in other

Figure 5.2
Source: Alon Brik/shutterstock.com.

ways punish their very young children. This is not surprising since mothers are usually providing most of the hands-on daily childcare while the fathers are providing most or all of the financial childcare.

Although becoming clinically depressed or murdering one's child are certainly not common, the increase in conflict and decline in marital happiness are common. Marital happiness declines because parenting is often more stressful, unrewarding, and exasperating than it is enjoyable, rewarding, and relaxing—especially when there is more than one child under the age of four. For example, in study with 900 employed mothers in Texas, taking care of their children ranked 16th out of 19 "pleasurable" activities.[62] Similarly, when parents rated their daily activities in terms of which ones were both pleasurable and rewarding, spending time with their children ranked third after doing volunteer work and praying.[63] Most parents rated their jobs as the most rewarding daily activity. And as previously explained, the quality of the co-parenting relationship is worse and parents are more likely to separate when one of the children has emotional or behavioral problems.

Conflict between the parents can also arise because having children puts an additional financial burden on the family. Importantly, these conflicts do not necessarily end after the children leave home. Even well into their adult years, a number of children continue to rely on their parents for money. In recent years, there has been an increase in "**boomerang**" **children**—young adults who go back home to live with their parents after graduating from college and even after obtaining a job. For example, in a study of families from four different racial groups, parents often argued with their adult children and with one another over how much financial aid to give the children.[64] Even parents in their 60s and 70s can still be arguing with one another over financial issues related to their children. For example, the number of Americans older than 65 filing for bankruptcy tripled from 1991 to 2018.[65] More than one-third of these bankrupt parents said that helping their adult children financially had contributed to their own financial demise—for example co-signing loans that their adult children failed to repay or helping them buy a house. Historically children were an economic asset to their parents because they helped with the farm work or with the family business. As the nation became more industrialized and college educations became more of a necessity, children became a financial burden instead of an asset. Children were no longer expected to contribute to the family financially. One sociologist explains this historical shift more bluntly: "Children are economically worthless but emotionally priceless."[66]

The parents' relationship with one another is further strained if one of their children has emotional, behavioral, or chronic health problems.[48,67] These problems include attention deficit disorders, depression, anxiety, and severe childhood asthma. Moreover, being happily married does not guarantee that co-parenting will go well with a temperamentally difficult child. Ironically the more happily married couples had a worse co-parenting relationship than the less happily married couples when their four-year-old had a difficult temperament.[46] This might be because the happily married parents had a greater decrease in joy and intimacy than less happily married couples which, in turn, makes co-parenting even more difficult. This is not to say that most parents regret having children. There is, however, an inevitable tradeoff—the pleasures of parenthood versus the additional strain on the parents' relationship with one another.

Overall then, a satisfying relationship between the parents, cooperative co-parenting, and mothers keeping the parenting "gate" open promote stronger relationships between fathers and their children—more so for daughters than for sons.

Conclusion

The fact that most mothers and daughters communicate more comfortably, more personally, and more often than fathers and daughters is not in and of itself a terrible thing. What is unfortunate, however, is that fathers and daughters generally end up having far fewer personal, meaningful conversations with one another throughout their lives—seldom achieving the level of emotional intimacy that both of them might have otherwise enjoyed. Since, even as adults, many daughters do not seek advice from their fathers on personal matters, opportunities for creating a more meaningful relationship are lost. As Box 5.4 illustrates, daughters themselves can be treating their fathers in ways that prevent their relationship from being as relaxed, as joyful or as meaningful as it might otherwise become.

While many factors contribute to the quality of the father-daughter relationship, the mother is one of the most significant. She strengthens their relationship by encouraging the father's equal role in co-parenting and opening the parenting gate from the time their daughter is born and throughout childhood. The mother also strengthens the father-daughter relationship by not reversing roles with, or triangulating or becoming enmeshed with their daughter. As we will see in the next chapter, if the parents' relationship ends, the mother plays an even more powerful role in shaping the kind of relationship the father and daughter will have thereafter.

Box 5.4 Are the women in your family "equal opportunity" daughters?[68]

Compared to how often they do these things for or with their mother, have the daughters in your family given their father as many equal opportunities to get to know one another and build a close relationship?

> 0=never, very unequal 1=rarely, unequal 2=usually, fairly equal 3=almost always, completely equal

____ I share as much with him about what's going on in my life
____ I invite him to do things alone with me (eat out, exercise)
____ I ask him personal or meaningful questions about his life
____ I make sure he knows how much I value his opinion
____ I ask what's going on in his life besides his work
____ I ask him to do errands or just hang out with me
____ I talk with him about feelings, not just about opinions or ideas
____ I ask him for advice on personal matters (not money, school, or work)
____ I phone, text, or email just to him
____ I talk with him about our past together
____ I let him know what I'd like changed in our relationship
____ I act interested & appreciative when he asks about my life (not annoyed & disinterested)
____ I buy gifts for him that show how well I know him (not generic gifts)
____ I tell him I love and value him

Although mothers play a pivotal role, daughters are certainly not powerless when it comes to creating a more meaningful, more personal relationship with their father as the stories in Box 5.5 illustrate. Daughters need to set aside ample time alone with their fathers on a regular basis—time without any other family members present. Then daughters need to use that time to ask their fathers more personal, more meaningful questions about his past and his present life. Regardless of family dynamics that may have limited or damaged their relationship, daughters can seize the opportunity to create a stronger bond with their father—enriching both of their lives in the process.

Box 5.5 Daughters' enriching conversations with their fathers

BETH: As I got him to talk about his childhood, I realized my dad was a victim of vicious cycles in his own family. It's hard now to be angry with him over things he never learned how to do. The thing that glaringly stood out for me was how negative an impact my grandfather had on dad. My dad still seems to be trying to prove to his dead father that he can be successful.

JOANNE: His stories were so meaningful because I am struggling with the same questions as he did when he was my age. I also saw him as a young man remembering what it was like to fall in love.

MARIA: The more questions I asked, the more I saw my dad as a person who struggles through life as a man and a husband, not just as my father. When we were discussing his dreams, the look on his face and his tone of voice made me see him as a man with a lonely heart. It meant so much to have him open up to me.

AUTUMN: As we talked, I realized that we've both been wanting the same thing from our relationships all these years. But we never talked enough to figure that out.

JAMYLAH: When I first told my dad I wanted to spend a few hours alone with him to ask questions about his life, he laughed and seemed really nervous. But he did it. It ended up being the first time we've ever talked about his life for more than five minutes.

ZEENA: It was very moving when my dad said the nicest gift I ever gave him was deciding finally that I want to get to know him.

Review Questions

1   How does the mother-daughter relationship usually differ from the father-daughter relationship?
2   According to each of these theories, how and why does the father have an impact on his daughter: psychoanalytic, attachment, and family systems?

3 According to psychoanalytic theories, what is the "Electra complex" and how does it affect father-daughter relationships?

4 What portions of the original attachment theories do recent research studies uphold and which do they refute?

5 What does insecure and secure attachment mean and what common mistakes do many people make when they talk about the term attachment?

6 What was unique about family systems theory when it was first developed?

7 What factors influence how much stress or satisfaction parents experience in their relationships with their adult children?

8 Explain each of these concepts and explain how they relate to the quality of father-daughter relationships: triangulation, enmeshed, role reversals, personal boundaries?

9 What is individuation and what part does it play in father-daughter relationships?

10 What are ten of the behaviors on the Family Enmeshment Scale that indicate enmeshment?

11 What are the various components of maternal gatekeeping and how does gatekeeping influence father-daughter relationships?

12 How and why does the co-parenting relationship and marital happiness affect the father-daughter bond?

13 Which mothers are most likely to engage in gatekeeping?

14 What are the various factors that contribute to parenting stress and specifically how does parenting stress affect father-daughter relationships?

15 How do sons and daughters generally differ in terms of their relationships or communication with their father?

Questions for Discussion and Debate

1 In what ways have you seen mothers undermining father-daughter relationships—and in what ways strengthening them?

2 Why does it matter that mothers and daughters usually know one another better and communicate more easily than fathers and daughters?

3 How do you think most fathers feel about their daughters' talking more and spending more time with the mother and, as a result, knowing one another better? How would you feel if you were the father in that situation?

4 What advice would you give a close friend whose relationship with her father was being damaged by her being enmeshed with her mother?

5 What topics do you feel are the most difficult for teenage or young adult daughters to discuss with their fathers? How could fathers make it easier for their daughters to talk to them about those topics?

6 As the daughter, or the father, or a therapist working with the family, what would you do to try to stop the mother from gatekeeping when it was clearly damaging or straining the father-daughter relationship?

7 If a father believes that for the first five years of her life his involvement in his daughter's life is far less important than the mother's involvement, what would you say to him?

8 If you know a daughter who communicates better with her father and shares more personal information with him than she does with her mother, what do you think accounts for that? How would you feel if you were her mother? Her father? Why?

9 What advice would you give to new parents who both want the most meaningful relationship possible with their daughter?

10 How helpful do you believe family therapy is for improving most father-daughter relationships? Why?

11 If a daughter is becoming overly enmeshed with her mother, how might you go about helping the father, the daughter, and the mother change their family pattern?

12 What impact have you observed an unhappy marriage having on father-daughter relationships?

13 What could a teenage or adult daughter do if her mother's behavior or comments are undermining or limiting her relationship with her father?

14 Using the enmeshment checklist, how would you describe the level of enmeshment in the relationships in your own family network?

15 What information in this chapter was most upsetting or most relevant to you personally?

References

1 Trowell J, Etchegoyen A. *The importance of fathers: A psychoanalytic re-evaluation.* New York: Routledge; 2002.

2 Jung C. *Psychoanalysis and neurosis.* Princeton, NJ: Princeton University; 1970.

3 Bowlby J. *Attachment and loss.* New York: Basic Books; 1969.

4 Dagan O, Sagi-Schwartz A. Early attachment network with mother and father: An unsettled issue. *Child Development Perspectives* 2018; 12: 115–121.

5 Newland L, Freeman H, Coyle D. *Emerging topics on father attachment.* New York: Routledge; 2011.

6 Groh A, Fearon R, van Ijzendoorn M, Bakermans M, Roisman G. Attachment in the early life course: Meta-analytic evidence for its role in socioemotional development. *Child Development Perspectives* 2017; 11: 70–76.

7 Waters E. Are we asking the right questions about attachment? *Family Court Review* 2012; 49: 474–482.

8 National Institute of Child Health and Human Development Early Child Care Research Network. Does amount of time spent in child care predict socio-emotional adjustment during the transition to kindergarten? *Early Childhood Research Quarterly* 2004; 19: 203–230.

9 Kochanska G, Kim S. Early attachment organization with both parents: Infancy to middle childhood. *Child Development* 2012; 83: 1–14.

10 Grossman L, Grossman L, Kindler H, Zimmerman P. Attachment and exploration: The influences of parents on psychological security from infancy to adulthood. In: Cassidy J, Shaver P, editors. *Handbook of attachment*. New York: Guilford Press; 2008. 857–879.

11 Bowen M. *Family therapy in clinical practice*. New York: Jason Aronson; 1978.

12 Titelman P. *Differentiation of self: Bowen family systems theory perspectives*. New York: Routledge; 2015.

13 Alexander P. Parent-child role reversal scale. *Journal of Systemic Therapies* 2003; 22: 31–44.

14 Rossi A, Rossi P. *Of human bonding: Parent-child relations across the life course*. New York: de Gruyter; 1990.

15 Fingerman K, Whiteman S, Dotterer A. Mother child relationships in adolescence and old age. In: Reis H, Sprecher S, editors. *Encyclopedia of human relationships*. Thousand Oaks, CA: Sage; 2010. 48–52.

16 Golish T. Changes in closeness between adult children and their parents. *Communication Reports* 2012; 13: 79–97.

17 Proulx C, Helms H. Change in relationships with young adult sons and daughters. *Journal of Family Issues* 2008; 29: 234–261.

18 Mathews A, Derlega V, Morrow J. What is highly personal information? *Communication Research Reports* 2006; 23: 85–92.

19 Youniss J, Smollar J. *Adolescent relations with mothers, fathers and friends*. Chicago, IL: University of Chicago; 1985.

20 Kiecolt J, Blieszner R, Savla J. Long term influences of intergenerational ambivalence on midlife parents' psychological well-being. *Journal of Marriage and Family* 2011; 73: 369–382.

21 Shanahan L, McHale S, Osgood D, Crouter A. Conflict frequency with mothers and fathers. *Developmental Psychology* 2007; 43: 539–550.

22 Miller M, Lee J. Communicating disappointment. *Journal of Family Communications* 2001; 1: 111–131.

23 Freeman H, Almond T. Young adults' use of fathers for attachment support. In: Newland L, Freeman H, Coyl D, editors. *Emerging topics in father attachment*. New York: Routledge; 2011. 218–240.

24 Li C, Kerpelman J. Parental influences on young women's career aspirations. *Sex Roles* 2007; 56(1–2): 105–115.

25 Nielsen L. College daughters' relationships with their fathers: A fifteen year study. *College Student Journal* 2006; 54: 16–30.

26 Donovan E, Thompson C, LeFebvre L, Tollison A. Emerging adult confidants' judgments of parental openness. *Communication Monographs* 2016; 84: 179–199.

27 Afifi T, Afifi W, Morse C, Hamrick K. Adolescents' avoidance tendencies and physiological reactions to discussions about their parents' relationship. *Communication Monographs* 2008; 75: 290–317.

28 Kang Y, Ganong L, Chapman A, Coleman M. Attitudes toward parental disclosures to children and adolescents by divorced and married parents. *Family Relations* 2017; 66: 839–853.

29 Schrodt P, Shimkowski J. Feeling caught as a mediator of coparental communication and young adult children's mental health and relational satisfaction with parents. *Journal of Social and Personal Relationships* 2013; 30: 977–999.

30 Birditt K, Fingerman K, Zarit S. Adult children's problems and successes. *Journal of Gerontology* 2010; 65: 145–153.

31 Birditt K, Rott L, Fingerman K. "If you can't say something nice, don't say anything at all" Coping with interpersonal tensions in the parent-child relationship during adulthood. *Journal of Family Psychology* 2009; 25: 769–778.

32 Birditt K, Miller L, Fingerman K, Lefkowitz E. Tensions in the parent and adult child relationship: Links to solidarity and ambivalence. *Psychology and Aging* 2009; 24: 287–295.

33 Bianchi S, Robinson J, Milkie M. *Changing rhythms of the American family.* New York: Sage; 2006.

34 Pleck J, Masciadrelli B. Paternal involvement by U.S. residential fathers. In: Lamb M, editor. *The role of the father in child development.* New York: Wiley; 2010. 222–271.

35 Sandberg J, Hofferth S. Changes in children's time with parents. *Demography* 2001; 38: 423–436.

36 Bouchard G. How do parents react when their children leave home? An integrative review. *Journal of Adult Development* 2014; 21: 69–79.

37 Barrett E, Morman M. Turning points of closeness in the father daughter relationship. *Human Communication* 2012; 15: 241–259.

38 Puhlman D, Pasley K. The maternal gatekeeping scale. *Family Relations* 2017; 66: 824–838.

39 Austin B, Fieldstone L, Pruett M. Bench book for assessing parental gatekeeping in parenting disputes. *Journal of Child Custody* 2013; 10: 1–16.

40 Ganong L, Coleman M, Chapman A. Gatekeeping after separation and divorce. In: Drozd L, Saini M, Olesen N, editors. *Parenting plan evaluations: Applied research for the family court.* New York: Oxford University Press; 2016. 308–346.

41 Jia R, Schoppe-Sullivan S. Relations between coparenting and father involvement in families with preschool-age children. *Developmental Psychology* 2011; 47: 106–118.

42 Elliston D. Withdrawal from coparenting during early infancy. *Family Relations* 2008; 47: 481–499.

43 Sasaki T, Hazen N, Swann W. Do involved dads erode moms' self-confidence? *Personal Relationships* 2010; 17: 71–79.

44 Sweeney K, Goldberg A, Garcia R. Not a mom thing: Predictors of gatekeeping in same sex and heterosexual parent families. *Journal of Family Psychology* 2017; 31: 521–531.

45 Feinberg M, Kan M, Hetherington E. The longitudinal influence of coparenting conflict on adolescent maladjustment. *Journal of Marriage and Family* 2007; 69(3): 687–702.

46 Cook J, Schoppe-Sullivan S, Buckley C, Davis E. Are some children harder to coparent than others? *Journal of Family Psychology* 2009; 23(4): 606–610.

47 Kerns S, Prinz R. Coparenting children with attention deficit disorders and disruptive behavior disorders. In: Drozd L, Saini M, Olesen N, editors. *Parenting plan evaluations: Applied research for the family court.* New York: Oxford University Press; 2016. 243–279.

48 Osborne C, McLanahan S. Partnership instability and child wellbeing. *Journal of Marriage and Family* 2007; 69: 1065–1083.

49 Carlson J, Pilkauskas N, McLanahan S, Brooks-Gunn J. Couples as partners and parents over children's early years. *Journal of Marriage and Family* 2011; 73: 317–334.

50 Schoppe-Sullivan S, Altenburger L, Lee M, Bower D. Who are the gatekeepers? Predictors of maternal gatekeeping. *Parenting Scientific Practices* 2015; 15: 166–186.

51 Feldman S, Nash S, Aschenbrenner B. Antecedents of fathering. *Child Development* 1983; 54: 1628–1636.

52 Gottman J, Levenson R. Marital happiness and childrearing. *Marriage and Family* 2008; 62: 737–745.

53 Rothman R. Marital satisfaction across the transition to parenthood. *Journal of Family Psychology* 2008; 22(1): 41–50.

54 Papp L, Cummings M, Goeke-Morey M. For richer, for poorer: Money as a topic of marital conflict in the home. *Family Relations* 2009; 58: 91–103.

55 Gilbert D. *Stumbling on happiness*. New York: Vintage; 2005.

56 Twenge J, Campbell W, Foster C. Parenthood and marital satisfaction: A meta analytic review. *Journal of Marriage and Family* 2003; 65: 574–583.

57 Paulson J, Bazemore S. Prenatal and postpartum depression in fathers. *Journal of the American Medical Association* 2010; 19: 54–63.

58 Ramchandani P. Postpartum depression in fathers. *Lancet* 2005; 44: 144–155.

59 Mezulis A, Hyde J, Blark R. Father involvement moderates effects of maternal depression during child's infancy on child behavior problems in kindergarten. *Journal of Family Psychology* 2004; 18: 575–588.

60 Oberman M, Meyer C. *When mothers kill*. New York: New York University; 2008.

61 Hallers-Haalboom A. Wait until your mother gets home! Mothers' and fathers' discipline strategies. *Social Development* 2016; 24: 82–98.

62 Kahneman D, Krueger A, Schkade D, Schwarz N, Stone A. A survey method for characterizing daily life experience: The day reconstruction method. *Science* 2004; 306(5702): 1776–1780.

63 White M, Dolan P. Accounting for the richness of daily activities. *Psychological Science* 2009; 20: 1000–1008.

64 Descartes L. Put your money where your love is. *Journal of Adult Development* 2006; 13(137): 147.

65 Thorne D, Lawless R, Foohey P. *Bankruptcy booms for older Americans*. Los Angeles: University of California: Consumer Bankruptcy Project; 2018.

66 Zelizer V. *Pricing the priceless child: The changing social value of children*. Princeton, NJ: Princeton University Press; 1994.

67 Schermerhorn A. Offspring ADHD as a risk factor for parental marital problems. *Twin Research and Human Genetics* 2012; 15: 700–713.

68 Nielsen L. *Between fathers and daughters: Enriching and rebuilding your adult relationship*. Nashville: Turner Publishing; 2008.

Chapter 6

Divorced or Separated Fathers and Their Daughters

Daughters are less likely than ever before not to spend the first 18 years of their lives living in the same home with their fathers. In the past most daughters who were separated from their fathers during childhood either had fathers who had died, abandoned the family, or been forced to live away from home in order to earn money for the family.[1] But in 2009 for the first time in U.S. history, 40% of children were born out of wedlock—most of whose parents separate before their child's fifth birthday. Another 35% are separated from their fathers because their parents are divorced.[2] As the sobering statistics in Box 6.1 illustrate, the typical or average American daughter will spend part of her childhood living apart from her father because her parents have separated. For reasons that are explained in this chapter, after parents separate, most father-daughter relationships are stressed, weakened, or eventually end altogether.

Box 6.1 Who are American children living with?[3]

51% married mother & father
4% unmarried mother & father
14% mother & stepfather
12% single mother, divorced
11% single mother, never married
5% neither parent
2% mother & her boyfriend
1% single father, never married
1% single father, divorced
1% father & stepmother
0.5% father & his girlfriend

This chapter explores a number of provocative and complicated questions. How and why do most father-daughter relationships change after parents separate? Why is the daughter's relationship with her father generally more damaged than the son's? Which daughters are the most likely to be living apart from their fathers? What can we do to support and strengthen these relationships?

Father-Daughter Relationships at Greatest Risk

Certain groups of daughters are much more likely than others to spend part or all of their childhood living apart from their fathers. At greatest risk are daughters whose parents are poorly educated and consequently have extremely low incomes or live in poverty and those whose parents are not married when the children are born. Because education, income, and non-marital births are closely linked to race, Asian American and non-Hispanic white daughters are the most likely to live in the same home with their father throughout childhood.

In regard to education, college educated parents are the most likely to get married and to stay married.[4] Only 25% of college graduates are divorced, compared to 40% of non-college graduates. Almost half of non-Hispanic white and 64% of Asian American parents have college degrees, compared to only 29% of Hispanic, 24% of black, and 22% of Native American parents. College educated parents also have higher incomes and are older when they get married and have their first child. Half of white families have a family income above $61,349, compared to $46,882 for Hispanic and $38,000 for black and Native American families. Asian American families have the highest incomes with half of these families earning more than $80,720. Only 12% of white and Asian American children live in poverty, compared to 34% of black and Native American and 28% of Hispanic American children. Overall then, non-Hispanic white and Asian American daughters are the most advantaged in terms of living with their fathers throughout childhood.

With respect to their parents being married when the children are born, non-Hispanic white and Asian American children are again the most advantaged.[4] When their children are born, 90% of Asian Americans and 70% of non-Hispanic whites are married, compared to only 20% of African Americans, 33% of Native Americans, and 40% of Hispanic Americans. Since income, race, education, and out of wedlock births are all closely linked, children in certain states are the most likely to grow up living apart from their fathers. For example, 51% of the children in New Jersey and Connecticut are living with their married parents, compared to only 32% in Mississippi and Louisiana—two of the states with the highest minority populations and highest rates of poverty, out of wedlock births, and high school dropouts.[5]

Two changes in divorce rates are worth noting. First, in the past women who were more educated than their husbands were more likely to end up divorced than women who were less educated than their

Figure 6.1
Source: Kamira/shutterstock.com.

husbands.[6] This is no longer the case. In fact when both spouses have equal levels of education, they are less likely to get divorced than when one is more educated than the other. Second, although there are fewer divorces now than in the past, this is not because more parents are staying together. It is largely because 40% of parents never get married. When they separate, as most do, these are not counted as divorces. In short, children today are more likely than in the past to spend part or all of their childhood living apart from their father.

Given the large numbers of children living apart from their fathers, it is especially important to ask: What factors help fathers and daughters maintain a good relationship after the parents separate? And why are daughters generally affected more negatively than sons when their parents separate?

The Impact of Parental Separation on Daughters

Although their parents' separation is a painful, stressful, unsettling experience for most children, the vast majority do not develop long lasting, serious problems after the separation. This does not mean, however, that separation has no impact. Indeed, compared to children from intact families, these sons and daughters are two to three times more likely to develop problems in regard to: depression, aggression, delinquency, teenage pregnancy, school failure, academic under-achievement, drug, alcohol and nicotine use, stress related illnesses, romantic relationships, and divorce.[7] More important still, daughters generally pay a higher price than sons in these respects, as we will now see.

Quality of the Father-Daughter Relationship

Perhaps the greatest damage from the parents' separation is its negative impact on a daughter's relationship with her father. Compared to sons, daughters are more likely to pay this price—with repercussions that can last a lifetime. In extreme cases, their relationship ends altogether. Most young adult daughters wish their fathers had spent more time with them after the divorce. Most also wonder if their father loves or misses them.[8,9] When fathers try to reconnect with their young adult daughters after years of spending very little time together, daughters say the relationship is awkward and superficial.[10]

During the teenage years, daughters with separated parents are more likely than sons to feel rejected and unloved by their father.[11,12,13] It is worth noting that some research suggests that black daughters are more likely than white or Hispanic daughters to maintain good relationships with their fathers after their parents separate. In this study, boys of all races were closer to their fathers than girls were—with the exception of black girls.[14] Similarly, for women aged 18 to 88, the black daughters were closer to their fathers than were white daughters.[15]

As young adults, compared to sons, daughters generally feel their relationships with their fathers are more damaged after their parents' separation. Daughters are more likely to feel that their fathers do not want to spend time with them.[16] They are also more dissatisfied than sons are with the quality of their relationship with their father.[17–19] Daughters are less likely than sons to feel that their relationships with their fathers has improved over the years since their parents' separation.[20] They are also less apt than sons to consider their father to be one of their best friends.[21] In a 20 year study that followed 175 children of divorce, three times as many adult daughters as sons felt their relationship with their dad had deteriorated.[22] Similarly, in a 30 year study that followed 72 children of divorce, compared to sons, adult daughters felt their relationships with their dads were more damaged.[23] Even in their early 30s, daughters from divorced homes are more likely than sons to have conflicts with their fathers.[24]

Interestingly, years after their parents' divorce, when adult children have their first child, sons feel their relationships with their fathers improved while daughters do not.[20] Similarly, while they were pregnant and nine months after their baby was born, daughters of divorce still had more conflict and less support from their fathers than daughters with married parents.[25] In other words, the birth of a grandchild does not appear to draw fathers and daughters closer when they have distant, troubled relationships.

Sexual Behavior and Romantic Relationships

In addition to the damage to the father-daughter relationship, daughters with separated parents are also more likely to engage in risky sexual behavior and to have less satisfying romantic relationships. As teenagers, daughters who have not lived with their fathers since early childhood are eight times more likely to become pregnant than daughters from intact families. In contrast, girls whose parents separated later in childhood are only two times more likely to have a teenage pregnancy.[26] This suggests that the more years a daughter lives with her father, the less likely she is to become pregnant as a teenager. Girls with separated parents also have sex with more people before the age of 19, have more unprotected sex, and are coerced into having sex more often than girls from intact families.[27] To test whether the loss of fathering time in divorced families was the actual cause of the daughter's riskier sexual behavior, researchers compared younger and older sisters in the same family.[28] Since younger sisters had spent less time living with their fathers, if father absence was the cause of riskier sexual behavior, then younger sisters would engage in riskier behavior. And that is what the researcher found to be true. The older sisters not only reported having better relationships with their fathers, they also engaged in less risky sexual behavior.

Young adult daughters also have more satisfying romantic relationships and better marriages if they maintain a close relationship with their father after the parents separate. In college, these daughters have more emotionally intimate, more communicative, more trusting, and more secure relationships with their boyfriends.[9,29,30,31] As married women, they feel that their marriages are more emotionally intimate.[32] It is also worth noting that female undergraduates whose parents have high conflict relationships have worse relationships with their boyfriends when their parents are married than when they are divorced.[33] This suggests that when the parents have a contentious relationship, daughters are less negatively affected when their parents separate than when they stay married.

Daughters' romantic relationships also tend to more damaged than sons' relationships by their parents' separation. Compared to sons, daughters are less trusting and less satisfied with their romantic relationships and communicate more poorly with their romantic partners.[30,34] For example, young adult sons and daughters from divorced families were more likely than those from intact families to have unsatisfying, unstable romantic relationships.[35] But this was truer for daughters than for sons. Satisfying romantic relationships included being able to communicate well, to express affection, and to feel secure and confident about the relationship. Similarly, for young adults from divorced families who were engaged, daughters were less confident than sons that their marriage would succeed.[36]

Daughters and sons with separated parents are more likely to divorce than their peers with married parents. In part this is because they get married and have children at a younger age and are less educated and less well off financially—all of which contribute to higher divorce rates. A daughter's risk of divorce increases 70% if her parents are divorced and skyrockets to 190% if both she and her husband have divorced parents.[37] Again though, daughters are less likely to divorce if they have maintained close relationships with their fathers. In other words, the quality of the father-daughter relationship seems to be a more reliable predictor than her parents' marital status of whether a daughter's marriage will succeed.

Emotional and Psychological Well-Being

Daughters with separated parents are also more likely to have anxiety disorders and to be clinically depressed, which, in turn, increases their odds of developing eating disorders.[38] For example, girls whose parents separated when their daughter was under the age of two had more emotional and behavioral problems in elementary school than girls whose parents separated when their daughter was three to five years old.[39] The girls' problems included being depressed and anxious, bullying, fighting, kicking and biting, lying, disobeying teachers, and being disliked by peers. This study echoes the research discussed in earlier chapters showing that the father's involvement in the early years of his daughter's life has far-reaching consequences.

Two studies serve to illustrate the interplay between depression, parental divorce, and the quality of adult children's marriages. Sons and daughters with divorced parents were more depressed in mid-life (average age 52) than those with married parents.[40] But if they were married, they were not any more depressed than people from intact families. In other words, if a daughter with divorced parents is married at mid-life, she is no more likely to be depressed than a daughter from an intact family. Unfortunately, though, daughters with divorced parents are less likely to be happily married and are more likely to be divorced. Similarly, in a study that followed 13,000 children from birth to age 33, at the age of 33 sons and daughters who had maintained close relationships with their fathers after their parents separated were more likely to be happily married and less likely to be depressed than those whose relationships with their fathers were not close.[41] Again though, the father's impact was greater for daughters than for sons.

Physical Well-Being

Having a close relationship with her father is beneficial for the daughter's physical health, as explained in an earlier chapter. These benefits including being less likely to be obese or grossly underweight and less likely to use alcohol, nicotine, and other drugs—all of which can have lifelong repercussions on a daughter's health.

Since daughters with separated parents generally have worse relationships with their fathers than girls from intact families, it is not surprising that they have more physical health problems. For example, when the divorced father is well educated, the less involved he is with his children, the more likely they are to be obese.[42] Interestingly this was not true for less educated fathers. This suggests that well-educated fathers may be providing their children with healthier foods or encouraging more exercise than less educated fathers. In college, the daughter's health is also linked to the quality of her relationship with her divorced father. Students with close relationships with their dads have fewer stress related illnesses such as insomnia, headaches, chest pains, and intestinal problems.[43] In a sample from nine universities, regardless of whether their parents were married or separated, daughters who felt loved by and close to their fathers had better outcomes in regard to 6 of 12 risky behaviors that pose a threat to their health.[44] These risky behaviors included binge drinking, drunk driving, using drugs, misusing prescription drugs, having unprotected sex, and having sex with someone they had just met. It is worth noting that the quality of their relationships with their mothers was only linked to 2 of the 12 risky behaviors. Similarly, adults in their early 30s from divorced homes used marijuana more frequently than their peers from intact families, though they were not more likely to drink.[24]

In sum, three findings have clearly emerged in the research. First, daughters with separated parents have more social, physical, psychological, and relationship problems than those with married parents. Second, daughters are more likely than sons to have these problems. Third, these problems are closely linked to the quality of sons' and daughters' relationships with their fathers. This helps explain why daughters generally have more problems than sons, since the father-daughter relationship is more damaged. Given the importance of their relationship after the parents separate, we now turn our attention to these questions: What factors affect the quality of father-daughter relationships after the parents separate? Why are some fathers and daughters able to maintain good relationships while others are not?

Damaging Beliefs: Divorce Woozles

As explained in Chapter 1, societies or individuals sometimes hold beliefs about fathers that are not true—beliefs that are based on "woozled" data. These woozles lead to damaging stereotypes and wrong-headed assumptions that influence our behavior and our attitudes towards certain groups of people. So before we explore the research, take the quiz in Box 6.2.

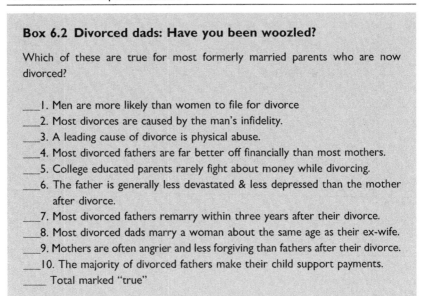

Box 6.2 Divorced dads: Have you been woozled?

Which of these are true for most formerly married parents who are now divorced?

____1. Men are more likely than women to file for divorce

____2. Most divorces are caused by the man's infidelity.

____3. A leading cause of divorce is physical abuse.

____4. Most divorced fathers are far better off financially than most mothers.

____5. College educated parents rarely fight about money while divorcing.

____6. The father is generally less devastated & less depressed than the mother after divorce.

____7. Most divorced fathers remarry within three years after their divorce.

____8. Most divorced dads marry a woman about the same age as their ex-wife.

____9. Mothers are often angrier and less forgiving than fathers after their divorce.

____10. The majority of divorced fathers make their child support payments.

_____ Total marked "true"

Which statements do you believe are true? It would not be surprising if you marked all ten as true, given the many woozles our society has embraced about divorced men. As we will now see, however, the first six statements in the quiz are false. Only the last four statements are true. Imagine then the negative impact it might have on her relationship with her father if the daughter believes all ten statements are true.

Contrary to the negative stereotypes about divorced fathers, research provides several somewhat surprising facts about most divorces.[45,46] Women generally adapt more quickly and are less depressed than men after they separate. In part this may be because the wife is generally the one who initiates the divorce. Two-thirds of all divorces are initiated by the wife. In most of these marriages, the husband was not abusive, alcoholic, drug addicted, dysfunctional, cruel, mentally ill, or unfaithful. The main reason most women give for wanting to end the marriage is that the relationship is not fulfilling, joyful, or satisfying. This is not to say that women are to blame for most divorces. It is simply to say that women are more likely to leave an unhappy relationship. Indeed a number of men say they were not aware that the problems in the relationship were so serious that their wives were contemplating divorce. Wives also adapt better because they have confided in friends about the upcoming separation and created a supportive network. This does not mean that wives do not feel sad, depressed, or overwhelmed after the separation. It simply means that fathers suffer as much or more than mothers—mainly because the fathers are separated from their children and have to vacate the family home. Not surprisingly then, fathers are far more likely than mothers to resort to heavy drinking or drugs, develop stress related physical problems, and become clinically depressed. Divorced women are no more likely than married women to commit suicide. But divorced men are more than twice as likely as married men to kill themselves.[45]

Another damaging divorce woozle is the belief that fathers are far better off financially than mothers after they divorce—and that this inequity is largely the father's fault. Obviously this woozle can have a negative impact on daughters who believe that fathers take advantage of mothers financially and that this is probably true for her father as well. This woozle was born over 30 years ago, based on one study by the sociologist Lenore Weitzman. Weitzman's study gained national attention by claiming that a woman's standard of living fell by 73% and a man's rose by 42% after their divorce.[46] Leaving aside that she used a small, non-representative sample of relatively wealthy, white California families, many scholars disagreed with and disproved her conclusions.[47] For example, a Loyola law school professor who reviewed Wieztman's study deemed it "Ph.D. poppycock."[47] Ten years after its publication, Weitzman finally conceded that her analysis was flawed.[48] But by then, her damaging woozle had been on the loose for a decade and had become deeply embedded in the public's beliefs.

Contrary to the woozle, the financial situations of mothers and fathers are quite similar after their divorce. In the largest federally funded study ever conducted on the topic, the researchers compared each parent's taxable income after child-related tax deductions as well as additional money spent for the children's health insurance and other expenses beyond child support payments.[48] For example, assume the mother earns $24,000 and the father earns $36,000. He will pay roughly $9,000 in child support to the mother which is not tax deductible and then pay $8,700 in income taxes. The mother pays no tax on the $9,000 of child support income and pays only $2,600 in income tax because she receives $3,700 worth of tax deductions since the children live with her. After accounting for all of these factors, divorced fathers were left with only $25 a month more than the mothers. According to other studies, a divorced father's standard of living generally declines by about 8%.[49]

Finally, there is the "deadbeat dad" woozle: the belief that most fathers refuse to pay child support even though they have the money. This woozle falls apart when we look at the data.[50,51] Only 20% of divorced fathers fail to pay any child support. Moreover, 45% of divorced fathers pay for their children's health insurance, 40% voluntarily buy them clothes, 60% give gifts, 10% pay for childcare or summer camps, and 20% pay for medical expenses beyond health insurance. The majority of fathers who do not pay child support are men who were never married to their child's mother. The vast majority of these fathers are impoverished, poorly educated men with high rates of incarceration, substance abuse problems, and mental or emotional problems. Because most of these men have such low incomes, only 20% of their children would be lifted out of poverty if their fathers were able to pay child support.[50]

In sum, many popular beliefs about divorced fathers are woozles—untrue or only partially true beliefs that can inadvertently contribute to weakening father-daughter relationships.

Shared versus Sole Physical Custody

Custody Laws and Terminology

After parents separate, decades of research have been consistently clear on one point: the best way to protect and maintain children's relationships with their fathers is to maximize the time they spend together in ways that enable them to interact across a wide range of activities in the children's daily lives. When their time is restricted to every other weekend or mid-week visits, their relationships are unlikely to thrive and often flounder—too often ending altogether as the father becomes more like an uncle than a parent.

Before exploring this research, we have to understand the difference between **legal** custody and **physical** custody. **Legal custody** refers to each parent's legal rights to have access to information and to make decisions about their children's health, education, and religious upbringing. For example, a parent with "sole" legal custody can take the children out of public school, enroll them in a private, religious school, refuse to give permission for them to participate in sports, or refuse to have them vaccinated, even though the other parent strongly objects.

Physical custody is an entirely different and separate matter from legal custody. The physical custody agreement or "parenting plan" designates how much time children will spend with or live with each parent and on what schedule. In **sole physical custody** (SPC), children live primarily or exclusively with one parent, typically spending every other weekend, a few hours on alternate Wednesday nights, and a few weeks of vacation or holiday time with their "non-residential" parent. Since the mother almost always (90%) has sole physical custody, most children are only allowed to spend 20–25% of the time with their father until they turn 18. At that age, the legal and physical custody arrangements end. In contrast, in **joint physical custody** (JPC) arrangements, children live with each parent at least 35% and often 50% of the time throughout the year. A joint physical custody agreement is also referred to as "shared parenting." The average amount of parenting time granted to fathers varies greatly from state to state.[51] For example, in California the average parenting plan gives children 120 days a year with their fathers (33% of the parenting time). In contrast, in Tennessee, the average parenting plan only gives children 80 days a year with their fathers (22% of the parenting time).

It is worth noting that in a 2017 survey involving more than 600 judges, those who held traditional gender role beliefs about mothers' and fathers' roles in the family awarded much more parenting time to mothers than to fathers.[52] In contrast, those judges who held less traditional views awarded fathers more parenting time. Likewise, in a 2013 survey of 227 people summoned for jury duty, the vast majority believed that judges were biased against fathers in custody cases. Even though they themselves believed that parenting time should be divided more equally, they felt that most judges would grant most of the parenting time to mothers.[53]

In almost all states, joint (shared) legal custody is the norm. It is automatically granted unless one parent is proven too unfit to take part in the decision-making. It is the physical custody plan—the parenting time—that causes the most conflict between the parents. Physical custody is also the center of the national debate over revising custody statutes to allow children to have more fathering time. The central question is whether children benefit most from living with each parent at least 35% of the time year round and throughout the school week in joint physical custody (JPC)—or whether they benefit most by living mainly or exclusively with just one parent in sole physical custody (SPC).

The issue of shared parenting/joint physical custody is more important for daughters than for sons in several respects. First, as we have already seen, daughters' relationships with their fathers suffer greater damage than sons' relationships after their parents separate. Second, daughters generally spend less time with their fathers and are less likely than sons to live in a shared parenting family. Third, daughters are more likely than sons to want—or to have wanted—more time with their fathers. Even as adults, many daughters mourn the loss of their fathers. Given this, if JPC is beneficial for children, it is likely to be especially beneficial for daughters.

Box 6.3 Shared physical custody: Have you been woozled?

Which statements are true for the majority of separated parents? "Shared parenting" means the children live with each parent at least one-third of the time.

_____ 1. Most mothers want fathers to have shared physical custody.

_____ 2. Shared parenting only works for well-educated, higher income parents.

_____ 3. Most state custody laws give both parents almost equal parenting time.

_____ 4. Most children in shared parenting families feel unsettled and "homeless."

_____ 5. Most shared parenting plans fail after a year or so.

_____ 6. Shared parenting is not beneficial for children under the age of four.

_____ 7. Parents must have a close, cooperative relationship for shared parenting to succeed.

_____ 8. Shared parenting kids are more stressed & anxious because they live in two homes.

_____ 9. Sons benefit more than daughters from shared parenting.

_____ 10. Most children are opposed to shared parenting.

_____ Total marked "true"

Before exploring the research on shared and sole physical custody, take the "Shared Parenting" quiz in Box 6.3. How many did you mark as "true"? Since there are so many woozles surrounding the issue of shared physical custody, it would not be surprising if you believe all ten statements are true. But as we will now see, all ten statements are false.

Joint versus Sole Physical Custody: Outcomes for Children

The three research questions at the heart of the debate are: (1) Do most children benefit more from JPC than from SPC? If so, in what ways? (2) If JPC children do have better outcomes, is it largely because their parents are richer and more educated, have better parenting skills, and have far more cooperative, friendly relationships with much less conflict than SPC parents? (3) If parents are "forced" by court orders or by negotiations with their lawyers to share the physical custody, do their children still benefit?

Over the past three decades 60 studies have compared children's well-being in sole versus shared physical custody families.[54,55] The results can be grouped into five broad categories of child well-being: (1) academic or cognitive outcomes; (2) emotional or psychological outcomes; (3) behavioral outcomes which include teenage drug, nicotine, or alcohol use; (4) physical health or stress related physical outcomes; and (5) the quality of parent-child relationships.

Compared to SPC children, JPC children had better outcomes on all measures in 34 studies, equal outcomes on some measures and better outcomes on others in 14 studies; equal outcomes on all measures in six studies; and worse outcomes on one measure, but equal or better on all other measures in six studies. In the 25 studies that considered family income, JPC children still had better outcomes on all measures in 18 studies, equal on some measures and better on other measures in four studies, equal outcomes in one study and worse outcomes on one but equal or better on other measures in two studies. In the 19 studies that considered parents' levels of conflict, JPC children again had better outcomes on all measures in nine studies, equal to better in five studies, equal in two studies, and worse outcomes on one but better outcomes on the other measures in three studies. In the nine studies that considered the quality of parent-child relationships at the time of separation, JPC children had better outcomes on all measures in five studies, equal or better outcomes on other measures in two studies, and worse outcomes on one of the measures in two studies.

The greatest advantage for JPC children was better family relationships. In 22 of 23 studies that assessed family bonds, JPC children had closer, more communicative relationships with both parents. The second greatest advantage for JPC children was better physical and mental health. In 13 of 15 studies that addressed physical health, JPC children had fewer psychosomatic, stress-related physical problems. Forty-two studies assessed children's emotional health: depression, life-satisfaction, anxiety, and self-esteem. In 24

Figure 6.2
Source: Iakov Filimonov/shutterstock.com.

studies, JPC children had better outcomes. In 12 studies, there were no significant differences between the two groups. In six studies, the results were mixed depending on the children's gender and which measure of emotional well-being was being assessed.

As teenagers, JPC children also had better outcomes. Twenty-four studies assessed one or more of these behaviors: drinking, smoking, using drugs, being aggressive, bullying, committing delinquent acts, getting along poorly with peers. In 21 studies, JPC teenagers had better outcomes on all measures. In three studies, the results were mixed because the differences between JPC and SPC teenagers depended on gender or on which measure was being assessed.

What about children's relationships with their grandparents—and why should we care? In all four studies that addressed this question, JPC children had closer relationships with their grandparents than SPC children. This matters because children who have close relationships with their grandparents tend to be more emotionally and behaviorally well adjusted.

Especially when the family is experiencing the initial stress of the parents' separation, strong relationships with grandparents can be a protective factor for children.

In six of the 60 studies, JPC children had worse outcomes than SPC children on one of the measures of well-being. In one study, JPC teenage boys had somewhat worse relationships with peers than SPC boys—but JPC girls had better peer relationships. In the second, highly conscientious teenagers were more anxious in JPC than in SPC, but less conscientious, more "laid back" teenagers were less anxious in JPC. In the third, if parent conflict was still high eight years after the divorce, the girls, but not the boys, were more depressed in JPC. In the fourth study, teenagers who did not have good relationships with their fathers were more depressed in JPC. Two studies focused exclusively on children between the ages of zero and five. In both studies, the vast majority (80%) of the parents had never been married or lived together. In the one study, the 22 toddlers in JPC were less persistent at tasks than the SPC toddlers. In the second study, toddlers who "overnighted" with a non-residental parent from 20% up to 50% time had lower scores on the measure of behaving "securely" with their mothers when stressed. But most of these toddlers lived mainly with their fathers, not with their mothers, which would explain why they behaved less securely around their mothers.

It is extremely important to note that JPC parents do not generally have significantly less conflict or more cooperative relationships than SPC parents.[53] This conflict includes isolated incidents of physical aggression (hitting, pushing, slapping, biting, pinching) that may have infrequently occurred in their relationship, especially around the time of their separation. JPC parents are not as likely as SPC parents, however, to have a history of physically violent behavior towards one another—the kind of behavior that endangers parents and children while the parents are together as well as after they separate. Violent parents are highly unlikely to have JPC arrangements because custody laws prohibit JPC when parents are physically abusive, negligent, or otherwise unfit to provide adequate care for their children.

In sum, even after considering the parents' levels of conflict, the quality of their relationships with children, and family income, JPC children had better outcomes. Even though the effect sizes in these studies were generally small, it is clear that joint physical custody where the children live with each parent 35% or more time in a shared parenting family is beneficial for children of all ages. But other factors also influence the quality of father-daughter relationships after parents separate, as we will now see. Before we explore those factors, take the quiz in Box 6.4 to assess your beliefs about divorced fathers and daughters. Despite the popularity of many of these beliefs, the first five statements are false and the second five statements are true. Let us now find out why.

Box 6.4 Divorced fathers and their daughters: Fact or fiction?

According to recent research and statistics, which of these statements is true?

___1. After their parents separate, daughters are usually less distressed than sons.

___2. Most daughters are satisfied with how much time they spend with their divorced dad.

___3. Daughters generally get along better with their dad after he remarries.

___4. Daughters under the age of three are overly stressed if they spend overnight time in their father's care after the parents separate.

___5. Most daughters have long lasting mental health issues after their parents divorce.

___6. Formerly married fathers generally pay their full child support after a divorce.

___7. Most daughters blame the divorce more on their fathers than on their mothers.

___8. Daughters generally dislike their stepmothers more than their stepfathers.

___9. The main reason fathers spend so little time with their daughters is that they remarry.

___10. After divorce, the daughter's relationship with the dad is generally more damaged than the son's.

___ Total marked true

Parents' Damaging Disclosures

As explained in earlier chapters, mothers generally share more personal information with their daughters than with their sons and share more than fathers do with their children. After parents separate, therefore, mothers must be especially careful not to disclose information that might damage the daughter's relationships with her father. This means not disclosing information about the divorce, or about financial issues, or about the father that might lead the daughter to think less of or distance herself from her father. Whether living together or separated, children feel stressed and depressed when their parents share negative information about one another with them. The children feel forced to align with one parent against the other.[56,57] Both sons and daughters feel anxious and caught in the middle when their mothers talk to them about the divorce or about their father.[57] But the daughters are more distressed, more depressed and develop more stress related illnesses than the sons.[53,58,59] It is also worth noting that even well-educated mothers can disclose damaging information about the father that increases the daughter's stress and depression.[23]

A series of studies by one research team illustrate the kinds of disclosures that take a toll on children, regardless of their age and regardless of whether their parents are separated or still together.[60-63] When parents badmouthed or argued with each other, their young adult children only felt stressed if they were placed in the middle of the dispute. As long as they did not feel caught in the middle, the negative things their parents told them about one another sometimes helped them understand why their parents got divorced. Interestingly, when their parents were antagonistic and put the children in the middle, young adults with married parents felt more stressed than those with divorced parents. Importantly though, when they had good relationships with their parents, they felt less caught in the middle even when their parents were saying negative things about one another. Interestingly, in married and in separated families, the young adults were more upset when their mother was verbally aggressive towards the father than when the father was verbally aggressive to their mother.

Enmeshment and Role Reversals

Damaging disclosures often go hand in hand with two other situations that damage father-daughter relationships: enmeshment and role reversals. Both of these situations generally take a greater toll on daughters than on sons. Enmeshment and role reversals increase the odds that the daughter will become anxious, stressed, and depressed because she is overly involved in being her mother's emotional caretaker, confidante, and ally after the parents separate.

As explained in an earlier chapter, **enmeshment** means that a parent and child are overly involved in one another's lives in unhealthy ways that prevent the child from developing his or her own identity or from becoming autonomous.[64] Enmeshment is more common for mothers who do not have careers and who base their self-worth almost exclusively on their relationships with their children. Mothers are far more likely than fathers are to have enmeshed relationships with children—especially their daughters. After the parents separate, a mother is also more apt to turn to one of her children, usually the daughter, for emotional support and friendship.

Parents who are enmeshed with their children also tend to "parentify" or "reverse roles" with them. **Role reversals or "parentification"** mean the parent burdens the child with the responsibilities of being a confidante, best friend, protector, or advisor. These children are providing the kind of emotional care for their mothers that the mothers should be providing for the children. These children are in many ways parenting their own parent, hence the term parentification.

Sons can become enmeshed or reverse roles with their mothers, as can fathers and daughters. But these situations are far more common between mothers and daughters, putting daughters at far higher risk than sons of becoming stressed, anxious, and depressed.[23,65,66,67,68] As one young adult daughter put it: "I was more her mom than she was mine."[69] Because daughters are more likely than sons to provide emotional support and be confidants for their mothers before the parents separate, it is unlikely that father-daughter role reversal or enmeshment will occur after the parents separate. Daughters whose mothers reverse roles or become enmeshed with them are more likely to become anxious and depressed, especially if their relationships with their fathers become weaker after the parents separate.

Box 6.5 Fathers and daughters reflect on the divorce

BURT, AGE 42: My daughter lived with me for five years because she and her mom didn't get along. But when she turned 16, she said she wanted to go live with her mother—just see me every other weekend. I was in shock. Of course I didn't force her to keep living with me. But she seems to grow more and more distant. When I ask what's wrong, she says "nothing." Is there a point where I should stop seeing her until she starts treating me better?

ADAM, AGE 62: I think I have forgiven myself for not being as good a father as I should have been. But then I fall apart and feel guilty all over again whenever I see fathers and daughters laughing together—or when I think of my daughter getting married without my being there. I long for the day when she will forgive me and answer my phone calls and letters.

WEI LIN, AGE 44: I know I made mistakes with my daughter after my divorce. I've tried to apologize. But she still returns the gifts I send for her children's birthdays. I'm desperately searching for a tool kit to fix our relationship. But after all these years, even now as a grandfather, I don't know how to stop the aching.

ANNA, AGE 18: My dad is not used to talking about relationships. But we started talking about the divorce and one comment really cut straight to my heart. When we were discussing his dreams, he said he wonders if he will ever marry again. The expressive look on his face and tone of his voice showed me how much the divorce had really crushed him. For the first time I saw my dad as a man with a lonely heart. Yes he is strong and independent and successful. But he is also weak and lonely and sad and insecure.

JADA, AGE 19: I asked him what had made him saddest after the divorce. I thought he would say it was when I ruined his 40th birthday by refusing to be there. Instead, he said the saddest thing was not being allowed to be part of my day to day life. I never thought it bothered him that I lived with mom full time. I was always under the impression that he never thought about me. I was also surprised that he still had wedding pictures of him and mom. Mom has always given me the impression that dad never cared about their life together.

RACHEL, AGE 17: Finally allowing my dad to tell me his side of the divorce made me uncomfortable because I've tried so hard to maintain a positive image of my mother. After much thought, I've decided that it's still possible for me to admire her even though I see how much suffering she caused him.

Maternal Gatekeeping

In addition to enmeshment, role reversals, and negative disclosures, some mothers behave in ways that metaphorically "close the gate" between the father and child. As discussed in the previous chapter, whether intentional or not, a mother's "gatekeeping" behaviors weaken and complicate the children's relationship with their father.[70] After parents separate, **gatekeeping** behaviors might include refusing to let the children have pictures of their father in the mother's home, frequently texting or calling the children whenever they are with their father, or withholding important information about the children from the father.[71]

The mothers who are the least likely to "close the gate" between the children and their father have a number of things in common.[72,73] They generally had good relationships with their fathers while they were growing up and have less sexist gender role beliefs about fathers and mothers being equally involved in their children's lives. After divorce, a mother is also less likely to close the gate when her friends believe that being a "good" mother means keeping the father actively involved in the children's lives.[74] Then too, how well the mother adapts to the separation may influence gatekeeping. After separating, compared to men, women tend to hold onto grudges longer, ruminate more about the failed relationship, and stay angrier longer.[72,75,76] Understandably, emotions such as these may make it more difficult for a mother to open the gate between the children and their father.

Parental Alienation

When carried to the extreme, gate-closing behavior can contribute to children becoming alienated from their other parent—sometimes resulting in the end of their relationship. **Parental alienation** describes a situation where the gatekeeping after the parents separate is so extreme that a child who formerly had a good relationship with a parent begins resisting or refusing contact with that parent for no apparent or logical reason. In extreme cases, an alienated child may refuse all contact with their disfavored parent and with members of that parent's extended family.[77-80]

Understandably, there are children who resist or refuse to spend time with a parent who is emotionally or physically abusive, negligent, unloving, or otherwise unfit to take care of them. But in cases of parental alienation, before the parents separated, the child had a good relationship with the parent who is now being rejected for irrational, petty, superficial, or fabricated reasons. For example, a daughter may claim that her father never spent time with her and never did anything nice or fun with her despite irrefutable, abundant evidence (family pictures, vacation videos, birthday presents) that she is wrong. The child may also begin to complain about or to exaggerate trivial behavior that was never a problem before the alienation began. For example, the daughter may refuse to spend time with her dad because she says he spends too much time on the phone or is late to pick her up from soccer games. One way to determine whether a child's reasons for rejecting a parent are legitimate is to ask: Would the parent's behavior be a reason to allow a child to push that parent away if the parents were still living together? For example, if the parents were still married, would a mother allow the daughter to distance herself from her dad just because he was late to her soccer games or talked too much on his cellphone?

In most cases the alienating parent is the one the children live with most or all of the time—typically the mother. The rejected parent is generally, though not always, the father. Whether intentional or not, the favored parent encourages and allows the child to refuse to spend time or to reject their other parent altogether. For example, the mother may say it is not her responsibility or that she has no way to force her daughter to continue spending time with her father, even though this is in violation of the custody agreement. Instead of making it clear to her daughter that she does not approve of and will not allow this kind of behavior, the mother reinforces or permits it.

Clearly not all children become alienated even in the most extreme situations. Indeed, one sibling may resist the alienating parents' efforts, while the other sibling succumbs. Then too, many children do not realize they were

Figure 6.3
Source: Altanaka/shutterstock.com.

victims of parental alienation until they are adults who can reflect on the past with greater maturity and insight. Estimates of how many children are subjected to alienating behavior and how many actually become alienated range from 13% to 25%.[81]

It is important to realize that even infants and toddlers can begin to become alienated from their father if the mother's gatekeeping behavior is persistent and extreme.[82] For example, when a toddler is leaving the mother to spend time with the father, the mother may act overly anxious, cry, start arguments, or appear distressed. Or the mother may not have the child's belongings ready when the father arrives. This then creates a sense of chaos and confusion that can make the child unwilling to leave with the father. She might also not help the young child overcome the normal anxiety that most toddlers exhibit when they are leaving one caregiver for another. Sensing the mother's desire to have the child stay with her, very young children may resist going with their father by clinging to the mother, crying, fretting, and hitting. Consequently, the father is put in the awkward and stressful position of trying to sooth the unhappy resistant child and dealing with the distressed, mother.

When a child becomes alienated from a parent, the consequences are generally long-lasting and reach beyond the parent-child relationship.[83,84] Even though these children may appear well adjusted in terms of being successful at school and being well behaved, as they age, they are at higher risk of developing relationship and emotional problems. Having been allowed or encouraged to reject a parent for irrational reasons instead of being helped to work through the problems in the parent-child relationship, these children tend to behave in the same unhealthy ways in their friendships and romantic relationships. They tend to have unrealistic expectations of other people, lack the skills to resolve relationship problems, show little empathy or compassion to forgive others for their mistakes, and reject people for trivial or irrational reasons. In short, they treat people much the same as they treated their rejected parent. Not surprisingly, as they age, they are more likely to become depressed, suicidal, lonely, and anxious and to have troubled relationships throughout their lives.

The Diagnostic and Statistical Manual of Mental Disorders has not yet listed parental alienation as a disorder or a syndrome. It has, however, added a new condition called "child affected by parental relationship distress" (CAPRD).[85] These children display the same kinds of problems and their parents behave in similar ways to children who have "parental alienation syndrome" (PAS). Given the damaging and long-lasting impact of parental alienation, "gate-closing" behaviors that appear to be distancing the children from one of their parents—typically their father—should not be dismissed as trivial or short-lived problems.

The father's remarriage

Box 6.6 Stepmothers: The father-daughter struggle

SUZANNE, DAUGHTER, AGE 21: Currently I'm struggling with dad's just having gotten married. I feel he has his own life now and I'm not part of it. When I told him how I felt, he explained that he has always focused his life on us girls. And now that we're in our twenties, he wants to focus on creating a fulfilling relationship with his wife. I realized too that this is the first time I've seen the romantic side of him. He was never like this with my mom. He showed me the video of his recent marriage and said how sad he was that I refused to attend. That made me feel pretty bad about myself.

ALICE, DAUGHTER, AGE 35: I appreciate the fact that my dad's wife never tried to act like a mother to me. I'm too old for that and it would have made things worse. She gives me and dad time to ourselves without her always being there. This has helped strengthen my relationship with him.

JOSH, AGE 60: My thirty-year-old daughter wants me to drive into the city to take her to dinner or take her shopping several times a month. But she refuses to come to my home or to call on the home phone because she doesn't want anything to do with to my wife. Should I lay down the law and insist she spend time with me and my wife?

SAMUEL, AGE 46: Now that I've remarried, I'm more relaxed with my daughter because I'm a happier man. I'm not so uptight and grouchy. My wife never interferes or criticizes me as a father. That has boosted my self-confidence and helped me be an even better dad to my daughter.

A final challenge to father-daughter relationships is the father's remarriage. The father's remarriage can of course have an impact on father-son relationships. For example, in a nationally representative study with nearly 2,000 formerly divorced fathers, adult sons and daughters felt closer to their father if was still single than if he had remarried.[86] But the challenges and the damage are far greater for fathers and daughters.[87]

In a meta-analysis of 21 studies, the most well-adapted adults after their divorce were those who fell in love again and remarried.[88] A successful second marriage also seems to benefit the children as well. For example, in a study with a sample size of 8,000, children had better achievement scores in math and social studies when their separated parents were in a stable relationship or had remarried.[89] The benefits of a happy second marriage were greater for daughters than for sons. Nevertheless, after the father remarries, the father-daughter relationship generally becomes more strained.

The impact of the father's remarriage on his relationship with his daughter depends on a number of factors.[87–90] First is the daughter's age.

Younger children generally adapt better than teenagers; and children of all ages adapt better when their mother has adjusted well to the parents' separation. When the stepmother has no children, there also tends to be less stress on the father-daughter relationship. But since most stepmothers do already have children or have a child during the second marriage, jealousy and competition between step or half siblings can further strain father-daughter relationships. The daughter may feel her father devotes too much time, attention, and money to his new family. Or she may feel that her father is being a better parent to the new children than he is—or was—to her. The daughter may also resent the stepmother if the father stops spending as much time with her after he remarries.

What daughters may not realize is that their fathers are also struggling with their own unique set of issues related to remarrying.[84,87] The father often feels it is his responsibility to create close relationships between all family members—especially his wife and daughter. Both the father and his wife may also feel pressured to create one big happy family rather than allowing relationships to develop slowly on their own—and accepting the fact that blended family members may not ever develop more than a cordial, superficial relationship. Burdened by unrealistic or conflicting expectations from his wife, daughter, and extended family, the father often struggles to balance everyone's opposing needs.

There are generally six challenges confronting stepfamilies—challenges that are sometimes greater when the stepfamily forms when the children are adults.[84,87] First, stepparents are often hurt and angered because they are marginalized or rejected, remaining outsiders despite years of effort to build bonds. Second, children may adapt poorly because they feel less loved or less welcomed in their parents' new home. Or they may feel disloyal to their unmarried parent if they befriend the stepparent. Third, stepparents may be critical of their spouse for being too lax and overly solicitous to their children—for example, not exerting enough discipline or spending excessive amounts of money on them. Fourth, children may be upset because family rituals change. For example, the parent and stepparent may no longer host holiday events or may celebrate everyone's birthdays in different ways. Even the wedding ceremony itself may create bad feelings, in that young adults are more disapproving when the wedding is a larger, flashier, more expensive event than when it is a smaller, simpler, low key occasion.[91] On the other hand, they also may disapprove if their parents have eloped or have a civil ceremony with no family present. Fifth, either of the parents or the stepparents might assume that just because the children are now adults, they can be given "the truth" about the parents' former relationship. This is a mistake. As discussed earlier, even adult children are upset when parents disclose negative things about one another. These five challenges exist regardless of the age of the children—and are especially daunting for fathers and daughters, for reasons already discussed in this chapter.

Box 6.7 Reconciliation between fathers and daughters

ARTHUR, AGE 54: Because of all the anger surrounding the divorce, my teenage daughter and I had no contact for seven months. For some reason she finally agreed to come to her grandmother's house to celebrate Christmas with all of us there. We somehow managed to begin again. Two week later there was a phone message from my daughter giving me her email address, ending with "I love you, Daddy." I sobbed like a baby. I have been on Cloud Infinity since.

RAMON, AGE 50: I stopped hearing from my 16-year-old daughter for three years. Then at 6:00AM, October 13, 2002, she woke me up from a deep sleep with a phone call. Initially, I thought someone was playing a cruel trick on me. But when she told me her middle name and the dog's name, I knew it was her. I started crying. We talked for an hour. She told me she was tired of being angry. She told me not to let her mother or her other sister know that we were going to start seeing each other again.

MARIA, AGE 22: I never thought I'd get any response. But my dad said my contacting him was the best gift I had ever given him. Now I think it was a mistake to take my stepfather's name. I never really thought about how my dad was hurt by that. I always had this vision of him as some opinionated, overbearing, stubborn tyrant. But he actually apologized to me for being a lousy father after the divorce. It had always been unthinkable that he might admit his failures. Now I know he actually does care—he always did. Seeing mom constantly upset by him had a profound effect on the way I felt about him. I have to focus on my issues with him—not mom's.

TANIKA, AGE 24: After three years of refusing to talk to my dad, a professor of mine convinced me to contact him. As our relationship slowly began again, I decided to talk to him about the breakup of our family. I got to tell him through my tears that I was really mad at him for a long time when he was battling his alcoholism. This was hard but it felt so good to get it out. He apologized. I couldn't believe it. I looked him directly in the eyes and told him I wasn't mad anymore. We both choked up then.

Sixth, later life remarriages can create stress between fathers and daughters over financial and health care matters. The daughter may resent her stepmother for decisions regarding the father's health care. Or she may be angry that her father and his wife do not consult her regarding his care for medical conditions or the decision to place him in a nursing home. The daughter may also resent her father for giving his wife, and not his children, health care power of attorney—which means his wife has exclusive legal authority to make end of life decisions for him. After he remarries, financial matters can also create stress between older fathers and daughters. How much money or what possessions is the father going to leave his second wife and their children? Is the father paying less for his daughter's or his grand-children's college educations because the money is being spent on his wife or their children? As the old saying goes, "When people say, 'it isn't the money, it's the principal of the thing,' you can be sure *it is* the money."

Interestingly, getting the whole stepfamily together to discuss their differences is *not* the best way to improve relationships—especially not the father-daughter relationship.[84,87] Indeed this is often the most destructive approach. Instead, therapists need to work separately with the father and daughter to help them strengthen their relationship—and to acknowledge the fact that the daughter's negative reactions to the remarriage may largely stem from her unresolved issues with her dad, not from issues with her stepmom. For example, the daughter may have felt ignored or unloved by her father and needs help expressing her grief and anger to him. The father may not realize that for years his daughter has longed for a closer relationship and more time *alone* with him—time without any other family members around, time that facilitates bonding and communicating. Simultaneously, but separately, therapists should work with the father and his wife to resolve their issues about their new roles in the stepfamily, the stepmother's feelings of sadness and rejection, and the father's feelings of always being stuck trying to meet the needs of the two females he loves most. The focus should not be on the daughter's relationship with her stepmother, but on the father's separate relationships with his daughter and his wife.

Conclusion

Box 6.8 Daughter sues father for college tuition[92]

In 2007 Dana Soderberg went to court to force her father to reimburse her for tuition at Southern Connecticut State University. Her parents, Howard and Deborah Soderberg, divorced in 2004. They agreed that the father would pay for the educations of their three children. Subsequently the daughter persuaded her father to sign a written contract obligating him to pay her college tuition until she was 25, as well as other expenses such as books and car insurance. As part of the agreement, she was supposed to apply for student loans which her father would then repay. But when Dana started her senior year, her father refused to pay the bills. She procured a $20,000 loan co-signed by her mother and finished school. After graduating, she sued her father for breach of contract. Her father argued that she had violated the contract by not applying for loans, by not attending school full time, and by not providing him with any receipts. He also claimed she dropped courses and spent the refunded money on non-educational items. The judge ruled that the father had to pay $47,000 for Dana's student loan, interest, attorney fees, and car insurance payments.

Whether the parents were ever married to one another or not, when they separate the father-daughter relationship generally becomes more complicated, more stressful, and more challenging. Unfortunately too many of their relationships are never restored to what they had been when the parents were together—and many end altogether. While a number of factors influence the quality of father-daughter relationship after the separation, the fact remains that fathers' relationships with their sons are generally less damaged. This damage in turn seems to largely explain why daughters pay a greater price than sons do for their parents' separation. As our society becomes more aware of those factors that help or hinder father-daughter relationships when parents live apart, we will hopefully provide fathers and daughters with more of the resources that will help preserve and strengthen their bond.

Review Questions

1   What percentage of daughters are growing up in the various types of married and unmarried American families?
2   What are ten popular but untrue beliefs about divorced fathers and what research or statistics refute each of these beliefs?
3   What are five popular but untrue beliefs about the typical American divorce and what research of statistics refute each?
4   Which daughters are at highest risk of having divorced parents and why are they at risk?
5   What is the long term impact of divorce on most daughters?
6   How much time are most fathers and daughter spending together after the parents' divorce?
7   What do each of these terms mean and how are they related to the quality of father-daughter relationships after divorce: joint legal custody, residential custody, shared parenting, parenting plans, co-parenting?
8   What are some of the reasons why fathers are not spending more time with their daughters after divorce?
9   What do each of these terms mean and how do they influence the father-daughter relationship: gate-keeping, role reversals, enmeshment, parentification, PAS, parental alienation?
10   How does shared parenting compare to sole mother residence in terms of its impact on daughters and on the father-daughter relationships?
11   What are the major objections raised to shared physical custody and what research refutes each?
12   What are five myths about shared physical custody and what research refutes each?
13   How are fathers affected by divorce compared to mothers?
14   How can financial issues damage father-daughter relationships after divorce?

15 How do we distinguish between parental alienation and the rational fear or rejection of a parent?
16 What are five of the major factors that weaken father-daughter relationships after divorce?
17 How can mothers strengthen father-daughter relationships after divorce?
18 Which fathers are the most and the least likely to pay child support?
19 How can the father's remarriage damage or complicate his relationship with his daughter and how might the damage be prevented?
20 How does the legal system sometimes work against father-daughter relationships?

Questions for Discussion and Debate

1 How much and what kind of information should parents share with their teenage or adult daughter about the reasons for their divorce?
2 If a teenage or adult daughter tells you that her father was a very good parent before the divorce, but that she no longer wants a relationship with him because he cheated on her mother, what would you say to her?
3 What are the pros and cons of the daughter living equal time with both parents after their divorce? If you were the daughter or if you were the parent, what residential custody arrangement would you want?
4 If the parents are not very cooperative or if one of the parents was unfaithful during the marriage, how do you feel about shared physical custody for their daughter?
5 What could our society do to increase the odds that fathers will spend more time with their daughters after the parents' divorce?
6 What advice would you give a divorcing father with a teenage daughter? How would your advice differ if she was in college?
7 If you are a man dating a woman whose parents are divorced, what would you be most concerned about given what you have read in this chapter? What information would you consider most important to learn about her family?
8 In terms of your relationship with your daughter after a divorce, would you rather be the mother or the father? Why?
9 What advice would you give the father and the daughter after the parents' divorce in order to preserve or strengthen their relationship?
10 As a professional whose work involves divorced fathers and their daughters, specifically what could you do to help the fathers feel welcomed, included, and valued as parents?
11 If her mother or her father is saying or doing things that are weakening the father-daughter relationship, what would you advise an adolescent or adult daughter to do?

12 How do you feel about a divorced father's being asked to give money for his daughter's college education or her wedding when she has had little or nothing to do with him since her parents' divorce?

13 As a divorced father who is engaged to be married, what would your expectations be for your daughter and your future wife in terms of their relationship with each other?

14 If a daughter feels her father is ignoring her for his new wife and other children, what would you advise her to do? Conversely, if parental alienation is occurring, what would you advise the father to do?

15 If you were going before a judge for a decision about where your daughter will live now that you are divorced, would you rather be the mother or the father? Why?

References

1 Griswold R. *Fatherhood in America.* New York: Basic Books; 1993.

2 Census Bureau. *Population estimates in United States.* Washington, DC: U.S. Department of Labor: Census Bureau; 2017.

3 Census Bureau. *Single parent households.* Washington, DC: Department of Labor; 2007.

4 Guzman G. *Household income: 2016.* Washington, DC: U.S. Census Bureau; 2017.

5 Wilcox B, Zill N. *Marriage and divorce rates nationwide.* Charlottesville, VA: University of Virginia; 2015.

6 Schwartz C, Hanb H. The reversal of the gender gap in education and trends in marital dissolution. *American Sociological Review* 2014; 79: 605–629.

7 Stewart A, Brentano C. *Divorce: Causes and consequences.* New Haven, CT: Yale University; 2006.

8 Finley G, Schwartz S. Father involvement and young adult outcomes. *Family Court Review* 2007; 45: 573–587.

9 Harvey J, Fine M. *Children of divorce: Stories of loss and growth.* New York: Routledge; 2010.

10 Braithwaite D, Baxter L. You're my parent but you're not. *Journal of Applied Communication Research* 2006; 34: 30–48.

11 Stamps K, Booth A, King V. Adolescents with nonresident fathers: Are daughters more disadvantaged than sons? *Journal of Marriage and the Family* 2009; 71(3): 650–662.

12 King V, Soboleski D. Nonresident fathers' contributions to adolescent well-being. *Journal of Marriage and Family* 2006; 68: 537–557.

13 Sobolewski J, King V. The importance of the coparental relationship for nonresident fathers' ties to children. *Journal of Marriage and Family* 2005; 67: 1196–1212.

14 King V, Harris K, Heard H. Racial diversity in nonresident father involvement. *Journal of Marriage and the Family* 2004; 66: 1–21.

15 Krampe E, Newston R. Reflecting on the father: Childhood family structure and women's paternal relationships. *Journal of Family Issues* 2012; 33: 773–800.

16 Fabricius W. Listening to children of divorce. *Family Relations* 2003; 52: 385–396.

17 Harvey J, Fine M. *Children of divorce*. New York: Routledge; 2010.

18 Frank H. Marital status, conflict and post divorce predictors. *Journal of Divorce and Remarriage* 2004; 39: 105–124.

19 Peters B, Ehrenberg M. The influence of parental separation on father-child relationships. *Journal of Divorce & Remarriage* 2008; 49: 78–108.

20 Scott M, Booth A, King V. Post-divorce father-adolescent closeness. *Journal of Marriage and Family* 2007; 69: 1194–1209.

21 Greenwood J. Parent child relationships after mid to late life parental divorce. *Journal of Divorce and Remarriage* 2012; 53: 1–17.

22 Ahrons C. Family ties after divorce. *Family Process* 2007; 46: 53–65.

23 Hetherington M, Kelly J. *For better or worse: Divorce reconsidered*. New York: Norton; 2002.

24 Windle M, Windle R. Parental divorce and family history of alcohol disorder: Associations with young adults' alcohol problems, marijuana use and interpersonal relations. *Alcoholism Clinical and Experimental Research* 2018; 42: 1084–1095.

25 Bouchard G, Doucet D. Parental divorce and couples' adjustment during the transition to parenthood. *Journal of Family Issues* 2011; 32: 507–527.

26 Ellis B, Bates J, Dodge R. Father absence and teenage pregnancy. *Child Development* 2003; 74: 801–821.

27 Ellis B, Schlomer G, Tilley E, Butler E. Impact of fathers on risky sexual behavior in daughters. *Development and Psychopathology* 2012; 24: 317–401.

28 DelPriore D, Scholmer G, Ellis B. Impact of fathers on parental monitoring of daughters and their affiliation with sexually promiscuous peers. *Developmental Psychology* 2017; 53: 1330–1343.

29 Kilmann P. Attachment patterns for college women of intact vs. non-intact families. *Journal of Adolescence* 2006; 29: 89–102.

30 Mullett E, Stolberg A. Divorce and its impact on the intimate relationships of young adults. *Journal of Divorce and Remarriage* 2002; (38): 39–59.

31 Schaick K, Stolberg A. Paternal involvement and young adults' intimate relationships. *Journal of Divorce and Remarriage* 2001; 36: 99–121.

32 Haaz D, Kneavel M, Browning S. The father-daughter relationship and intimacy in the marriages of daughters of divorce. *Journal of Divorce and Remarriage* 2014; 55: 164–177.

33 Braithwaite S, Doxey R, Dowdle K, Fincham F. The unique influences of parental divorce and parental conflict on emerging adults in romantic relationships. *Journal of Adult Development* 2016; 23: 214–225.

34 Herzog M, Cooney T. Parental divorce and interparental conflict. *Journal of Divorce and Remarriage* 2002; 37: 89–109.

35 Lee S. Parental divorce, relationships with fathers and mothers and children's romantic relationships in young adulthood. *Journal of Adult Development* 2018; 25: 121–134.

36 Whitton S. Effects of parental divorce on marital commitment. *Journal of Family Psychology* 2008; 22: 789–793.

37 Bartell D. Influence of parental divorce on romantic relationships in young adulthood. In: Fine M, Harvey J, editors. *Handbook of divorce*. New York: Routledge; 2006: 339–361.

38 Maine M. *Father Hunger: Fathers, daughters and the pursuit of thinness.* New York: Gurze; 2004.

39 Japel C, Tremblay R, Vitaro F, Boulerice B. Early parental separation and psychosocial development of daughters 6–9 years old. *Journal of Orthopsychiatry* 1999; 39: 49–60.

40 Carrier H, Utz R. Parental divorce among young and adult children: Long term analysis of mental health and family solidarity. *Journal of Divorce and Remarriage* 2012; 53: 247–266.

41 Flouri E. *Fathering and child outcomes.* Hoboken, NJ: John Wiley; 2005.

42 Menning C, Stewart S. Nonresident father involvement and adolescent weight. *Journal of Family Issues* 2008; 29(12): 1673–1700.

43 Fabricius W, Luecken L. Postdivorce living arrangements, parent conflict and physical health for children of divorce. *Journal of Family Psychology* 2007; 21: 195–205.

44 Schwartz S, *et al.* Perceived parental relationships and health risk behaviors in college attending adults. *Journal of Marriage and Family* 2009; 71: 727–740.

45 Kposowa A. Marital status and suicide in the National Longitudinal Mortality Study. *Journal of Epidemiology and Community Health* 2000; 54: 254–261.

46 Weitzman L. *The divorce revolution.* Boston: Free Press; 1985.

47 Tobin S. The divorce revolution: Book review. *Loyola of Los Angeles Law Review* 1987; 20(1640): 1649.

48 Weitzman L. The economic consequences of divorce are still unequal: Comment on Peterson. *American Sociological Review* 1996; 61: 537–538.

49 McManus P, DiPrete T. Losers and winners: Financial consequences of divorce for men. *American Sociological Review* 2001; 66: 246–268.

50 Stirling K, Aldrich T. Child support: Who bears the burden? *Family Relations* 2008; 57: 376–389.

51 Coltin B. *Fathering time after divorce by state.* New York: Custody Exchange Organization; 2018.

52 Miller A. Expertise fails to attenuate gendered biases in judicial decision making. *Social Psychological and Personality Science* 2018; (1): 8.

53 Votruba A, Braver S, Ellman I, Fabricius W. Moral intuitions about fault, parenting and child custody after divorce. *Psychology, Public Policy and Law* 2014; 20: 251–262.

54 Jappen M. Children's relationships with grandparents in joint and sole physical custody families. *Journal of Divorce and Remarriage* 2018; 59: 359–371.

55 Nielsen L. Joint versus sole physical custody: Children's outcomes independent of parent-child relationships, income and conflict in 60 studies. *Journal of Divorce and Remarriage* 2018; 59: 247–281.

56 Afifi T, McManus T. Divorce disclosures and adolescents mental and physical health. *Journal of Divorce and Remarriage* 2010; 51: 83–107.

57 Afifi T, Afifi W, Morse C, Hamrick K. Adolescents' avoidance tendencies and physiological reactions to discussions about their parents' relationship. *Communication Monographs* 2008; 75: 290–317.

58 Koerner A, Wallace S, Lehman S, Lee S, Escalante K. Sensitive mother to adolescent disclosures after divorce. *Journal of Family Psychology* 2004; 18: 46–57.

59 Koerner S, Kenyon D, Rankin A. Growing up faster? *Journal of Divorce and Remarriage,* 2006; 45: 25–41.

60 Schrodt P, Shimkowski J. Feeling caught as a mediator of coparental communication and young adult children's mental health and relational satisfaction with parents. *Journal of Social and Personal Relationships* 2013; 30: 977–999.

61 Schrodt P, Ledbetter A. Parental confirmation as a mitigator of feeling caught and family satisfaction. *Personal Relationships* 2012; 19: 146–161.

62 Schrodt P, Afifi T. Communication processes that predict young adults' feelings of being caught and family satisfaction. *Communication Monographs* 2007; 74: 200–228.

63 Shimkowski J, Schrodt P. Coparental communication as a mediator of conflict and young adult children's mental well-being. *Communication Monographs* 2012; 79: 48–71.

64 Bowen M. *Family therapy in clinical practice*. New York: Jason Aronson; 1978.

65 Leudemann M. Mothers' discussions with daughters following divorce. *Journal of Divorce and Remarriage* 2006; 46: 29–55.

66 Jurkovic G, Thirkield A, Morrell R. Parentification of adult children of divorce. *Journal of Youth and Adolescence* 2001; 30: 245–257.

67 Silverberg S. Sensitive mother to adolescent disclosures after divorce. *Journal of Family Psychology* 2004; 18: 46–57.

68 Braithwaite D, Toller P, Durham W, Jones A. Stepchildren's perception of contradictions in communication of co parents. *Journal of Applied Communication Research* 2008; 36: 33–55.

69 Mayseless O. I was more her mom than she was mine. *Family Relations* 2004; 53: 78–86.

70 Ganong L, Coleman M, Chapman A. Gatekeeping after separation and divorce. In: Drozd L, Saini M, Olesen N, editors. *Parenting plan evaluations: Applied research for the family court*. New York: Oxford University Press; 2016. 308–346.

71 Austin B, Fieldstone L, Pruett M. Bench book for assessing parental gatekeeping in parenting disputes. *Journal of Child Custody* 2013; 10: 1–16.

72 Cannon E. Parent characteristics and antecedents of gatekeeping. *Family Process* 2008; 47: 501–519.

73 Krampe E, Newton R. Father presence questionnaire. *Fathering* 2006; 4: 159–189.

74 Markham M, Ganong L, Coleman M. Mothers' cooperation in coparental relationships. *Family Relations* 2007; 56: 369–377.

75 Hilton J, Frye K. Psychological adjustment among divorced custodial parents. *Journal of Divorce and Remarriage* 2004; 41(1): 30.

76 Duck S, Wood J. Sex and gendered patterns in relational dissolution. In: Fine M, Harvey J, editors. *Handbook of Divorce*. New York: Routledge; 2006: 169–188.

77 Clawar S, Rivlin B. *Children held hostage: Identifying brainwashed children, presenting a case, and crafting solutions*. Chicago, IL: American Bar Association; 2013.

78 Lorandos D, Bernet W, Sauber S. *Parental alienation: The handbook for mental health and legal professionals*. Springfield, IL: Charles Thomas; 2013.

79 Warshak R. Parental alienation: Overview, management, interventions and practice tips. *Journal of the American Academy of Matrimonial Lawyers* 2015; 28: 181–213.

80 Warshak R. Ten parental alienation fallacies that compromise decisions in court and in therapy. *Professional Psychology, Research and Practice* 2015; 46: 235–249.

81 Harman J, Leder-Elder S, Biringen Z. Prevalence of parental alienation drawn from a representative poll. *Children and Youth Services Review* 2016; 66: 62–66.

82 Ludolph P, Bow J. Complex alienation dynamics and very young children. *Journal of Child Custody* 2012; 9: 153–178.

83 Baker A, Sauber R. *Working with alienated children and their families.* New York: Routledge; 2012.

84 Warshak R. *Divorce poison: How to protect your family from bad-mouthing and brainwashing.* New York: Regan Books; 2010.

85 Bernet W, Wamboldt M, Narrow W. Child affected by parental relationship distress. *Journal of the American Academy of Child and Adolescent Psychiatry* 2016; 55: 571–579.

86 Miller C. Repartnering following divorce: Impact on fathers and their adult children. *Journal of Marriage and Family* 2013; 75: 697–712.

87 Papernow P. The remarriage triangle: Working with later life recouplers and their grown children. *Psychotherapy Networker Magazine* 2016; January: 49–53.

88 Kramrei E, *et al.* Post divorce adjustment and social relationships: Meta-analytic review. *Journal of Divorce and Remarriage*, 2007; 46(145): 166.

89 Sun Y, Li Y. Post divorce family stability and adolescents' academic progress. *Journal of Family Issues* 2009; 30: 1527–1539.

90 Papernow P. Recoupling in mid-life and beyond: From love at last to not so fast. *Family Process* 2018; 57: 52–69.

91 Baxter L. Empty ritual: Young adult stepchildren's perceptions of the remarriage ceremony. *Journal of Social and Personal Relationships* 2009; 26: 467–487.

92 Nolan C. College grad sues father to recoup tuition costs. *The Connecticut Law Tribune* 2010; June 29: 2–3.

Chapter 7

Fathers and Daughters in Minority Families

Although the research and issues presented in previous chapters are applicable to father-daughter relationships regardless of race, there are circumstances and cultural differences that affect African, Hispanic, Asian, and Native American fathers and daughters in unique ways. This chapter explores those differences and acknowledges the challenges that are the most likely to confront father-daughter relationships in each group.

In a nation of almost 3.3 million people, in 2017, 61% of the American population was non-Hispanic white, 18% Hispanic, 13% black, 6% Asian American, 1% Native American, and 3% multiracial.[1] By 2020, 51% of the children under the age of 18 will be members of racial minorities, rising to 64% by 2060.[2] By 2045, the American population will be 49% non-Hispanic white, 25% Hispanic, 13% black, 8% Asian, and 4% multiracial. In short, the majority of American children are members of racial minority groups—which will also be true for all age groups within the next two decades.

The number of multiracial children has risen faster than any one racial group. Multiracial children's numbers tripled from 1980 to 4% in 2017.[3] These numbers are especially impressive since the U.S. Supreme Court did not rule until 1967 that interracial marriages were legal nationwide. Reflecting this shift, in 2000 31% of Americans opposed interracial marriages, compared to only 10% in 2015. The biggest increase was marriage between black and white adults, which increased from 5% in 1980 to 18% in 2015. Most multiracial children (42%) have one Hispanic and one white non-Hispanic parent.

Racial Disparities: Family Income, Non-marital Births, and Incarceration

As discussed in Chapter 6, certain groups of daughters are much less likely than others to grow up living in the same home with their father throughout childhood because their parents have separated—a situation that, for reasons already explained, tends to weaken father-daughter relationships. Asian American and non-Hispanic white daughters are the most likely to have college educated parents, to have parents who are married when their children are born, and to live above the poverty level. Regardless of the parents' race, each of these factors is closely linked to how likely children are to grow up in the same home with their father.

Box 7.1 Mean* family incomes[1]

	White	Asian	Hispanic	Black
Under $10,000	3.6%	3.4%	7.5%	11.6
$10,000 to 19,999	6.6	5.6	12.9	13.7
$20,000 to 24,999	4.6	3.6	8.1	6.7
$25,000 to 34,999	9.3	7.2	14.6	12.3
$35,000 to 39,999	4.7	3.1	6.1	5.6
$40,000 to 49,999	9.1	7.4	9.6	9.3
$50,000 to 59,999	8.4	7.3	8.9	8.2
$60,000 to 74,999	11.6	10.4	10.1	9.3
$75,000 to 84,999	6.7	7.0	5.1	4.9
$85,000 to 99,999	8.2	7.5	4.8	5.8
$100,000 to 149,999	16.1	20.4	7.6	9.0
$150,000 to 199,999	6.0	9.4	2.2	2.2
$200,000 and above	5.3	7.5	1.5	1.4

* The "mean" is the mathematical "average" for each group.

There are also considerable differences among racial groups in regard to family income.[4] In 2016, half of all Asian American families had household incomes above $80,720, compared to $63,155 for non-Hispanic whites, $46,882 for Hispanics, and $38,555 for blacks and Native Americans. Nearly 12% of non-Hispanic white and Asian American, 28% of Hispanic, and 34% of black and Native Americans children are living in poverty.

Because poverty and incarceration in all racial groups are closely connected, daughters in certain racial groups are far more likely to have incarcerated fathers since their fathers are far more likely to have grown up in poverty. Black and Native American children are 2.5 times more likely to live in poverty and 6.4 times more likely to have incarcerated fathers than non-Hispanic white children. Nearly 20% of black and Native American fathers are or have been incarcerated, compared to only 2% of Asian and 3% of non-Hispanic white fathers.[5]

Box 7.2 Median* family incomes, education, and marital status[1]

Parents with graduate degree	$100,000
Parents with college degree	$92,000
Parents with some college	$61,000
Parents with high school degree	$49,700
Parents without degree	$31,200
Married parent families	$73,000
Single parent families	$30,300

* The "median" is the point where half of the families earned less and half earned more than this amount.

Box 7.3 Racial differences in poverty, income, incarceration, and marital status[1,4]

	Total number of children % of population	% in poverty	Median family income	College educated parents	Parents without HS degree	Imprisoned father	Born out of wedlock
white	37,928,000 (51%)	12%	$61,349	49%	4%	3%	28%
Hispanic	18,156,000 (25%)	28%	$46,882	29%	29%	15%	53%
Black	10,156,000 (14%)	34%	$38,555	24%	10%	20%	72%
Asian	3,561,000 (5%)	12%	$80,720	64%	8%	2%	17%
American Indian	626,148 (1%)	34%	$38,300	22%	10%	18%	67%
Multi-race	3,100,000 (4%)	*					

*no data available.

These racial differences in income, incarceration, and out-of-wedlock births are important because they have a profound impact on father-daughter relationships, as we will see in Chapter 8. At the same time, however, we must keep three facts in mind. First, the vast majority of fathers in every racial group have never been in prison, are not living in poverty, and are either living with or married to the mother of their children. Second, incarceration, poverty, and non-marital births are linked more closely to parents' educational levels than to their race. In every racial group, the least educated people are the most likely to have children out of wedlock, to become mothers as teenagers, to live in poverty, and to be incarcerated. All of these factors work against fathers maintaining close relationships—or having any relationship—with their children. The key factor, however, is education, not race. Third, even though non-Hispanic white fathers are the most likely to be married to or live with the mothers of their children, this does not mean that most other fathers are disengaged or disinterested in their children.[6]

We turn our attention then to the unique situations and cultural differences in father-daughter relationships in African, Hispanic, Asian, and Native American families.

Colorism: The Impact on Daughters

Before discussing African American and Hispanic American fathers and daughters separately, we should note one important issue that they share in common: dealing with colorism. Racism is a form of discrimination based on being a member of a particular racial group. In contrast, **colorism** is a form of discrimination based on the lightness or darkness of a person's skin in all racial groups, with the exception of non-Hispanic whites. For example, very dark skinned people of Hispanic, or African, or East Indian descent will encounter more colorism than very light skinned members of their race. Colorism is based on the belief that lighter shades of skin are preferable and more desirable than darker shades. African and Hispanic Americans are the most likely to encounter colorism in the U.S. given the diversity in their shades of skin and their physical features. In fact, people of Hispanic descent have different words to describe their shades of skin. *Blanco* (white) refers to people with very light skin and European features who are often mistaken for non-Hispanic white Americans. In contrast, *indio*, *negro*, and *moreno* refer to Hispanic people with darker shades of skin and more indigenous features.[7]

Like racism, colorism can have a negative impact on the self-confidence and self-esteem of darker skin children. For example, teenagers with very dark skin are often less confident and more depressed than lighter skinned members of their race.[8] Darker skinned children also feel more discriminated against by adults and by their peers than lighter skinned members of their race.[9] Hispanic American daughters who are mistaken for African Americans are more likely to feel depressed, rejected, or stigmatized than those who are perceived as Hispanic.[10]

Given the potentially negative impact of colorism, Hispanic and African American fathers can play an especially important role in their daughters' feelings about their appearance. Fathers can promote their daughters' self-esteem by never showing favoritism towards their lighter skin daughters or towards daughters with more Caucasian features. For example, in some

Puerto Rican families, fathers favored the daughter with very light skin over the daughter with very dark skin.[11] The sisters with darker skin were more dissatisfied with their appearance, especially if people outside the family perceived them as African Americans. Similarly, in some African American families, lighter skin daughters felt they received higher quality parenting from their mothers than darker skin daughters, while the reverse was true for sons.[12] This finding is especially important because there were nearly 800 teenagers in the study.

Colorism can also take a toll on young adult daughters. For example in a study with Latina college students, the darker skin daughters who were born outside the U.S. were more dissatisfied with their appearance than the darker skin daughters born in the States.[13] The immigrant parents were less likely than the other parents to have talked to their daughters about colorism. In contrast, in non-immigrant families, the darker skin daughters received more reassurance from their parents that their darker skin was just as desirable as lighter skin.

Fathers may be especially helpful to their daughters in this regard. For example, in some black families, it was the women who sent daughters the message that lighter shades of skin were the most desirable or most favored in the family.[14] This attitude undermined the self-confidence of dark skinned daughters, contributed to rivalry between the sisters, and weakened the daughters' relationships with one or both parents. In contrast, fathers can squelch colorism in the family and teach their daughters how to deal with this form of discrimination in society. As one young adult daughter explained: "My father always told my sister and I that we're beautiful, with natural hair like African silk, and you are beautiful the way you are. I guess that is because he knew how society is" (p. 595). Another daughter explains:

> My younger sister was prancing through the house and she was like, "Vivica and I are the lightest ones, Vivica and I are lightest ones. We're the prettiest ones" ... I remember my father, he came running inside because he's dark and my older sister is dark and he was upset. He was just like, "No! You know you don't say this." ... "Don't make her feel bad because she is the darkest." (p. 596).

In addition to helping their daughters deal with colorism, fathers can help them cope with other issues related to race, as we will now see.

African American Fathers and Daughters

Unique Aspects of Their Relationships

Compared to other fathers, black father-daughter relationships are unique in several ways, beginning with the father's parenting style.[15] Black fathers tend to be stricter and to use physical punishment more often than other fathers. They also tend communicate less with their children than non-Hispanic white fathers, especially about personal topics. This does not mean, however, that black children feel any less loved by their fathers. In intact families black daughters felt just as close and just as loved by their fathers as white daughters.[16,17] Similarly, for teenagers living in single mother families, black teenagers were less likely than white teenagers to talk to their fathers about dating or other personal issues. The black teenagers, however, felt closer to their fathers than the white teenagers.[18] Likewise, even though black female undergraduates described their fathers as less nurturing than white and Hispanic daughters, they felt just as loved and felt they received just as much mentoring and advice from their fathers.[19]

The Father's Impact

Box 7.4 Serena Williams: International tennis champion and her father[24]

Internationally famous tennis champion, Serena Williams, has had a close relationship with her father since early childhood. In an African American family with five daughters, Serena's dad Richard started her playing tennis at the age of five. He also coached and home schooled her and her award winning tennis star sister, Venus. At the age of 33, Serena was playing a match to become the first player in 27 years to sweep all four Grand Slams in the same season. But her father was unable to attend due to poor health.

As Serena describes his role in her life:

> He's been the most important person in my career ... I miss him all the time. I call him. I try to reach out to him a lot. He calls me. He watches my matches. He still tells me things that I'm not doing right. My playing tennis was his idea. It's changed sports. It's changed history. Who would have thought that he could have raised two black girls to play a sport that African Americans haven't typically done well in? Every time I stand out there, I think that I wouldn't be here if somebody didn't have that vision for me. I don't know if I would have a vision like that for my kids ... He always says, "Don't put pressure on yourself. Be happy with what you have."

African American daughters often attribute their success, self-reliance, determination, and self-confidence to their fathers. As adults, a number of these daughters have written books about their fathers' contributions to their lives: *Color him father*,[20] *Father songs*,[21] *Daughters of men:*

African American women and their fathers,[22] and *Our black fathers.*[23] For example, as the story in Box 7.4 illustrates, the internationally famous tennis champion, Serena Williams, attributes her success largely to her father.[24]

Even though the majority of black daughters are living with their single mothers, they still benefit from having strong relationships with their fathers. In respect to drug and alcohol use, as sixth graders, these daughters are less likely to use drugs, regardless of their mother's educational level or the quality of their relationship with her.[25] As teenagers, they are less likely to drink.[26] In fact, the quality of the father-daughter relationship was a better predictor of teenage drinking than whether or not the parents lived together. Moreover, when teenagers from low income, single mother families are using drugs or are involved in delinquent behavior and their fathers began spending more time with them, their drug use and delinquency decreased—more so for black than for white or Hispanic adolescents.[27] Again, the additional fathering time was beneficial regardless of the quality of their relationships with their mothers.

As for academic performance and confidence, daughters with supportive fathers were more engaged in school and had more confidence in their academic abilities.[28] Their interest in science courses was closely linked to feeling close to their father—more so for black than for white daughters.[29] In college, regardless of whether their parents were separated or together, daughters who had a loving, supportive father credited him with teaching them how to succeed and how to prevail in difficult situations.[30] Even those whose fathers were not college educated and who could not afford to help pay for their daughter's college education felt that their father's emotional support was crucial to their self-confidence and perseverance. Interestingly too, daughters whose fathers had been involved in their athletic activities felt this had been an important way for him to teach her how to overcome obstacles in life.

Black daughters who have close relationships with their fathers are also less likely to engage in risky sexual behavior—which, in turn, decreases their chances of becoming teenage mothers or contracting incurable sexually transmitted diseases. Daughters whose fathers talk with them about sex are more likely to ask their boyfriends about their sexual past.[31] As teenagers they are also more likely to use birth control, to have sex with fewer partners, and to prevent disease by having their partners wear condoms.[32,33] And daughters who grew up in low income, single parent families who had good relationships with their fathers waited longer before first having sex or before having a child—regardless of their race.[34] As discussed in an earlier chapter, condom use is especially important for African American and Latina daughters because they have the highest rates of cervical cancer later in life—a cancer that can be prevented either by getting vaccinated against

Figure 7.1
Source: LeShay Shaw.

the HPV virus before becoming sexually active or by using condoms to prevent the transmission of the virus.[35]

Black daughters who are close to their fathers are also less likely to be victims of dating violence.[36] To be clear, "violence" did not mean rape or battering. It meant pushing, shoving, slapping, throwing things, cursing, or being threatened verbally. This finding is especially important because black daughters are the most likely to be victims of dating violence. In a large study with 2,450 teenage girls in Pittsburgh, black girls were more likely than white girls to be the victims and the perpetrators of dating violence.[37] Given this, black fathers may be especially helpful in teaching their daughters how not to express their anger physically with boyfriends and how to prevent becoming victims of dating aggression.

The father also has an impact on his daughter's self-esteem and on her psychological and emotional well-being. In a study with almost 2,000 black teenage girls in a Midwestern city, those who were close to their fathers were less depressed and less likely to be suspended from school.[38] The father-daughter relationship had a greater impact than did support from other adults, mentoring, or religious connections. Likewise, in single mother homes, teenage daughters were less likely to be depressed and to misbehave at school when they were not angry at or alienated from their fathers.[39] Interestingly too, not feeling angry or mistrustful of their dads mattered more than the actual amount of time they spent with him. Other studies with teenagers confirm that daughters are less depressed, less anxious, and less stressed when they have supportive relationships with their father.[40] Interestingly, girls in father absent homes say they feel less feminine than daughters who live with both parents.[11] The father-absent daughters felt they were too masculine in terms of being too verbally and physically aggressive.

In sum, even though most black daughters do not grow up in the same home with their fathers, supportive fathering still has a positive impact on her emotional, behavioral, academic, sexual, and psychological well-being.

Hispanic American Fathers and Daughters

Cultural Uniqueness

While African Americans have historically been the largest racial minority in the U.S., that is no longer the case for people under the age of 18. The 44 million Hispanic Americans account for 15% of the general population and 25% of the population of children under the age of eighteen.[1,42,43] Outside of Mexico, the U.S. has the world's largest Hispanic population. Much of the increase in the Hispanic American population is a result of the high birth rate, not an increase in immigration. Most (66%) are citizens because they were born in the U.S. Another 17% are **naturalized citizens** who have lived in the States at least five years and passed the Civics and English language tests required for citizenship. The remaining 17% are undocumented immigrants—most of whom entered the country legally, but stayed on illegally after their temporary visas expired. Two-thirds of Hispanic immigrants are from Mexico, followed by 9% from Puerto Rico (an American territory whose residents do not have U.S. citizenship) and 3% from Cuba. The remainder come from various Spanish-speaking countries around the world, largely from Latin America.

It is important to acknowledge that Hispanic Americans are not a homogenous group in terms of income, education, and out of wedlock births.[44] For example, most Cuban Americans came to the U.S. as refugees seeking asylum from Castro's socialist regime in the 1950s. Most were well educated, spoke English, and were familiar with American culture through their social or business connections in Cuba. Interestingly, nearly 14,000 of these early Cuban immigrants were Jewish—educated people who had settled in Cuba after fleeing from Spain to escape religious persecution during the Inquisition. Most Cuban refugees settled in Miami, Florida, where they acquired considerable political and economic influence. Compared to other Hispanic Americans, Cuban Americans are the most well educated, have the highest incomes, and have the fewest children born out of wedlock. So when discussing Hispanic Americans, it is important to remember that they are not a monolithic, homogeneous group with similar family situations.

But despite these differences, regardless of their country of origin, Hispanic American families share common religious, cultural beliefs and family expectations that impact father-daughter relationships.[45] Latino families are centered around the concept of *familismo* where the immediate and extended family's needs are more important than any individual's needs. Family members depend heavily on one another for emotional and financial support and often sacrifice their individual needs for the family's benefit. Rather than openly disagree with one another, members are encouraged to maintain harmony by keeping their true feelings to themselves, and by being agreeable and polite in order to avoid conflict. The emphasis, especially for females, is to be passive and demure. Members are also expected to spend considerable time together and to maintain close relationships even with the extended family. Another aspect of *familismo* is introducing boyfriends and girlfriends to the parents. This is a sign of respect for the parents, not a sign that the relationship is serious. Especially for girls whose parents did not grow up in the States, *familismo* can feel constraining and sexist. It can also contribute to anger, resentment, depression, and guilt for those daughters who defy their parents' wishes and fail to live up to their expectations for a "good" daughter.

Compared to Hispanic American families, most other families are more individualistic, meaning that the primary focus is on each person as an independent individual. As they age, sons and daughters are expected and encouraged to become increasingly self-reliant and to live lives separate from their parents. In becoming more autonomous, the daughter who openly disagrees with her parents is not as likely to be considered disrespectful or selfish, as she would be in a Hispanic American family.

Latino families also typically embrace the concept of *machismo*. But contrary to what many non-Hispanics believe this term means, in Hispanic

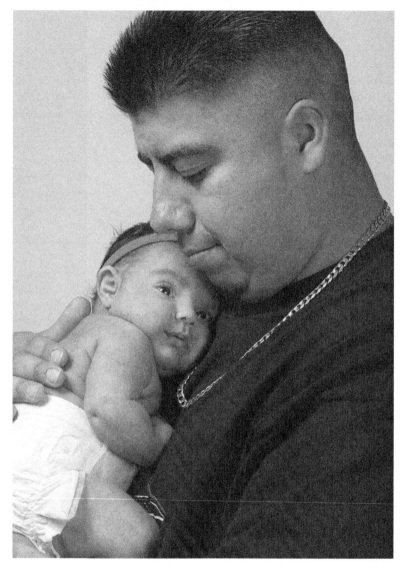

Figure 7.2
Source: Nate Allred/shutterstock.com.

culture machismo refers to a man's being responsible and dedicated to provide for and to protect all members of his family. Machismo is a positive
and desirable trait, not a negative one. Unfortunately being "macho" has
come to have a negative connotation as a hypersexual, aggressive, sexist,
possessive and insensitive man. The stereotype is that most Hispanic fathers
are too "macho" to express tender emotions, to treat their wives and

daughters with respect, or to be spiritual, communicative, sensitive, or empathic. In fact, it is more accurate to say that in all racial groups, some fathers are more "macho" than others.

It is true, however, that Hispanic families tend to adhere to more traditional gender roles than most white families. The mothers are largely in charge of the parenting and running the household. The fathers are more protective and strict, particularly with their daughters. Keep in mind, however, that the father's attitudes and behavior largely depend on how acculturated he has become. Immigrant fathers are generally more conservative and traditional than fathers born or raised in the States. For example, in a study with 735 infants from low income, Mexican American families, the most acculturated immigrant fathers were the most involved in the childcare.[46] Likewise, in poor Hispanic families with fifth grade children, the higher the mother's income, the more involved the fathers were in hands-on childcare.[47]

Compared to non-Hispanic fathers, Hispanic fathers generally expect their children to be more respectful, more submissive, and more obedient—especially their daughters. Daughters communicate on a much more personal level and spend much more time with their mothers than with their fathers. Although this is also true in non-Hispanic families, this mother-daughter connection is generally stronger in Hispanic families. Fathers and daughters seldom talk about personal issues. Such intimacy is not considered either a necessary or a desirable component of good fathering. For instance, Cuban American daughters described a good mother-daughter relationship as one where they talked a lot about personal things and kept many things secret from the father.[48]

Nevertheless, many Latina daughters wish their fathers were more communicative. For example, in a study with more than 7,100 teenagers from married families, Hispanic daughters were more dissatisfied than black or than white daughters with the quality of their relationships with their fathers. They were also more likely to be clinically depressed than the black or the white daughters. Regardless of race, daughters with poor father-daughter relationships were the most likely to be clinically depressed.[49] Other Hispanic adolescent girls have also said that they want "more" from their relationships with their fathers. But most also said it would be uncomfortable to have more personal conversations with him.[50]

The Father's Impact

With respect to their daughter's sexual behavior, Hispanic fathers clearly have an impact. Since fathers and daughters are not expected to communicate about personal things, mothers are generally in charge of talking about sexual topics. Unfortunately, Latina mothers are much less likely than white mothers to talk about sex or contraception with their daughters.[51,52] This is especially true for immigrant mothers.[53]

The fact that fathers are less likely than mothers to talk to their daughters about sex does not mean they never do so or that they necessarily have extremely conservative views about premarital sex. For example, in interviews with 20 Mexican American immigrant fathers in Los Angeles, protecting their daughter from a sexually dangerous society and improving her future through education were far more important than her virginity per se.[54] Although fathers who had grown up in rural areas had the most conservative views, most fathers did not have especially restrictive attitudes. Alfredo, a construction worker with a 13-year-old daughter, said: "I tell my daughter the day you are going to have sexual relations, do it. Not now, of course, when you get older. No problem, but use your brain, because you have a brain" (p.1123). Diego is a 36-year-old father with an 11-year-old daughter who says:

> I would tell my daughter to talk with her partner a lot about sex, that she should tell him what she wants, what she would like to do, how she would like to do it, about her fantasies and that she should have a lot of communication with him. (p.1123).

Fidel, father of three daughters, explained: "It is not so much that they are going to lose their virginity. It would hurt me that any *cabron* [asshole] would be the one with whom they would lose it!" (p.1125). Forty-year-old Sebastian, father of two daughters, said:

> Look, I have talked with my oldest daughter about it, and I have been telling her that I would like you to give it (her virginity) to the person that you love. The first time should be a wonderful experience, something that you long for, something that you desire. (p.1126)

So while some of these fathers said that they lacked the knowledge, self-confidence, or comfort to talk with their daughters about sex, others were very forthright and outspoken.

The fact that Hispanic fathers and mothers talk less to their daughters about sex than other parents do is disturbing because Latinas are more likely than other girls to become mothers as teenagers.[55] The rates of teenage pregnancy, births, and abortion have decreased by nearly 70% for all racial groups since 1991. But Latinas are still twice as likely (16%) as non-Hispanic whites (7%) and somewhat more likely than blacks (15%) to become teenage mothers.[56] Latino teenagers are only somewhat more likely to be having sex (36%) than white teenagers (31%) but less likely than African American teenagers (46%). It appears then that Latinas are more likely to get pregnant, not because they are more likely to be virgins, but because they are less likely to use contraceptives.

As their fathers are no doubt aware, Latina daughters are more likely than other teenage girls to date men who are significantly older—and more likely to intentionally become pregnant as teenagers.[57] Some researchers speculate that Latinas from exceptionally conservative families may intentionally become pregnant as teenagers as a way to leave home to live with their boyfriends.[51] Whether or not this speculation is true, Latinas from father absent homes are the most likely to become teenage mothers and those who have good relationships with their fathers are the least likely.[58,59,60]

Interestingly, how verbally aggressive Latina college women were with their boyfriends was more closely linked to their mother being verbally aggressive than to their father's verbal aggression.[61] Daughters whose mothers were verbally aggressive towards their fathers (name calling, slamming doors, smashing things, sulking) were more likely to treat their boyfriends in these aggressive ways. But there was no link between the daughter's verbally aggressive behavior and her father's verbal aggression towards the mother.

The father also has an impact on his daughter's emotional and psychological well-being. Latinas who have supportive relationships with their fathers have fewer externalizing and internalizing problems.[62] For example, in a study with more than 7,000 children, Latinas were more likely than black or than white girls to be depressed and dissatisfied with their relationships with their fathers.[49] But girls of all races who had good relationships with their fathers were the least depressed.

The father's impact on his daughter's emotional health is especially important because Latinas are more likely than any other group of daughters to attempt or commit suicide, regardless of their country of origin or their family's income.[63] Between 1991 and 2007, Hispanic teenage girls were twice as likely as white or black girls to attempt suicide—with their highest rate (21%) being in 1995 and lowest rate (12%) in 1991. For example, in a Minnesota study with 3,178 Latina students in 9th and 12th grade, 34% had thought about killing themselves in the past year.[64] Sixteen percent of these 9th graders and 7% of 12th graders attempted suicide. Daughters with emotionally or physically absent fathers were more suicidal than those with good father-daughter relationships.

In the most comprehensive study to date, 122 Latinas who attempted suicide and 110 with no history of suicide were studied over a period of five years.[63] The researchers considered family income, family cohesion, and the quality of the daughter's relationship with each parent (communication, affection, emotional support, and conflict). The suicidal and non-suicidal daughters were similar in almost all of these regards, except suicidal girls were less likely to be living with their fathers and less likely to have a supportive, communicative, low-conflict relationships with their parents. Suicidal daughters were also more likely to have stay at home mothers. The researchers speculated that unemployed mothers probably had more conservative cultural values than employed mothers. The mother's conservative values might then have created more tension between mother and daughter that contributed to depression. Suicidal daughters felt there was a greater gap between their values and their parents' values. And their parents were more likely to be dealing with immigration issues and economic hardship. The daughters' suicide attempts were less a desire to die than a desire to escape these stressful family situations. It appears that when parents heavily emphasize traditional gender roles and discourage their daughter's autonomy, she is more likely to fell anxious, depressed, and suicidal. Especially during her teenage years, her desire to become more self-reliant and to focus on her own needs may lead to more depression and suicidal thoughts.

Overall then, Hispanic American fathers have considerable influence on their daughters' emotional and psychological well-being, as well as on her sexual behavior.

Asian American Fathers and Daughters

Although Hispanic Americans are the largest minority group, Asian Americans are the fastest growing.[43] Between 1980 and 1990 the Asian American population in the U.S. increased by 98%, comprising 6% of the nation's population in 2017. Most have emigrated from China, followed by the Philippines, Vietnam, and Korea.

Asian American fathers are distinct from non-Asian fathers in several respects.[43] They are the most educated, with 64% having college educations compared to 49% of white, 29% of Hispanic, 24% of black, and 22% of American Indian fathers. Put differently, an Asian American daughter is four times more likely than a black or a Hispanic daughter to have a father with a college degree. Half of Asian American families have incomes above $80,720, compared to $61,348 for white, $46,882 for Hispanic, $38,555 for black, and $38,330 for Native American families. Almost 40% of Asian American families have incomes above $100,000 a year, compared to only 27% of non-Hispanic white families.

Asian American fathers are also the least likely to ever be incarcerated (2%) and the most likely to be married when they have children (83%). This means, Asian American children are ten times less likely than black or Native American children to have an incarcerated father and three times less likely to be born out of wedlock. Asian children are also more likely to be biracial (20%) than are black or Hispanic American children.[65]

Still, we should not stereotype Asian American families as an "ideal" minority. For example, 12% of Asian American children are living in poverty. Most of these parents recently immigrated and do not speak fluent English. Many Asian fathers are also under financial and emotional pressure to take care of the extended family financially. They are expected to have their elderly parents live with them, especially in Vietnamese and Filipino families.[66] As we have seen in earlier chapters, when fathers experience these kinds of ongoing stress, their relationships with their daughters often suffer.

Father-Daughter Relationships

Asian American father-daughter relationships are distinct in several ways.[66] These fathers tend to be less physically affectionate, less communicative, less emotionally expressive, and less lenient than non-Asian fathers. As is true with most Hispanic fathers, Asian fathers generally allow their sons more freedom than their daughters. This may help explain why Asian and Filipino American daughters have more conflict than sons do with their fathers.[67] When it comes to discussing sex, Asian fathers are especially reserved. For example, Asian American college students and high school students are less likely than other students to have ever talked with either parent about sex.[18,68] Their parents also have more conservative attitudes about premarital sex than do non-Asian students' parents. They are far less likely to

Figure 7.3
Source: Tom Wang/shutterstock.com.

have talked with their father about dating or about sex (17%) than white (38%), Hispanic (40%), and black (31%) teenagers.

Fathers who have recently immigrated from Asian countries and are not yet well-acculturated have more strained relationships with their children than fathers who were born or lived in the states for years—but more so for daughter than for sons.[66,67,69] The clash of social and cultural values between the conservative father and his more liberal Americanized children often creates stress and conflict—especially during the teenage and young adult years when children are dating and seeking more independence. And if the father is a more recent immigrant who is struggling financially, his children are more likely to have a stressful relationship with him than if he is doing well financially.[70]

In terms of their daughters' academic or vocational success, Asian fathers who have recently immigrated have higher educational expectations than do recently immigrated Hispanic fathers.[71] In that regard, it is worth noting that in Shanghai, China, a dramatic shift is taking place in father-daughter relationships.[72] Traditionally in China, the father's relationship with the son has taken precedence over his relationship with his daughter. While the son would carry on the family name, the daughter would marry and become a member of her husband's family. But nowadays in Shanghai—which is the most economically and educationally advanced city in China—many fathers are becoming highly involved in their daughters' lives. Increasing numbers of Shanghai fathers consider their most important role to be providing emotional and financial support and helping their daughters excel in school. Unlike men in rural areas of China, Shanghai men with these less sexist gender beliefs are sometimes ridiculed as being henpecked and unmanly, as evidenced by the book, *I'd rather be dead than be a Shanghai man*.[73] But Shanghai dads are defying these traditional stereotypes in support of their daughters. For example, in one Shanghai study, 76% of daughters said they felt close to their father and felt he was extremely supportive of their academic accomplishments and future career goals.[72] These fathers embodied the saying "*wang nü cheng feng*," which means to "hope for the daughter to become a Phoenix." This adage is related to Greek mythology where the phoenix is revered as a long-lived bird that regenerates or is born again, rising from the ashes of its predecessor.

While some Asian fathers hope their daughters will rise like the Phoenix, others hope their daughters will rise "like the dragon," as illustrated in the story of Chloe Kim, the internationally famous teenage Olympic snowboarding champion and her father.[74] As Box 7.5 explains, Chloe's father Jong Jin Kim came to the States from South Korea in 1982. In Korean culture, to become a dragon is to wait 1,000 years and then to evolve from a simple snake into a magnificent dragon who rises to the sky with a gold pearl in its mouth.

> **Box 7.5 Chloe Kim, Olympic gold medalist, and her immigrant father[74]**
>
> At the 2018 Winter Olympics 17-year-old Chloe Kim, an Asian American whose parents emigrated from South Korea in 1982, achieved international fame by winning the Gold Medal in snowboarding. But her father, Jong Jin Kim, also won international applause by being widely heralded as a stellar father who had committed himself wholeheartedly to his daughter's athletic career. As an immigrant in Southern California, he worked minimum wage jobs until he saved enough money to attend college where he eventually earned a degree in engineering. Having introduced Chloe to snowboarding when she was only four, Jong Jin Kim eventually gave up his job as an engineer to help her pursue her Olympic dreams. Chloe and her dad spent days away from the rest of the family throughout her childhood, as he drove long hours through the night, with Chloe asleep in the back seat, taking her to snowboarding competitions in the mountains. On the day of her Olympic competition, he texted her: "Today is the day *imugi* turns to dragon." In Korean culture, to become a dragon is to spend 1,000 years as a simple snake before finally rising to the sky to become a dragon with a gold pearl in its mouth. At the Olympics, Jong Jin Kim cheered for his daughter, shouting *"Imugi"* which loosely translates to mean "serpent-like lesser dragon." "I can't express how much I love my dad," Chloe told the *Boston Globe*. "I always get teary-eyed when I talk about him because he's so great."

Asian American father-daughter relationships are far less likely than Hispanic, black, or Native American relationships to face the challenges of poverty, out of wedlock births, or incarceration. But both Asian and Hispanic fathers who have recently immigrated face many of the same challenges in their father-daughter relationships.

Native American Fathers and Daughters

Native Americans are the smallest minority group, accounting for only 1% of the population. Understandably then, there are very few research studies about these fathers' relationships with their children. Among the strengths of Native American families are their supportive extended family networks and rich cultural heritage. Nevertheless, these families are the most likely to encounter certain situations that can undermine fathers' relationships with their chldren.[75] Compared to other Americans, Native children are the most likely to live in poverty (34%), to be born to unmarried parents (67%), to have incarcerated fathers (22%), and to be taken away from their parents and put into foster care. Their parents are also 51% more likely than other Americans to die from alcoholism.

Compared to other American children, Native Americans have more problems across a wide range of measures of well-being—all of which, as described in earlier chapters, are related to father absence or to the quality of the father-daughter relationship. These teenagers are the most likely to try to kill themselves (16%), with suicide being the second cause of teenage death and with daughters being twice as likely as sons to attempt suicide. They have the highest school dropout rates (50%) and are three times more likely to be arrested. Violence, murder, and suicide account for 75% of teenage deaths. They also have the highest rates of teenage binge drinking and alcohol addiction, with daughters often having higher rates than sons.[76] Native American daughters are also the most likely to be victims of physical and sexual violence and to drop out of school because they are pregnant.

It is important to remember, however, that the majority of Native Americans do not live in poverty, are never incarcerated, and are not alcoholic, violent, or suicidal. But, like African American children, the majority of Native American children do not grow up in the same home with their father, which poses a risk to father-daughter relationships.

Father-Daughter Relationships

One of the few studies to focus on fathers and daughters describes many unique aspects of their relationship.[77] Compared to other fathers, these fathers are more likely to worry about their daughters being physically or sexually abused—which is a legitimate concern since their daughters are more likely than other teenage girls to be abused. They are less comfortable than other fathers talking about sex with their daughters which is unfortunate given the high rates of teenage pregnancy.

Fathers with close connections to their tribal communities strive to impart spirituality and traditional tribal cultural values to their daughters.[78] These fathers and daughters feel their relationship is strengthened by participating together in tribal ceremonies. Fathers often remind their daughter in times of stress or difficulty to draw on these ceremonial experiences as sources of strength. As one Navajo father explains:

> At one time, my eldest daughter came to me about the stresses of school work. I explained to her that her strength had always been inside her because she successfully went through 4 days of her Kinaaldaa ceremony and that she should apply her understanding of her strength to her school to overcome her difficulties. She graduated with honors and just completed her freshman year at the university. (p. 922)

Supporting her academic success is an especially important role for the Native American father since their children often struggle and fail to succeed in college because they feel isolated, stereotyped or discriminated against.[78]

Only 20% graduate from college. Many fathers encourage their daughters academically by reminding them that their behavior and accomplishments reflect on the entire community as well as the extended family. Then too, fathers can help their daughters reject negative stereotypes of Native Americans and develop a more positive cultural identity. For example, in middle school, many of these daughters are sensitive to the simplistic and negative stereotypes about "Indians" as people who "dress up in costumes" for the entertainment of others.[79] Having fathers who help them appreciate the rich complexity of their history and culture can be a powerful resource for daughters.

In respect to their daughter's drug and alcohol use, Native American fathers also have an impact. Teenage daughters who have close relationships with their fathers are less likely to drink and use marijuana.[76] This study is especially important because the sample was large and nationally representative and because it factored in the parents' drug use, welfare status, and marital status. Although the research is scarce, it is clear that Native American daughters benefit from strong relationships with their fathers. We turn our attention now to a much larger group of fathers and daughters who are living in immigrant families.

Immigrant Families

Before discussing immigrant families, keep in mind that immigrants are not the same as refugees. Refugees are granted legal asylum because they are fleeing immediate or imminent danger in their own countries, most of which are torn asunder by war or by catastrophic natural disasters. Most refugees (63%) are from the Congo, Iraq, Syria, Somalia, and Myanmar.[42] Immigrants and refugees as alike in two regards: First, they cannot be deported once they are granted legal entry. Second, they must undergo a complicated, demanding application process and wait several years before being allowed to enter the U.S.

Immigration patterns have changed dramatically since 2010.[80] Since 2010 41% of immigrants have come from Southeast Asia—primarily China and India. Nearly half of the Asian immigrants (45%) have college degrees. In 2017, there were 43.7 million foreign-born people in the U.S., comprising 13.5% of the population. The number of documented and undocumented immigrants has been relatively stable since 2010. Prior to 2010, 51% of immigrants were of Latin American origin, with 26% being from Mexico. But since 2010, 58% have immigrated from Asia and only 28% from Latin American countries or Mexico. Even though most immigrants are from Mexico (11.5 million), their numbers declined from 2010 to 2016.

Since 2010, immigrants have been more educated than native-born Americans. Nearly 52% have college degrees compared to only 32% of native-born Americans, and only 29% of immigrants only have a high school degree, compared to 37% of native-born residents. Moreover, 26% of immigrants have graduate degrees, compared to only 12% of native residents. It is also worth noting that in some states where there are lower numbers of immigrants, the native born residents are far less educated than the immigrant residents. For example, in Ohio 62% of the immigrants are college graduates compared to only 28% of the native-born residents. The greatest increase in immigrants (87% gain since 2010) was in North Dakota.

The focus of this section on immigrant families is on Hispanic families because they are by far the largest group of immigrants. But three important facts about Asian American immigrants merit close attention. First, for more than a decade, Asian Americans have been the most educated and fastest growing group of immigrants. Second, the current welcoming attitudes and policies towards Asian immigrants are in stark contrast to the racism and discrimination levied against them in the past. In the late 1800s Chinese families were forbidden to immigrate. Other Asian immigrants were demonized as the "**Yellow Peril**," a term coined in California because white workers feared losing their jobs to Asian immigrants.[81] More disturbing still, after Japan attacked Pearl Harbor in 1941, the U.S. government imprisoned 125,000 Japanese American citizens in internment camps, fearing that they would aid the Japanese in the war.[82] Forced to leave their jobs and their homes, families were only allowed to bring what they could carry with them to these prisons. In addition to financial ruin, the emotional and physical toll on these children, their parents, and the elderly grandparents often lasted years beyond their return home. In an attempt to conceal what the government had done, the U.S. Army censored the photographs of these imprisoned families taken by Dorothea Lane, one of the greatest photographers of the twentieth century. These disturbing pictures were finally released in 2007.[83]

There are Japanese American daughters who have written memoirs about their childhood experiences in these internment camps. One daughter describes the emotional, financial, and physical toll that years of imprisonment took on her father and on his relationship with her and her brother.[84] Another, who was imprisoned at the age of seven with her family at the Manzanar prison camp in California, wrote a memoir that was later made into a movie about her family's ordeals and her father's mental and emotional breakdown.[85] In 2002, the book and the movie were distributed to 8,500 public schools in California in an effort to raise children's awareness. The point is that Asian Americans have not been spared the kinds of severe discrimination faced by other racial minorities.

Third, the immigration policies and discrimination that Asian immigrants experienced in America's past are similar in many ways to what Hispanic immigrant families are experiencing today—situations that can have a profoundly negative impact on father-daughter relationships. During the 1970s, illegal immigration from Hispanic countries increased dramatically as families fled brutal dictatorships and collapsing economies in Latin America. In response to the so-called "Brown Peril" from Mexico and Latin America, in 1986 Congress made it illegal for employers to hire undocumented immigrants and increased Border Patrol by 50%. Simultaneously, however, Congress granted amnesty to the three million immigrants who were already living in the US. Then in 2012 Congress passed the **Deferred Action for Children Act (DACA)** which allowed 2.1 million undocumented children over the age of 14 who had lived in the U.S. at least five years to remain in the country without threat of deportation, free to attend college and procure jobs.[86] But DACA did not grant citizenship to the "dreamers," the young adults who dreamed of being granted citizenship. As of January 2019, the fate of the dreamers remains uncertain.

Counting people from every country who have immigrated to the U.S. since 2012, 47% have college degrees. This is largely because immigration from Asian countries has increased so rapidly since 2012 and these are generally the most well-educated immigrants. At the other extreme, 29% of those who have immigrated since 2012 have not graduated from high school and nearly half are not proficient in English—most of whom are from Hispanic countries. Although immigrants from all countries comprise only 14% of the total U.S. population, 26% (88 million) of children under the age of 18 have at least one immigrant parent. Almost all (88%) of these children are American citizens because they were born in the U.S. even though their parents were born elsewhere. Two-thirds of their parents are documented immigrants who cannot be deported because they are in the States legally. Only 17% are undocumented residents who can be deported if apprehended. In 2016, 17% of the U.S. labor force were immigrant workers.

This section is exclusively focused on Hispanic families for two reasons. First, they are by far the largest immigrant group. Keep in mind, however, that Asian Americans are the fastest growing immigrant group. Indeed, the number of immigrants from Hispanic countries has been declining since 2001 largely because the economies in their native countries have grown stronger and dictatorships have declined. Second, almost all of the research that is relevant to father-daughter relationships in immigrant families is based on Hispanic families.

Unique Characteristics of Hispanic Immigrant Families

Regardless of their country of origin, Hispanic immigrants share a number of common characteristics. These commonalities, in turn, affect their father-daughter relationships in similar ways.[42,43,86]

Most live in California (10.7 million), Texas (4.7 million), New York (4.5 million), Florida (4.2 million), and New Jersey (2 million). But the largest growth has occurred in North Carolina (247% growth), Georgia, Nevada, Arkansas, and Utah. Most emigrated from Mexico. Their median family

income in 2015 was $49,560 compared to $54,995 for non-immigrant families. While the vast majority are not living in poverty, their poverty rates are
higher (21%) than the national average (13%).

In order to understand the impact that immigration status can have on
father-daughter relationships, we need to understand a few fundamentals
of immigration law. If one parent is an American citizen or is a legal
permanent resident or holding a "green card" that allows them to work
in the U.S., then there is no danger of being deported. If one parent is a
U.S. citizen, and the other parent and children live in another country,
they are allowed to apply to immigrate to the U.S. under the Family
Reunification Act. The average wait between applying and being allowed
to enter is six years. Waits are longer for Mexican emigrants because so
many apply and only 7% of immigrants are allowed to come from any
one country. Consequently, some parents and children are separated for
years while awaiting the decision.

Children born in the U.S. automatically become citizens even if their
parents are illegal residents who can be deported if apprehended. It is
estimated that there are 4.5 million "citizen children" in the US.[81] From
2005–2013, 3,165,426 unauthorized immigrants were deported which affected
about 1,582,711 citizen children. Moreover, many citizen children are in
"mixed status" families which means some members are documented while
others are not. For example, one sister might be a citizen while the other is
not. Or one parent might have a green card while the other does not. In
these situations, all family relationships can be stressed by the possibility
that one family member could be deported if apprehended by **Immigration
Control Enforcement (ICE)** agents.

When a child's undocumented parent is arrested, the outcomes are
uncertain. The parent can be held in detention centers for days or weeks and
then either returned home to await future immigration hearing or immediately deported. Since federal law only allows judges to cancel 4,000 deportation orders a year nationwide, very few parents are allowed to stay. Since
2009, ICE has been required to fill approximately 34,000 beds a day in
detention centers at the cost of $120 to $160 a day per person. The majority
have not committed any crime and many are mothers or pregnant women.
When their parent is detained or deported, children are placed with a relative, family friend, or foster parents. In 2016, approximately 15,000 of these
children were in foster care.[81] In 2018, however, President Trump passed a
"zero tolerance" executive order that resulted in thousands of children being
taken away from their parents as they attempted to enter the country
illegally.

If a child's undocumented parent is apprehended and ordered to leave the
country, there are three options.[81] First, both parents can return to their
country of origin with their children—many of whom have spent most or all
of their childhood in the U.S. Second, the documented parent can remain in

the States and raise the children alone, while the undocumented parent is deported. Third, both parents can return to their native country and leave the children in the care of another family member or in the foster care system.

Father-Daughter Relationships

Daughters and sons living with an undocumented parent are at increased risk of developing emotional, psychological, and behavioral problems—many of which are linked to their disrupted relationships with their fathers.[81] As the story in Box 7.6 illustrates, many of these problems arise even if the parents are not arrested or deported.

Box 7.6 The daughter of a deported, immigrant father[82]

Agustina is a 15-year-old daughter who attempted suicide while her father's deportation case was under review. He was deported to Mexico.

> I know the chances of him coming back in less than a year are slim ... I was supposed to have my *quinceanera* this December and I was really excited about it. But my parents can't afford a *quinceanera* anymore 'cause my mom is sending money to my dad.

Asked why she tried to kill herself, she says:

> I was feeling betrayed. Like I already had issues with my parents and I was already hurt because my dad was leaving. Then my counselor left and she was the one person I could talk to. And then my ex-boyfriend starting dating my best friend ... Because, everything with the legal issues, I just felt like my parents were not paying as much attention to me as much as to the legal issues with my dad. It was like the last straw when I attempted suicide (pp. 208–210).

If their parent is arrested, detained, or deported, children are often traumatized, especially if they are too young to understand what is happening or if the arrest is sudden and unexpected.[81] These children often have persistent feelings of loneliness, sadness, distress, and anxiety. Even when the detained parent is allowed to return home, children may become withdrawn and develop physical problems related to stress—for example, insomnia or stomach problems. Trying to relieve their daughters' stress, some Mexican American fathers try to distract them with humor—for example, making jokes about ICE officers. Other fathers choose a more direct and serious approach by explaining the harsh realities to their daughters.[87]

Children also become more stressed if they have to move out of their home to live with other relatives after a parent is arrested. Most undocumented immigrants have steady full time jobs. But after an arrest, the family income generally declines by half. Only one-third of these families fully recover financially after the apprehended parent returns home. One-fourth have to move in with relatives. Others are evicted because landlords do not want to attract the attention of the police.[81]

The consequences for these daughters and sons—especially for their relationships with their fathers—can be profound and far-reaching.[45] There is the daily stress due to constant vigilance about not saying or doing anything that might reveal the family secret. They are also burdened with negative stereotypes about immigrants that can undermine their self-esteem and make them self-conscious, defensive, and excessively shy or quiet. Feeling the constant pressure of behaving well at school or in any public places so as not to attract any attention to the family, they are more likely to become anxious, depressed, and suicidal. While they are more likely than other students to be well behaved at school, their self-control arises from the fear that misbehaving might lead to result in a parent being deported. Not surprisingly, daughters of undocumented immigrants have higher suicide rates than all other American daughters.[63]

To avoid being arrested, many undocumented immigrants keep their children close to home and discourage them from being involved in school or social activities. These children are under constant, emotional and physical stress in an effort to protect their undocumented parents or siblings. Children who witness a parent's arrest by ICE are often traumatized by ongoing nightmares, flashbacks, and symptoms of post-traumatic stress disorder even after their arrested parent returns home. Moreover, some children are not aware that one or both of their parents are undocumented until they become teenagers and need permission to get a driver's license further adding to their stress.

Immigrant Hispanic families face many challenges that shape the kinds of relationships that fathers are able to create with their daughters. Especially in families where one or both parents are undocumented, daughters' relationships with their fathers can be especially stressed, fragile, and unstable.

Conclusion

Minority families are not a homogenous, monolithic group who can be stereotyped and categorized in simplistic ways. Fathers and daughters in minority families do, however, face a number of similar challenges to their relationships—above all, the increased risk that these daughters will live apart from their fathers at some point during their childhood. Especially in immigrant families where there can be a wide gap between fathers' and daughters' cultural values, and where many parents may be undocumented, father-daughter relationships can be strained. Simultaneously minority families can bolster and enrich father-daughter relationships through their large kinship networks, strong commitments to the family, and appreciation for their unique culture, history, and identity. Regardless of race or culture, the overriding message is that strong, loving father-daughter relationships enrich daughters' lives and bestow benefits throughout her lifetime.

Review Questions

1 What percent of Americans belong to each racial group?

2 Citing specific percentages, how do the racial groups differ in terms of: education, income, out of wedlock births, and incarceration?

3 For each racial group, what negative stereotypes or negative beliefs are not supported by the research?

4 How are most African, Hispanic and Asian fathers' relationships with their daughters and their parenting styles different from those of non-Hispanic white fathers?

5 For each racial group, citing specifics, how do fathers affect these aspects of their daughters' lives: academic, drug & alcohol use, sexual behavior, teenage pregnancy, depression, and self-confidence.

6 How and why do father-daughter relationships in first generation immigrant families generally differ from those in non-immigrant families?

7 What problems are unique to undocumented immigrant families and what impact do these have on father-daughter relationships?

8 Define each of these terms and explain how each can influence father-daughter relationships: colorism, Latina, acculturation, *machismo, familismo, moreno, indio.*

9 Specifically how have recently immigrated families changed in the past decade in terms of immigration rates, countries of origin, and income and educational status?

10 In respect to their racial group, which daughters are most at risk in terms of these problems: growing up in poverty or in a fatherless home, depression and suicide, teenage pregnancy, drug and alcohol use, dropping out of high school, having an alcoholic or an incarcerated father.

11 Why are Asian Americans not the "ideal" minority in terms of how they have been treated historically and problems they presently face today?

12 Define these terms and explain why they can have or did once have a negative impact on father-daughter relationships: the yellow peril, DACA, ICE, internment camps, citizen children, mixed status family, undocumented immigrant, green card.

13 Where do most immigrant families live in the U.S. and how has the profile of recent immigrants changed over the past decade?

14 Citing specific percentages, how have the number of interracial marriages and interracial children changed over the past few decades?

15 In terms of communicating with their daughters and their parenting styles, what are the strengths and the weaknesses for fathers in each racial group?

Questions for Discussion and Debate

1 In regard to father-daughter relationships, which racial group would you most and least want to belong to? Why?

2 How do you feel about parents who have children without ever getting married? Why?

3 What issue do you feel is most important for each racial group in terms of maintaining and strengthening their father-daughter relationships?

4 As a member of each of the racial groups discussed in this chapter, which stereotypes would you find most offensive and which do you feel are the most damaging to father-daughter relationships?

5 When you think about Serena Williams' and Chloe Kim's relationships with their fathers, what advice would you give to other fathers?

6 What could American society do to decrease the problems faced by undocumented immigrant families?

7 What characteristics or cultural beliefs in each minority group do you feel strengthen their father-daughter relationships?

8 As a Hispanic or African American father, how could you help your daughters cope with "colorism" or the jealousy between your own daughters related to colorism?

9 Looking back in American history, what events, laws or societal attitudes surprised or upset you most in regard to minority families and immigrant families?

10 What specific beliefs of yours were most challenged by the research presented in this chapter? Where or how did those particular beliefs originate in your own life?

References

1 Census Bureau. *Population estimates in United States*. Washington, DC: U.S. Department of Labor: Census Bureau; 2017.

2 Frey W. *U.S. to become minority white*. Washington, DC: The Brookings Institute; 2018, March 14.

3 Bialik K. *Key facts about race and marriage*. Washington, DC: Pew Research Center; 2017.

3 Guzman G. *Household income: 2016*. Washington, DC: U.S. Census Bureau; 2017.

5 Bureau of Justice. *American Indian and Alaska Natives in local jails*. Washington, DC: Bureau of Justice Statistics; 2017.

6 Connor M, White J. *Black fathers: An invisible presence in America*. New York: Routledge; 2011.

7 Uhlmann E. Prejudice based on skin color among Hispanics in the United States and Latin America. *Social Cognition* 2002; 20: 198–225.

8 Fegley S. Colorism embodied: Skin tone and psychological well-being in adolescence. In: Overton W, Muller U, editors. *Body in mind, mind in body*. Mahway, NJ: Erlbaum; 2008. 281–312.

9 Greene M, Way N, Pahl K. Perceived adult and peer discrimination among Black, Latino, and Asian American adolescents. *Developmental Psychology* 2006; 42: 218–238.

10 Ramos B, Jaccard J. Dual ethnicity and depressive symptoms: Being Black and Latino in the United States. *Hispanic Journal of Behavioral Sciences* 2003; 25: 147–173.

11 Landale N, Oropesa R. White, Black, or Puerto Rican? *Social Forces* 2002; 81: 231–254.

12 Landor A. Exploring the impact of skin tone on family dynamics and race related outcomes. *Journal of Family Psychology* 2013; 27: 817–826.

13 Telzer E, Garcia H. Skin color and self perceptions of Latinas. *Hispanic Journal of Behavioral Sciences* 2009; 31: 357–372.

14 Wilder J, Cain C. Teaching and learning color consciousness in black families. *Journal of Family Issues* 2012; 32: 577–604.

15 Hattery A, Smith E. *African American families today: Myths and realities*. New York: Rowman & Littlefied; 2012.

16 Harper S, Fine M. Noncustodial fathers' interactions with children. *Fathering* 2006; 4: 286–311.

17 Taylor K. *Black fathers*. New York: Doubleday; 2003.

18 King V, Harris K, Heard H. Racial diversity in nonresident father involvement. *Journal of Marriage and the Family* 2004; 66: 1–21.

19 Schwartz S, Finley G. Divorce variables as predictors of young adults fathering reports. *Journal of Divorce and Remarriage* 2005; 44: 144–164.

20 Colbert S, Harrison V. *Color him father: Stories of love and rediscovery of black men*. Philadelphia: Kinship Press; 2006.

21 Gayles G. *Father songs*. Boston: Beacon Press; 1997.

22 Vassel R. *Daughters of men: African American women and their fathers*. New York: Amistad; 2007.

23 Gaines H, Royston A. *Our black fathers: Brave, bold and beautiful*. Atlanta, GA: Five Sisters Publishing; 2017.

24 Robson D. This one's for dad. *Sportsworld com* 2015; August 31: 1–2.

25 Boyd K, Ashcraft A. Father-daughter relationships and drug refusal among African American adolescent girls. *Journal of Black Psychology* 2006; 32(1): 29–42.

26 Jordan L, Lewis M. Preventing alcohol use among African American adolescents. *Journal of Black Psychology* 2005; 31(131): 152.

27 Coley R, Medeiros B. Nonresident father involvement and delinquency. *Child Development* 2007; 78: 132–147.

28 Cooper S. Father-daughter relationship and academic engagement of African American adolescents. *Journal of Black Psychology* 2009; 35: 404–425.

29 Hanson S. Success in science among young African American women. *Journal of Family Issues* 2007; 28: 3–33.

30 Johnson M. Strength and respectability: Black women's negotiation of racialized gender ideals and the role of daughter-father relationships. *Gender and Society* 2013; 6: 889–912.

31 Brown D, Rosnick C, Bradley C, Kirner J. Does daddy know best? Exploring the relationship between paternal sexual communication and safe sex practices among African-American women. *Sex Education* 2014; 14: 241–256.

32 Hutchinson K, Cederbaum J. Talking to daddy's little girl about sex: Daughters' reports of sexual communication and support from fathers. *Journal of Family Issues* 2011; 32: 550–572.

33 Stanik C, Riina E, McHale S. Parent adolescent relationship qualities and adjustment in two parent African American families. *Family Relations* 2013; 62: 597–608.

34 Vigil J, Geary D. Parenting and women's life-history development. *Journal of Family Psychology* 2006; 20(4): 597–604.

35 Galbraith K. Parental acceptance and uptake of the HPV vaccine among African Americans and Latinos: A literature review. *Social Science & Medicine* 2016; 159: 116–126.

36 Green B, Davis C, Clark T, Coupet Q. The role of fathers in reducing dating violence victimization and sexual risk behavior among a national sample of Black adolescents. *Children and Youth Services Review* 2015; 55: 48–55.

37 Ahonen L, Loeber R. Dating violence in teenage girls: Parental emotional regulation and racial differences. *Criminal behavior and mental health* 2018; 26: 240–250.

38 Cooper S, Brown C, Metzger I, Clinton Y, Gurthrie B. Racial discrimination and African American adolescents' adjustment. *Journal of Child and Family Studies* 2012; 35: 1–15.

39 Coley R. Daughter-father relationships and adolescent psychosocial functioning. *Journal of Marriage and Family* 2003; 65: 867–875.

30 Trask A, Cunningham M, Lange L. The impact of social support on symptoms of psychological distress in African American girls. *Research in Human Development* 2010; 7: 164–182.

31 Mandara J, Murray C, Joyner T. Father absence and African American adolescents' gender role development. *Sex Roles* 2005; 53(207): 220.

32 Zong J, Batalova J, Hallock J. Frequently requested statistics on immigrants and immigration in the United States. *Migration Policy Institute* 2018; February 8: 1–34.

33 Camarota S, Zeigler K. *Immigrants in the United States: A profile using 2014 and 2015 census data.* 2017. Report No.: October, 2016.

34 Lansford J, Deater K, Bornstein M. *Immigrant families in contemporary society.* New York: Guilford; 2009.

35 Menjivar C, Abrego L, Schmalzbauer L. *Immigrant families.* New York: Polity Press; 2016.

36 Cabrera N, Hannon J, Taillade J. Predictors of coparenting in Mexican American families. *Infant Mental Health Journal* 2009; 30(5): 523–548.

37 Coltrane S. Father involvement in low income Mexican American families. *Family Relations* 2004; 53: 179–189.

38 Crocket L. Conceptions of good parent-adolescent relationships among Cuban American teenagers. *Sex Roles* 2009; 60(575): 587.

39 Videon T. Parent child relationships and adolescents' psychological wellbeing. *Journal of Family Issues* 2005; 26: 55–78.

50 Way N, Gillman D. Adolescent girls' perceptions of their fathers. *Journal of Early Adolescence* 2000; 20: 309–331.

51 Gillian M. The role of parents in pregnancy behaviors of young Latinas. *Hispanic Journal of Behavioral Sciences* 2007; 29: 50–67.

52 Sangi J, Ali N, Posner S, Poindexter A. Disparities in contraceptive knowledge between Hispanic and non-Hispanic whites. *Contraception* 2006; 74: 125–132.

53 Afable A, Brindis C. Acculturation and the sexual health of Latino youth: Literature review. *Perspectives on Sexual and Reproductive Health* 2006; 38: 208–219.

54 Gonzalez L. Fathering Latina sexualities. *Journal of Marriage and Family* 2004; 66(5): 1118–1130.

55 Guttmacher Institute. *U.S. rates of pregnancy, birth and abortion among adolescents and young adults continue to decline.* 2018. Report No.: September 7, 2017.

56 National Vital Statistics. *Births: Final data for 2016.* 2018. Washington, DC; January 31. Report No.: 67.

57 Abma J. Teenagers in the United States: Sexual activity, contraceptive use and childbearing. *Vital Health Statistics* 2004; 23: 1–48.

58 Ates A, Basham C. Teenage pregnancy among Latinas. *Hispanic Journal of Behavioral Sciences* 2007; 20: 554–569.

59 Biggs M. Factors associated with delayed childbearing in Latinas. *Hispanic Journal of Behavioral Sciences* 2010; 33: 77–103.

60 Frost J, Driscoll A. Adolescent Latino reproductive health: Literature review. *Hispanic Journal of Behavioral Sciences*, 2006; 23: 255–326.

61 Oramas L, Stephens D, Whiddon M. Influence of parental conflict resolution strategies on Hispanic college women's experiences with verbal aggression. *Journal of Interpersonal Violence* 2017; 32: 2908–2928.

62 Crean H. Conflict in the Latino parent-youth dyad. *Journal of Family Psychology* 2008; 22: 484–493.

63 Zayas L. *Latinas attempting suicide: When cultures, families and daughters collide.* New York: Oxford University Press; 2011.

64 Garcia C. Family and racial factors associated with suicide and emotional distress among Latino students. *Journal of School Health* 2008; 78: 487–495.

65 Hidalgo D, Bankston C. Blurring racial boundaries: Asian Americans. *Journal of Family Issues* 2010; 31: 280–300.

66 Chung A. *Saving face: The emotional costs of the Asian immigrant family myths.* New York: Rutgers University Press; 2016.

67 Park Y, Vo L, Tsong Y. Asian American parents and young adult children. *Cultural Diversity and Ethnic Minority Psychology* 2009; 15(18): 26.

68 Kim J, Ward M. Silence speaks volumes. Parental sexual communication among Asian American emerging adults. *Journal of Adolescent Research* 2007; 22: 3–31.

69 Koli J, Shao Y, Wang Q. Father, mother and me: Asian American immigrants. *Sex Roles* 2009; 60: 600–610.

70 Mistry R, Benner A, Tan C, Kim S. Family economic stress and academic well-being among Chinese American youth. *Journal of Family Psychology* 2009; 23: 279–290.

71 Fuligni A, Fuligni A. Immigrant families and the educational development of their children. In: Lansford J, Deckard K, Bornstein M, editors. *Immigrant families in contemporary society.* New York: Guilford Press; 2007. 231–250.

72 Zu Q, Yeung W. Hoping for a Phoenix: Shanghai fathers and their daughters. *Journal of Family Issues* 2018; 34: 184–209.

73 Qin L. *I'd rather be dead than be a Shanghai man.* Beijing, China: Zi Yuan; 2004.

74 Boren C. Chloe Kim's father wins gold as the ultimate Olympic dad. *Washington Post* 2018; February 13.

75 Center for Native American Youth. *Facts on Native American youth and Indian country.* Aspen, CO: The Aspen Institute; 2010.

76 Eitle T, Eitle D. Explaining the association between gender and substance use among American Indian adolescents. *Sociological Perspectives* 2015; 58: 686–710.

77 Reinhardt M, Evenstand J, Faircloth S. She has great spirit: insight into the relationships between American Indian dads and daughters. *International Journal of Qualitative Studies in Education* 2012; 25: 913–931.

78 Makomenaw M. Welcome to a new world: Experiences of American Indian tribal college and transfer students at predominantly white institutions. *International Journal of Qualitative Studies in Education* 2012; 25: 855–866.

79 Cooper K, Cooper S. My culture is not a costume: The influence of stereotypes on children in middle childhood. *Wicazo Sa Review* 2018; 31: 56.

80 Frey W. *Recent foreign born growth counters Trump's immigration stereotypes.* New York: Brookings Institute; 2017 October 2.

81 Zayas L. *Forgotten citizens: Deportation, children and the making of exiles and orphans.* New York: Oxford University Press; 2015.

82 Reever R. *Infamy: The shocking story of Japanese American internment camps in World War II.* New York: Picador; 2016.

83 Gordon L, Okihiro G. *Impounded: Dorothea Lange and the censored images of Japanese American internment.* New York: W.W. Norton; 2008.

84 Gruenewald M. *Looking like the enemy: My story of imprisonment in a Japanese American internment camp.* New York: New Sage Press; 2005.

85 Houston-Wakatsuki J, Houston J. *Farewell to Manzanar: The true story of a Japanese family's internment.* Los Angeles: New Lear; 1973.

86 Krogstad J, Passel J, Cohn D. Key facts about U.S. immigration policies and proposed changes. *Pew Research Center* 2017; February 26: 1–8.

87 Gallo S. Humor in father-daughter immigration narratives of resistance. *Anthropology and Education Quarterly* 2016; 47: 279–296.

Chapter 8

Destructive or Challenging Situations in Father-Daughter Relationships

Although all father-daughter relationships are challenging in their own ways, some situations pose more challenges than others. Still other situations are destructive, not only to the father-daughter relationship but to the daughter's immediate and long term safety and well-being. In terms of the overall numbers of people involved, poverty and the father's incarceration are the most likely to damage or destroy father-daughter relationships. In respect to the severity of their impact on the daughter, however, the father's addiction to drugs or alcohol or his sexually abusing his daughter have far more severe, long-lasting effects.

Though unlikely to permanently damage father-daughter relationships or cause harm to the daughter, other situations are nonetheless challenging. These situations include single fathers raising children, gay fathers or lesbian daughters, daughters conceived through sperm donation, military families, or the father's terminal illness. We begin with the three most widespread of these problems: poverty, incarceration, and substance abuse or addiction.

Poverty and Never Married Parents

Compared to other developed nations in the world, America has the highest rates of child poverty.[1] American children are more likely to live in poverty (21%) than children in the 20 other richest countries (13%), have a 50% greater chance of dying as infants, and a 57% greater chance of dying before the age of 19. Compared to other developed nations, the U.S. also has more incarcerated parents and more children born to unmarried parents who separate before their children are five years old—both of which are linked to poverty. In short, American children are more likely than children in other developed countries to grow up living in poverty in a home without their fathers.

The likelihood that a child will grow up living apart from her father in an impoverished family differs dramatically among racial groups.[2,3] In 2016, 12% of non-Hispanic white and Asian, 28% of Hispanic, and 34% of black and Native American children were living in poverty. To be clear, the majority of impoverished children are non-Hispanic whites. But Hispanic, black, and Native American families have higher rates of poverty than do white families. Impoverished children are also the most likely to spend most, or all, of their childhoods living apart from their fathers and to have fathers who are incarcerated at some point in their children's lives. For example black children are 2.5 times more likely than white children to live in poverty and 6.4 times more likely to have an incarcerated father.[1]

Box 8.1 Racial differences in poverty, incarceration, and non-marital births[3,4]

	Living in poverty	Incarcerated father	Non-marital births
Non-Hispanic white	12%	3%	28%
Hispanic American	28%	15%	53%
African American	34%	20%	72%
Asian American	12%	2%	17%
Native American	34%	18%	67%

In discussing poverty and family incomes, keep in mind that the median income is not the same as the average or mean income. The **median income** means that half of the incomes fall below this amount and half fall above it. For example, if a particular group has a median family income of $50,000, it does not mean that the majority of families in that group are earning $50,000. The "average" income is called the **mean income**. In America the **poverty level** is defined as a total income of $22,000 for a family of four.

Leaving race aside, 30% of all Americans over the age of 25 have a college education. Their average individual income is $56,000, rising to $82,000 with a graduate or professional degree. Individuals with only a high school degree earn an average of $31,000, and those without a high school degree earn only $20,000.[2] In 2016 half of all Asian American families had a household income above $80,720, compared to $63,155 for non-Hispanic whites, $46,882 for Hispanics and $38,555 for blacks.[2,3]

Parents living in poverty are less likely to be living together or married when their children are born, and less likely to still be together by time their children are five years old.[4] Because family income, non-marital births, and race are closely linked, 90% of Asian American parents are married when their children are born, compared to 70% of non-Hispanic white, 20% of black, 33% Native American, and 50% of Hispanic parents. There are also differences among racial groups in how likely the parents are to get married or to stay together as an unmarried couple. For example, when their child is born, only 28% of black parents are married and of those who are living together, only 13% are still together by their child's fifth birthday. In contrast, nearly 33% of Mexican Americans parents who are not married when their child is born eventually get married and 36% of the unmarried parents are still living together by their child's fifth birthday.[5] Again though, income and education, not race, are the strongest predictors of whether the parents are married or cohabiting when the children are born. Regardless of race, college educated parents are more likely to be married and less likely to divorce than less educated parents.

The most comprehensive study of families who are both poor and unmarried is the Fragile Families research project which is a large, nationally representative, ongoing study of poor, unmarried American parents in America's largest cities.[4] Eighty percent of these families are African or Hispanic American. Unmarried fathers are five years younger than married fathers when they have their first child, 27 versus 31 years old respectively. Nearly 50% of unmarried fathers have children with more than one woman. At the time their child is born, half of unwed parents are living together but only 30% are still together by their child's fifth birthday.

Several popular beliefs about these poor, unmarried fathers are not supported by the data from the Fragile Families study.[4] Even though they live apart, the majority of these fathers are involved with their children for the first few years of their lives—and many believe that they will eventually marry their child's mother, though this rarely happens. Many of these fathers feel they were pushed out of their children's lives by the mother's gatekeeping. In part, this may occur because more than half of all unwed mothers are in another romantic relationship within the first three years after their child's birth. Other fathers say they stop seeing their children because they first want to pull themselves out of poverty, which unfortunately rarely occurs.

Not only are children born to poor, unmarried parents the most likely to grow up living apart from their fathers, their fathers have the highest rates of violence, drug and substance abuse, mental illness, and incarceration. This combination of factors means that these daughters are the most likely to have a limited relationship or no relationship with their fathers.

Incarcerated Fathers

Father-daughter relationships also suffer when fathers are in prison for prolonged periods. Since incarceration is closely linked to poverty, and poverty is closely linked to race, daughters in certain racial groups are far more at risk of being separated from their fathers due to incarceration.[6,7] Most prisoners (59%) are non-Hispanic white; 38% are black, 2% are Native American, and 1.5% are Asian American. In the general population, only 1.5% of Asian American and 3% of white fathers are incarcerated compared to 20% of black and Native American and 15% of Hispanic fathers. Leaving race aside, for the 30% of fathers who did not finish high school, almost 40% will serve time in prison and 75% are unemployed.

Although no race is more likely to be in prison for having committed a violent crime, Native Americans have had the sharpest increases in incarceration rates, doubling from 1999 to 2014.[8] For children living in poverty in minority families, over 50% of their fathers and 10% of their mothers will serve time in jail before the child's fifth birthday.[9] Put differently, 1 in 3 African American daughters have a father in prison, compared to 1 in 6 Hispanic American daughters and 1 in 17 non-Hispanic white daughters. Nationwide, 1 in every 28 children has a father in prison—2.7 million children, or roughly 1.4 million daughters. On any given day, nearly 10% of black daughters versus only 1% of white daughters have a father in jail.

Until the 1970s, it was rare for children to be separated from their father because he was imprisoned.[6,10] In the 1970s only 2% of Americans were incarcerated compared to 11% today. There are seven times as many people in prison in the U.S. as in Western Europe.[10] Although crime rates have fluctuated over the past several decades, the rate of incarceration has steadily continued to increase. The combination of three factors seem to account for this dramatic increase: higher unemployment for poorly educated men, increased drug use, and far harsher penalties for dealing drugs. Drug related crimes that were once punished with probation, fines, or community service now carry a mandatory prison sentence—typically 10 to 12 years. Consequently, the number of inner city, poor, non-white fathers imprisoned for selling drugs soared. Only 10% of men in federal prisons and 50% in state prisons committed a crime that caused physical harm to anyone.

In addition to being physically separated from their children, incarcerated fathers have a number of other factors working against their relationships. When they leave prison, these fathers have more stress related disorders; and at the time they are imprisoned, they have more psychological, behavioral, and substance abuse problems than other fathers. Incarcerated fathers are also far less likely to be married or to have ever lived with their children's mother.

Fathers who somehow manage to maintain a connection to their children are less likely to return to prison.[6,11] Given this, it is especially unfortunate that most prisons do not offer programs or provide any environment that help fathers maintain relationships with their children. Unlike female prisons, male prisons rarely provide playgrounds or child friendly areas where children can comfortably visit their parents. Nor do most male prisons offer programs to help fathers improve their parenting skills and stay connected to their children. In short, there is a double standard for fathers and mothers who are imprisoned.

Although extremely rare, some prisons are making an effort to help fathers maintain some connection to their daughters by sponsoring father-daughter dances and fatherhood classes. In an Indiana prison in 2014, 37 daughters between the ages of two and 29 attended a father-daughter dance hosted in their father's prison.[12] Dressed in suits and ties, fathers greeted their dressed up daughters with a long stem rose and spent the afternoon dancing, eating, and talking together. This Indiana prison was also unique in offering child friendly spaces where fathers could spend time with their children playing games, doing crafts, or reading. The original idea for holding father-daughter dances in prison was conceived by Angela Patton in Richmond, Virginia, who runs Camp Diva which is designed to promote confidence and well-being in African American daughters.[13]

As we might expect, children whose fathers have spent time in prison are disadvantaged in several ways. In a national study with 15,587 children, those whose parents had ever been incarcerated were more likely to be arrested, run away from home, and be physically abused by someone they are dating.[14] Daughters whose fathers are in prison during her early teenage years are more likely to have children as teenagers.[15] Teenagers whose fathers have recently been sent to prison are more likely to start spending time with troubled and delinquent teenagers.[16] Young children are more likely to be physically aggressive if their father is in prison.[9] Surprisingly, in an analysis of 25 studies, daughters were more likely than sons to be involved in criminal activities if their fathers had been in prison.[17] This finding merits repeating given the large number of studies in this analysis: Daughters are at greater risk than sons of engaging in criminal behavior if their fathers have served time in prison.

As for young adults, those whose fathers have been incarcerated feel more socially excluded in terms of their social status and incomes, unless they manage to graduate from college.[18] Yet even those who do go to college report that without support from adults outside the family or from grandparents and older siblings, they would not have coped as well with their father's incarceration.[19]

In sum, father-daughter relationships suffer when the father is incarcerated, when the parents are not living together when the children are born, or when the family is living in poverty. When a family is faced with all three situations, which is often the case since the three are closely linked, father-daughter relationships are even more vulnerable. This, in turn, increases the odds that these daughters will develop the kinds of social, behavioral, academic, and psychological problems linked to father absence that have been discussed throughout this book.

Alcoholic Fathers

To understand more fully the situations of daughters with alcoholic fathers, a few basic facts about alcoholism are helpful.[20,21] Approximately 10% of American children have an alcoholic parent. Problem drinking that is severe, chronic and recurring is either referred to as **alcoholism** or as an **alcohol use disorder** (AUD). Approximately 15.1 million Americans have an alcohol disorder—9.8 million men (8.4% of all men) and 5.3 million women (4.2% of women). While not all heavy drinkers are physically addicted to alcohol, 25% of all people are born with a genetic predisposition to become addicted. Unfortunately only 6% of alcoholics receive help for their addiction.

The vast majority of children have parents who drink.[20,21] Nearly 70% of Americans have had a drink in the last year and 56% in the last month. Nearly one in four Americans over the age of 18 report binge drinking and 7% report heavy drinking in the past month. It is worth noting that college students are more likely to drink (58%) than other young adults their age (48%). In fact, roughly 20% of college students meet the criteria for AUD. This means that it is highly likely that a college-educated father drank during his college years.

Men are nearly twice as likely as women to be addicted to alcohol. This means that children are far more likely to have an alcoholic father than an alcoholic mother. Very few studies, however, have specifically explored the impact of the father's or the mother's alcoholism on daughters versus sons. The research is clear, though, that younger children and **adult children of alcoholics (ACOAs)** have more emotional, psychological, behavioral, academic, and physical health problems than their peers.[18–21] Several nationwide organizations, books, and internet sources now exist to help adult children of alcoholics deal with their ongoing problems.

The father's alcoholism has a negative impact on children in several ways. These fathers are more likely to have chronic, debilitating health problems. As a result, they often have trouble finding or keeping a job, which increases the family's financial stress. These fathers are also more likely to die or to suffer a serious, debilitating injury due to preventable accidents caused by being drunk. Indeed alcoholism is the third leading cause of preventable deaths and accounts for 31% of driving fatalities. Moreover, children with alcoholic fathers are subjected to more verbal conflict and more physical abuse—not only between the parents, but also between the parent and child. For example, teenagers with an alcoholic parent report more conflict between their parents than those without alcoholic parents.[22] The quality of parenting declined for the alcoholic and the non-alcoholic parent. The conflict and poor parenting may help explain why children whose parents drink heavily have more problems sleeping and are often sleep deprived, especially if it is the father who is the problem drinker.[23] As discussed in an earlier chapter, Native American children are at highest risk of having an alcoholic parent and of becoming alcoholics themselves as teenagers.

Looking specifically at the impact on daughters, one of the largest studies with 1,200 young adult daughters found a pattern among adult children of alcoholics (ACOAs).[24] Many of these daughters grew up feeling that they had to be perfect in order not to provoke the alcoholic parent or add to the family's high stress, instability, and conflict. Being hyper-vigilant about not angering or upsetting their parents, and focusing excessively on keeping the peace, daughters carry these patterns into their relationships outside the family. Box 8.2 describes the feelings and behaviors of many of these daughters. It is also worth noting that in a longitudinal study that followed 227 children from infancy to twelfth grade, daughters with an alcoholic parent were more likely to be victims of dating violence when they became teenagers.[25]

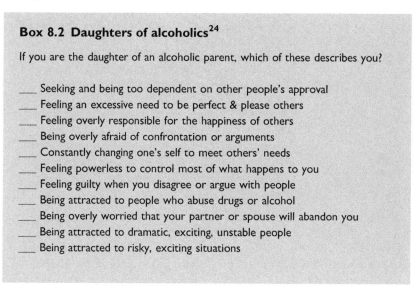

Box 8.2 Daughters of alcoholics[24]

If you are the daughter of an alcoholic parent, which of these describes you?

____ Seeking and being too dependent on other people's approval

____ Feeling an excessive need to be perfect & please others

____ Feeling overly responsible for the happiness of others

____ Being overly afraid of confrontation or arguments

____ Constantly changing one's self to meet others' needs

____ Feeling powerless to control most of what happens to you

____ Feeling guilty when you disagree or argue with people

____ Being attracted to people who abuse drugs or alcohol

____ Being overly worried that your partner or spouse will abandon you

____ Being attracted to dramatic, exciting, unstable people

____ Being attracted to risky, exciting situations

Other studies with female ACOAs confirm this pattern. Young adult daughters feel more stigmatized by their parents drinking problems than do sons.[26] Moreover, the daughters who did not talk about their parent's alcoholism were more depressed and had lower self-esteem than those who did talk about the problem. Interestingly too, daughters but not sons were more likely to drink, use marijuana, and have sex as teenagers if their fathers had been heavy marijuana users as teenagers. [27]

For sons and daughters who are in college, the impact of their parents' alcoholism may be less severe than for less educated young adults. For example, ACOAs were not more likely than other college students to be depressed or to drink.[28] And undergraduates who said their father had a drinking problems did not report feeling less attached to their father than did other students.[29] Interestingly though, when the mother was the alcoholic, these students felt less attached to their mothers and to their fathers. Likewise, adults in their early 30s were more likely to use marijuana if their mothers were alcoholics, but not if their fathers were alcoholics.[30] Moreover, when the mother was an alcoholic, daughters and sons whose parents were divorced had higher rates of marijuana use than those whose parents were still married.

Studies such as these underscore the point that a parent's alcoholism does not have a simple, direct, or predictable impact on children.

The impact of a parent's alcoholism on children's alcohol or drug use is not altogether clear. For example, teenagers whose fathers abused alcohol or marijuana were more likely to drink and use marijuana before the age of 15.[31] American Indian children with an alcoholic mother or father were more likely to have drinking problems between the ages of 11 and 20.[32] On the other hand, college students with alcoholic parents were no more likely to drink than other students.[21] Then too, teenagers were more likely to drink or use drugs if their father drank or used drugs when he was a teenager, but not if he drank or used drugs only as an adult.[33] Strangely, the reverse was true for mothers. Teenagers were more likely to drink or use drugs if their mother drank or used drugs as an adult, but not as teenager. Keep in mind, as discussed in an earlier chapter, that females between the ages of 12 and 20 are somewhat more likely than males to drink and to binge drink.[34] This suggests that an alcoholic parent might have a more negative impact on daughters than on sons, since teenage girls are more prone to drink.

The Opioid Epidemic

Although far more children are damaged by their parent's alcohol abuse than by their parents' drug abuse, the most rapidly growing addiction among adults is to opioids.[35,36] Nearly 2.5 million American adults are addicted to opioids, accounting for 42,249 deaths in 2016.[37] Most of these addicted adults are parents. Before the late 1990s, the most widely used addictive drugs were cocaine and heroin. Since then, opioids have become the front-runners. Initially created as prescription drugs to reduce severe pain, **opioids** are a class of drugs that include codeine, hydrocodone, oxycodone, and fentanyl. The highest rates of opioid deaths are in West Virginia—five times higher than the lowest death rates in Nebraska.[38]

Certain parents are far more likely than others to become addicted to opioids. Even though women are less likely than men to use opioids, women are just as likely as men to become addicted.[34] In fact, women start using opioids at an earlier age and become addicted faster than men.[39] For adults who are clinically depressed or have other mood disorders, the vast majority of opioid addicts are women (68%). Education, however, plays a stronger role than gender. Of those who are addicted, only 10% have graduate degrees, compared to 25% who attended or graduated from college, and 65% who never attended college. Regardless of education or gender, the overwhelming majority (80%) of addicts are non-Hispanic whites. In terms of father-daughter relationships, fathers should be far more concerned about their daughter than about their son becoming addicted to opioids as young adults.

There is too little research to draw conclusions about the impact of parents' opioid abuse on children.[40] Most studies fail to consider family income, the quality of parenting, and the parent's mental health. What we do know is that 7% of parents between the ages of 24 and 32 are addicted to opioids. Moreover, most of these addicts have no medical condition requiring pain killers.[41] A large number (44%) of these young parents have financial hardships, which is understandable since so few of them attended college. Nearly a third (28%) of opioid users have a history of prior drug use.

Children with an opioid addicted parent are more likely to be in foster care due to neglect or physical abuse. Nationwide, nearly 40% of children who are being raised by their grandparents and 30% of those in foster care have an opioid addicted parent—usually their mother.[42] For example, in Florida, as opioid prescriptions increased between 2012 and 2015, the number of children removed from their parents for child neglect increased by 32%.[43] Similarly, in North Carolina 40% of the 16,500 children in foster care have an opioid addicted parent.[44]

In the absence of more data, it is reasonable to assume that these children will experience many of the same kinds of emotional, behavioral, academic, and psychological problems as children whose parents are addicted to alcohol.

Sexually Abusive Fathers

Compared to fathers who abuse drugs or alcohol, physically abusive fathers are far less common and sexually abusive fathers are extremely rare. To be clear, this statement refers to biological fathers, not to stepfathers or to the mother's live-in boyfriend.

Before discussing father-daughter sexual abuse, we must be very clear what the terms incest and sexual abuse mean. While most people might assume these terms mean that the father has had sexual intercourse with his daughter, this is incorrect. **Incest** and **sexual abuse** are terms that refer to a wide range of sexual behavior other than sexual intercourse. These incestuous sexual behaviors include genital touching, fondling breasts, oral sex, and masturbation. Incest and sexual abuse also encompass any kind of sexual behavior with members of the extended family (i.e. cousin, uncle), stepfamily (stepsibling, stepfather), and non-biological relatives (adopted siblings). As we will now see, incest and sexual abuse rarely mean sexual intercourse and rarely mean any form of sexual behavior between the victim and a biological parent or fully biological sibling.

It is also extremely important to understand that very few incest studies categorize the behavior of biological fathers separately from the behavior of stepfathers and mothers' boyfriends. This means that many daughters who report being victims of incest are referring to their stepfathers or to their mother's live-in boyfriends, not to their biological father. It is also difficult to estimate how many male and female children are victims of the various kinds of sexual abuse. Most children, especially boys, are too ashamed to report or to admit the abuse. Moreover, historically American doctors and mental health professionals have been reluctant to believe that sexual abuse occurs in white, well-educated families, and have been less likely to recognize or report it.[45]

Keeping these limitations in mind, recent research has disclosed some surprising facts about sexually abused children.[46–48] It is estimated that one in six boys and one in four girls are sexually abused before the age of 18. Again though, sexual abuse includes a wide range of behavior other than intercourse. So most of these abused children did not have anal or vaginal intercourse with their abuser. Most abusers (67%) are people that the child knows, but they are not members of their immediate family network. Even within the family network, most abusers are members of the extended family (i.e. cousins, uncles) or the stepfamily. It is extremely rare for the abusers to be the biological parents or siblings of their victims. Most children (69%) are abused in their own home and 30% are abused by someone under the age of 18 (cousins, stepsiblings). Most adult abusers are under the age of 30. Nearly 40% of males and 6% of females were abused by a female.[47] In short, the odds of a daughter being sexually abused by her biological father—let alone having had intercourse with him—are extremely low.

As for the reliability of children's reports, not all are truthful. There are daughters who falsely accuse their biological fathers or other family members of having sexually abused them.[49] For example, when parents are going through a contentious divorce, sons and daughters are more likely to accuse their father falsely of having sexually abused them.[50] In these situations, the mother may invent and promote the false allegations in order to win sole custody of the children. Young children can be more easily duped than older children into falsely accusing their father of sexual or physical abuse or misled into believing that they "remember" incidents that never, in fact, occurred.

There are also cases where adult daughters are encouraged by a therapist to "recover" their buried memories of abuse, decades after the abuse allegedly occurred.[49] Through questionable **"recovery" techniques** such as hypnosis, dream analysis, and journal writing, the therapist leads the client to discover her repressed memories of sexual abuse. It is certainly true that daughters can repress memories of abuse for years. But it is also true that these types of "recovery" techniques can create memories of events that never occurred, as the cognitive psychologist Elizabeth Loftus has documented in her research.[49]

Men who engage in these kinds of sexually abusive behaviors with children generally share some common characteristics.[51,52,53] If he is the mother's boyfriend or the children's stepfather, his relationship with the mother is often not sexually or emotionally satisfying. Their relationship often involves high conflict and physical abuse. Childhood sexual abuse is also more common in low-income families and in families where the adults abuse alcohol or drugs. Abusers are also more likely to have been sexually or physically abused as children. This does not mean, however, that most abused boys become sexually or physically abusive men. The vast majority do not. What it does mean is that men who abuse children sexually are more likely to have been victims of abuse as children than men who never sexually abuse children.

In a meta-analyses involving at least 15 studies, sex offenders who were biologically related to the child differed from offenders who were unrelated biologically.[54,55] The unrelated offenders were more likely to have a history of prior sexual offenses, to abuse drugs and alcohol, and to have mental health problems. The offenders who were biologically related in any way to the abused child were more likely to have been sexually abused as children and to have had physically abusive or negligent parents.

Two other studies illustrate that it is extremely rare for a biological father to engage in any kind of sexual behavior with his daughter. In the first study with a sample of 2,034 students from six colleges, 51 daughters (2.5%) reported that their stepfather, mother's boyfriend, or biological father had sexually abused them.[51] Since the researchers did not categorize the biological fathers separately, we cannot know how many of these 51 daughters were abused by their biological father. It was clear to the researchers, however, from the information in the survey that most of the abusers were not the biological fathers. If the mother's relationship with her husband or boyfriend was physically abusive, the daughter was five times more likely to be abused. Likewise, daughters who did not have close relationships with their mother were more likely to be abused than those with close mother-daughter relationships.

In the second study, daughters' reports did make a distinction between biological fathers and other abusers.[51] In this sample of 1,261 young women (average age 22), any kind of sexual behavior between father and daughter was extremely rare. Although 241 daughters (18%) said they were sexually abused as a child, only 19 of the 1,261 daughters (1.5%) said her father was the one who sexually abused her. Of the 19 daughters who said their biological father was the abuser, only seven had sexual intercourse with him. In other words, only 0.5% of the daughters had sexual intercourse with her father and only 1% had engaged in any kind of sexual behavior with him.

Regardless of who their abuser was, daughters and sons who are sexually abused as children have more emotional, psychological, and health related problems.[46] Even as adults, they are more likely to abuse drugs and alcohol, to be clinically depressed and anxious, and to have difficulty trusting or enjoying their romantic relationships. They often carry feelings of guilt and shame into adulthood, years after the abuse occurred. We turn our attention now to family situations that are far less destructive and far more common than childhood sexual abuse.

Fathers in the Military

There are roughly two million American children living in military families.[40] In almost all (95%) of these families, the father is the parent who is in the service. A number of differences between military and civilian families contribute to the challenges facing these father-child relationships.[56,57] Military couples marry and have children at a younger age and relocate ten times more often than civilian families. Most of these children will change schools six to nine times. Their mothers are ten times more likely than civilian mothers not to work outside the home. Living only on the military father's income, many of these families face greater financial struggles than civilian parents of similar age and education.

Perhaps the greatest challenge to military fathers' relationships with their children is deployment. Since 2001, more than two million children have had a parent deployed, usually to war zones in Iraq or Afghanistan. More than 900,000 children have experienced multiple deployments, with an average separation of 12–15 months from their father. Nearly 320,000 men, most of whom are fathers, have returned from these two wars with traumatic brain

Figure 8.1
Source: Ethan Wilson.

injuries. Many more suffer ongoing combat related stress, depression and **post-traumatic stress disorder** (PTSD) after they return to their families. Approximately 5.5 million wives or relatives are caring for these wounded fathers.

Not surprisingly, compared to civilians, military children have higher rates of depression, anxiety disorders, behavioral problems, drug and alcohol use, and stress related illnesses (i.e. sleeping and eating problems, stomach aches).[56,58] For example, veterans' teenage children are more likely to smoke cigarettes and use drugs regardless of whether their father talked to them about drug use.[59] And children whose fathers have PTSD are more likely to have internalizing and externalizing problems.[60] Twelve- to 13-year-olds whose fathers had been deployed for less than 180 days in the past three years did not develop more problems. But if their father had been gone more than 180 days, the children developed more academic problems and became less self-reliant and more irresponsible.[61] As might be expected, those children whose parents are actively involved in their community and create close connections to other military families are less depressed and less anxious than those whose parents are more socially isolated.[62] Especially during times of stress or during the father's deployment, these parents provided their children with higher quality parenting, which helped them cope with the family stress.

It is not only the father's absence that has a negative impact on children, but the decreased quality of parenting when he returns.[57] For example, after being away from their children for 12 to 14 months, fathers returned home more physically and emotionally stressed—especially if they had served in a war zone. The fathers also had more strained relationships with their children and their wives. Especially when the children are under the age of seven and have gone through major developmental changes in his absence, fathers are stressed and worried about reconnecting.[63] Moreover, fathers who are deployed more than once to combat areas are at highest risk of developing PTSD. Even with the help of parenting programs, it is difficult for these fathers to improve their parenting skills and reconnect with their children largely due to the father's clinical depression.[64,65]

Studies have not compared father-daughter to father-son relationships in military families. But given the research presented in earlier chapters, it is reasonable to assume that the father's relationship with his daughter is usually more distant and more strained than with his son. By its nature, the military environment is more conducive to traditionally masculine activities and values where most fathers and sons can more easily find common ground. Then too, since most mothers in these families do not work full time or do not work at all, mothers and daughters may form closer bonds than they do in most civilian families. For many reasons then, military fathers are likely to face more obstacles than civilian fathers in their relationships with their children, especially with their daughters.

Single Fathers Raising Children

Another challenging situation for fathers is raising daughters on their own as divorced, never-married, or widowed men. Families headed by single fathers have changed in several regards since the 1960s.[66,67] There are currently almost two million fathers who are raising children on their own—four times more than in 1960. Of these, 44% are divorced, 19% separated but not yet divorced, 33% never married, and 4% widowed. In contrast, in the 1960s almost all of these fathers were raising their children alone because they were divorced. Of the 39 million families in the U.S., 27% are headed by single mothers and 5% by single fathers. Nearly 25% of these fathers are living with a girlfriend and 25% are living with a relative—usually with their mother. So most of these children are not growing up in households where their father is the only adult. The same is true for children living with single mothers. Another adult, typically the maternal grandmother or the mother's boyfriend, is usually living with the mother and children.

According to a recent review of the literature, single mother and single father families are more alike than they are different in terms of income, race, or previous marital status.[66] Still there are some differences. Daughters are less likely than sons to be living with a single father. In part this might be because mothers feel that sons need their fathers more than daughters do, or because sons are more difficult than daughters for single mothers to control. Single fathers also tend to have fewer children and to have older children than single mothers. Most children are living with their fathers because their parents mutually agreed to this arrangement, not because of court orders.

For those single fathers who were never married to their children's mother, several somewhat surprising findings have emerged from the large Fragile Families' Project.[68] The vast majority of parents in this study were poorly educated, lower income, minority parents who were not married when their children were born. When the children were three years old, those whose mother drank more than the father or whose mother was depressed were more likely to be living with their father. If the mother used drugs, the odds of living with the father increased by 70%. Children were also more likely to live with their father if he was more educated than their mother and if the mother had children who were fathered by different men.

Overall children fare just as well in single father as in single mother families.[49] Those in single father families are, however, somewhat more likely to use drugs and to have behavioral problems. This is not especially surprising, however, since sons are more likely than daughters to live with single fathers and boys tend to experiment more with drugs and to be more aggressive than daughters. In general, though, sons and daughters raised either by a single mother or a single father have similar academic, behavioral, and emotional outcomes. On the other hand, in a large national sample, children raised by their fathers had better physical health than those living with a single mother or with a remarried mother and stepfather.[69] This finding is noteworthy because the data came from 67,558 children in the 1999 and 2002 rounds of the National Survey of American Families. In terms of how well teenagers feel they communicate with their parents, 529 teenagers growing up in single father families gave him higher ratings than the teenagers with married parents.[70] They shared more with their single fathers about what was going on in their lives and went to him more often for help with personal problems.

It is also worth noting that daughters sometimes fare better in single father than in single mother homes. For example, in one California study the parents had been divorced on average for four years. Even after accounting for family income, the teenage girls who lived with their father were less depressed and less anxious than girls living with their mother.[71] And in a study with lower income families, teenage girls who lived with their fathers had higher achievement scores than girls living with their single mothers.[72]

Overall then, daughters who are living in single father homes fare as well—or sometimes better—than those living in single mother families. Keep in mind, however, that these single mothers and single fathers are generally not raising the child alone since there is usually another adult living in the home.

Gay Fathers

Some of the fathers who are raising children on their own are gay or bisexual. It is estimated that 6 to 14 million children have gay or lesbian parents.[73] We do not know how many sons or daughters are being raised by lesbian, gay, bisexual, transgender, or "queer" (**LGBTQ**) parents. We do know that the number of gay fathers who are raising children has increased and that society has become more accepting of LGBTQ families.[74] Still, the number of LGBTQ families is small because only 1.6% of adults over the age of 18 identify as gay or lesbian and only 0.7% identify as bisexual.[75] Most Americans would find these numbers shocking since most adults in the U.S. believe that 25% of the population is gay, lesbian, or bisexual.[76]

Four limitations must be kept in mind regarding the research on gay fathers and their children.[68,77] First, there is far less research on gay fathers than on lesbian mothers. Second, there is no research on gay fathers' relationships with their daughters versus sons. Third, there are too few studies to draw conclusions about the similarities or differences between gay and lesbian parents or the different impact they might have on sons compared to daughters. Fourth, virtually all of the research on gay fathers and their children is based on non-Hispanic white men who have more education and higher incomes than fathers in the general population.

Keeping these limitations in mind, families of gay fathers differ from those of lesbian mothers in several respects. Compared to lesbian mothers, gay fathers face more discrimination and receive less social support.[73,77] Partly this is because society is more accepting of and more comfortable around lesbians than around gay men. Society is also much more disapproving of gay men raising children than of lesbians raising children. Gay fathers also report that other gay men are often uncomfortable or unsupportive of gay men raising children. This discrimination and lack of support means that being a parent is probably more stressful and more challenging for gay fathers than for lesbian mothers.

Gay fathers become parents in one of four ways. The overwhelming majority become parents while in a heterosexual relationship. That is, most gay fathers were formerly married to the mother of their children. Others are either foster fathers or adoptive fathers. The smallest group are gay fathers who become parents through surrogacy, which involves medical and legal arrangements with the surrogate mother. Because this process is expensive and complicated, most of these fathers are well-educated men with relatively high incomes whose parents and siblings are usually supportive of their decision.[78] This might partly explain why, in one study of children born to gay fathers through surrogacy, the children had fewer internalizing problems than the children of lesbian mothers.[79]

It is also worth noting that African Americans are generally more disapproving of gay men than are non-Hispanic white Americans.[80,81,82] As a result, African American men are less likely than non-Hispanic white men to acknowledge to themselves or to others that they are gay or bisexual. These African American fathers may be under intense pressure, publicly living a heterosexual life—some as married men—while secretly having sex with other men. This situation, known as "the down low" or "living on the DL", may contribute to greater depression and more substance or alcohol abuse for these African American men.[80]

How do children fare in gay father families? Overall, these children are as well-adjusted emotionally, academically, and behaviorally as children raised by heterosexual parents.[73,77,83] For example, two years after being adopted, "high risk" children (those with more social, physical, or behavioral problems) were faring just as well in gay and lesbian families as in heterosexual families.[84] Importantly, the gay and lesbian parents were much more likely than heterosexual parents to have adopted children with high risk factors, such as being born prematurely or having lived with several foster families. Yet despite these additional disadvantages, these adopted children made near identical gains to those adopted by the heterosexual parents.

This is not to say that children raised by gay or lesbian face no greater obstacles than children raised by heterosexual parents. For example, eight-year-olds adopted by gay or lesbian parents reported feeling "different" from their peers and disliked being teased, bullied or ostracized by other children.[85] Especially during the teenage years when peer approval assumes such importance, children say their peers can be especially unkind or insensitive.[86] Most say they felt uncomfortable in certain social situations and felt some degree of peer rejection, discrimination, or ridicule growing up with LBGQ parents. For example, how do you introduce your father's male romantic "partner" to your teenage friends? If the father and his partner are married, do you refer to your dad's husband as your stepfather? When encountering openly hostile, homophobic people, is it best to lie about the fact that your father is gay?

Other children are stressed because they feel they have to be perfect in order to present the "ideal" image of their family to society.[68] There is the stress of being under intense scrutiny and feeling that any teenage problem—drinking or bad grades, for example—will automatically be blamed on the fact that their parents are not heterosexual. Many are also hesitant to talk to their parents about their teenage problems because they do not want to create additional stress for the family. Moreover, if a child is not heterosexual, he or she is often afraid to disclose this information, which increases stress and depression. They fear that their sexual orientation will be used as proof that LGBTQ parents cause their children to become gay or lesbian.

To help these children cope with their additional stresses, an organization called COLAGE (children of lesbian and gays everywhere) was created. This organization offers provides resources and advice for children and parents in LGBTQ families (www.colage.org).

These is also some evidence that children with gay and lesbian parents may not fare as well as those with heterosexual parents. For example, in a study with children between the ages of 18 and 39, those with gay or lesbian parents had more problems than those with heterosexual parents.[87] Only 23 of the 73 adult children with gay fathers had actually lived with their father. In contrast, almost all (159 of 175) of the children with lesbian mothers had been raised by her. Compared to the 2,540 children with married, heterosexual parents, lesbians' children had worse outcomes on 25 of 40 variables and gay fathers' children had worse outcomes on 11 of 40 variables. For example, children with heterosexual parents were less likely to have ever been clinically depressed or ever arrested. On the other hand, children of gay and lesbian parents were just as satisfied with their lives and were no more likely to drink, use marijuana, or be in poor health. It is also hard to draw conclusions from this study because a number of the variables where children of gay and lesbian parents did worse than children of heterosexuals were not related to mental health or behavior problems. For example, children with heterosexual parents were more likely to have voted in the last election, which was counted as a "better" outcome. More important still, unlike some of the children with gay and lesbian parents, none of the children with heterosexual parents had ever lived in foster homes and none of their parents were divorced. This matters because divorce and foster care are linked to worse outcomes for children, independent of their parents' sexual orientation.

Children with gay or bisexual fathers can, however, be negatively affected by how their father tells them about his sexual orientation.[88] The process of "coming out" is generally stressful for most fathers and for their children. In large part this is because society is much more disapproving of gay men raising children than of lesbians raising children. Some gay fathers who have children through surrogacy begin talking to their children about their origins in very general, simple ways when the children are as young as four.[89] At the other extreme, even in old age, some gay fathers never reveal their sexual orientation to their children or their grandchildren.[90] This is unfortunate since adult children feel less depressed and closer to their fathers when he tells them the truth—as do the fathers themselves.[88]

Overall then, children with gay fathers fare as well as those with heterosexual fathers, despite the additional challenges most of them encounter. Although these fathers and daughters encounter unique challenges that might at times put additional stress on their relationship, there is no reason to presume that their relationships are less loving or less meaningful.

Lesbian and Bisexual Daughters

A daughter's sexual orientation can also present unique challenges for father-daughter relationships. There are very few studies specifically about fathers' relationships with their gay or bisexual daughters. Most of the research simply discusses parents' relationships with their gay or lesbian children without distinguishing mothers from fathers or sons from daughters. The absence of research is not surprising, however, since nearly 97% of daughters and sons identify as heterosexual.[75] Still, it is clear that fathers play a powerful role in how well their daughters cope with not being heterosexual.

First, these fathers need to be aware that, compared to heterosexual daughters, their daughters are more likely to have emotional and psychological problems.[81] They are more likely to drink and to use drugs as teenagers and as adults. In fact, in surveys involving 12,493 people between the ages of 18 and 25, lesbian daughters were more likely than gays sons and more likely than heterosexual sons and daughters to drink or to drink heavily.[91] Gay and lesbian students were three times as likely to be clinically depressed or suicidal. On the other hand, fathers might take some comfort in knowing that their lesbian daughters will encounter less discrimination, harassment, rejection, and victimization than would their gay sons.[75] This might help explain why lesbians are less likely than gay males to attempt or commit suicide—especially as teenagers when suicide rates are at their highest.

Second, fathers who are accepting and supportive of their daughter disclosing her sexual identity reduce the odds that she will develop social, emotional, or psychological problems.[92] The most resilient, well-adapted LBGQ youth are those who have supportive families and friends. Indeed lesbian daughters have written about the role their fathers played in making them more resilient and making them feel loved and lovable.[93] The most vulnerable years for LBGQ youth are the earlier teenage years when other teenagers subject them to the worst rejection, harassment, and victimization. For example, in a sample of 351 black, Latina, and white lesbians, 50% reported having been depressed as teenagers; but this figure had dropped to 35% three years later.[94] Adolescence is the time when most LBGQ children first show symptoms of these mental health or drug and alcohol problems. So fathers should be especially alert and supportive during their daughters' teenage years, while reassuring her that her adult years will likely be less difficult.

Third, fathers should be prepared for the fact that daughters usually "come out" first to their mothers or their friends.[95] This is not surprising since, as discussed in earlier chapters, daughters generally share more personal information with their mothers than with their fathers. When daughters "come out" to a parent or friend and the response is negative, they often feel worse in the short run. But they are less depressed and feel better about themselves in the long run than those who hide or lie about their sexual orientation—which may help explain why the average age for coming out nowadays is around fourteen.[96] Unfortunately many parents, family members, and communities are extremely rejecting, as evidenced by the fact that 40% of homeless youth are LGBTQ.[92]

Fourth, fathers need to be aware and to acknowledge to their daughter that her sexual orientation is not a mental disorder. In 1973 the American Psychiatric Association (APA) removed homosexuality from the *Diagnostic and Statistical Manual of Mental Disorders*. Since that time, it has become clear that problems arise not because LGBTQ people are mentally ill, but because they are chronically stressed by the discrimination, abuse, and victimization they encounter in society. Their emotional and psychological problems often arise from three sources of chronic stress: direct personal experiences, the hypervigilance and expectation of being victimized or rejected, and the acceptance of society's negative attitudes which leads to internalized homophobia.[92] Fathers can help their daughters recognize and combat these three sources of stress.

Fathers should also be made aware of other factors that increase the risk that their daughters will develop problems related to their sexual orientation.[92] Daughters who are dating or in a relationship with another lesbian are less depressed and more well adjusted overall than daughters who are socially isolated from other lesbians or pretending to be heterosexual in their social lives. Daughters are also better adapted when they attend schools or are part of religious and community organizations that are supportive of sexual minorities and have a zero tolerance policy for bullying and discrimination.

In sum, these fathers can rest assured that the vast majority of their daughters will grow up to be emotionally, socially, and mentally well-adjusted adults. At the same time, however, fathers need to keep in mind that, as members of a sexual minority, their daughters are more at risk of developing the kinds of problems that arise from discrimination, harassment, rejection, and victimization.

Daughters of Sperm Donors

Compared to the research on lesbian or bisexual daughters' relationships with their fathers, the research on daughters who were conceived through sperm donation is virtually nonexistent. In fact, there are no statistics documenting how many American children are born to lesbian or to heterosexual mothers who conceived through sperm donation—either by an anonymous donor at a sperm bank or by someone the mother knows who agrees to donate his sperm. Based on national data from fertility clinics, in 2015 there were 76,930 babies born through assisted reproductive technologies.[97] The report does not indicate, however, how many babies were conceived through sperm donations versus other forms of technologically assisted reproduction.

There are studies, however, that provide an overview of the men who anonymously donate sperm to sperm banks.[98,99] Some donors are married heterosexual men with children. Others are unmarried heterosexuals or gay. Only about 20% of donors in the U.S. want to meet their offspring, though 40% say they would not object to meeting if the children desired and initiated it.[99] Others, however, are willing to meet the children if the children insist on it and if the children initiate the contact. In one study, men who donated sperm and women who donated eggs were equally likely to want to meet any children conceived through their donations, though we cannot generalize from just one study.[100]

Children conceived through sperm donation in the U.S. are different in several respects from their counterparts in other countries.[101] Unlike countries such as Norway and Britain, in the U.S. there is no legal limit placed on the number of donations that one donor can make. This means one sperm donor can father an unlimited number of children. This raises the risk that half-siblings might unknowingly have children together, which, in turn, can increase the number of genetic disorders. In that vein, in the Netherlands children have a legal right to know who their sperm donor is. So all sperm donors must provide their names. And in Vermont and Washington state, clinics are required to collect the sperm donor's medical history and to disclose it to the children if they ask.[102]

In the U.S. contact between donors and their children has increased for several reasons.[101] Some sperm donation clinics collect enough information from donors that their adult children can discover their identities through websites such as the Donor Sibling Registry.[103] Other children discover who their donors are while they and their unknown half-siblings are seeking help for rare genetically inherited health conditions. Still others discover their half-siblings through internet searches and together find their biological father.[98,104,105]

Given the scarcity of research studies, we cannot generalize about how most sperm donors or half-siblings with the same donor father react to their situations. What we can glean from books that have interviewed members of sperm donor families is that the reactions are varied.[98,104,106] Some half-siblings become friends, while others never want to meet. Some sperm donors who agree to meet their teenage or young adult children have very comfortable, satisfying meetings. Other contacts, however, are so unpleasant, disappointing, or stressful that the donor and the child regret having agreed to meet one another.

In the few published research studies, the experiences of sperm donor families are also mixed. In a study with young adults, when the parents avoided the topic of the donor conception, the children were more stressed than when the topic had been openly discussed.[107] While some families used the words "father" or "dad" to refer to the sperm donor, others either referred to him as the "donor" or never used any name to refer to him.[108] In explaining the situation to young children, some heterosexual married couples use humor, for example by explaining that "daddy ran out of tadpoles."[109]

How or when parents explain their conception to the children may also depend in part on the parents' sexual orientation. For example, in one study almost all (94%) of the 283 lesbian mothers had told their children about the sperm donor conception before they were ten years old, while 40% of the 458 heterosexual couples had not.[110] In fact 24% of the heterosexual couples did not tell the children until they were older than 18. In part heterosexual parents might wait longer because, as some couples have said, they do not want to undermine the father's confidence in himself by revealing to the children that he is not their biological father.[111] Interestingly though, in a study with 44 young teenagers (average age 14), most of them were indifferent rather than upset when their heterosexual, married parents told them they had been conceived through egg or sperm donation.[112] On the other hand, for 19 children aged 7–13 living with unmarried mothers, those who had negative feelings about their sperm donor were less securely attached to their mothers.[113]

Overall then, we know very little about children who are conceived through sperm donation. Based on the scant data available, these sons and daughters do not seem to be experiencing serious or long-lasting problems. Based on what we know from the child development literature, we can assume that being raised by loving parents matters far more to children and is more closely linked to their well-being than the manner in which they were conceived.

Fathers with Terminal Illnesses and the Impact of the Father's Death

One of the most difficult situations confronting fathers and daughters is coping with a father's terminal illness and, even if the death is expected, adjusting to his death.

Most daughters will experience their father's terminal illness or his death before their mother's because American men generally die seven years before women.[114] Most likely her father and mother will die from heart disease or cancer, which account for 50% of all deaths over the age of 60 in the U.S. With today's advanced medical technology to detect disease at earlier stages, a parent's death is generally not sudden or unexpected. Consequently, most daughters and sons are aware—or will eventually be aware—that their father has a terminal disease or a serious medical condition that will shorten his life.

It is unlikely that a daughter and her father will experience his having or dying from Alzheimer's disease (AZ) since two-thirds of the afflicted are women.[115,116] Although 5.7 million Americans have AZ, it almost always occurs late in life. Roughly 11% of men and 16% of women over the age of 70 have AZ, though the numbers increase rapidly for women over the age of 85. There are 16.1 million family members providing care for a parent or spouse with AZ, which means that many daughters are providing some, or sometimes all, of the care for their parent. "Early onset" Alzheimer's means the symptoms appear before the age of 65. This disease affects only 4% of the population, but progresses far more rapidly than later onset dementia. Estimates are that 200,000 to 500,000 Americans have early onset dementia, but most are unaware of their condition because the symptoms are still too mild.

Still, there are daughters whose relationships with their fathers are profoundly affected by his having Alzheimer's—especially if it occurs during her childhood. Very little has been written about the experiences and needs of children whose parents have early onset dementia.[116] Many of these children are still teenagers or younger when their parent becomes afflicted. For example, in one case where the 50-year-old father had early onset dementia, the daughter was only 16 and the son only 11. Clearly children at this young age with a middle aged parent are far less emotionally equipped than middle

Figure 8.2
Source: KonstantinChristian/shutterstock.com.

aged children with elderly parents to deal with the debilitating cognitive and behavioral symptoms of dementia.

Even for fatal illnesses that are far more widespread than dementia, very few studies have focused specifically on terminally ill fathers' relationships with their daughters. We can however, extrapolate from studies of sons and daughters with parents who are terminally ill or dying. Not surprisingly, adult caregivers who have a close relationship with their frail, sickly parent are less stressed and less depressed than those who have distant or strained relationships.[117] The quality of parent-child relationships may help to explain why more adult children are providing care for their widowed father than for their divorced father.[118]

It is not clear whether the father's death has any great impact on daughters than on sons. For example, in one small study where fathers died early in their children's lives, daughters were more likely than sons to be clinically depressed as adults.[119] Adult sons and daughters also reacted differently when their father or mother had died of lung cancer or a stroke caused by smoking.[120] The daughters were more likely than the sons to stop smoking after their parent died of a smoking related disease. After their parent died, however, daughters were more likely than sons to develop stress related health problems. The researchers speculated this happened because daughters became more depressed than sons. On the other hand, in a large national survey with 8,865 adults, sons were more depressed and had more physical health problems than daughters after their father died, while the reverse was true after their mother died.[121] Moreover, sons and daughters whose mothers or fathers had killed themselves were more likely to become suicidal than children whose parents had died from any other cause.[122] But in another large nationally representative study with 19,015 participants, daughters were no more likely than sons to be suicidal if their parent had committed suicide. Moreover, the father's suicide had no greater or lesser impact than the mother's suicide on the children's suicide attempts. Overall then, the quality of the parent-child relationship probably plays a great role in how children react or adjust to the death than does the gender of the parent.

Box 8.3 The father's terminal illness and impending death

Lise Funderburg, a multiracial journalist, created a deeper relationship with her African American father after he was diagnosed with terminal cancer. Having grown up in an integrated Philadelphia neighborhood, she had never understood why her father was so strict, demanding, and elusive. But after his diagnosis, when she was in her 40s, they made many pilgrimages together to his hometown in rural Jasper County, Georgia. Through those journeys, Funderberg discovered a father full of warmth, humor, and disarming candor. It was only then she understood that his strict, elusive parenting came from growing up in poverty and his terrible experiences growing up in the violent, racist South. After his death she wrote about their relationship in her memoir, *Pig Candy*, referring to the candied bacon he had loved as a child.[128]

Daphne Merkin, a highly respected writer for *The New Yorker*, wrote an article in which she reminisced about the profound impact of her father's death. She writes that she wishes she had gotten to know him better while he was alive. And she reminisces that shortly before he died, as he was holding her hand, he told her he hoped some day she would write about him. Even years after his death, she tenderly writes about missing him and envisioning him sitting in his study with his bald head covered with a flat, black crocheted yarmulke.[129]

Daughters whose fathers die relatively young generally remember their fathers fondly, despite the pain the daughter had to endure at an early age. But in essays written by adult daughters, the age at which their fathers died mattered less than the quality of their relationship in terms of how his death affected the daughter.[123–125] In these essays the daughters who had close relationships with their fathers had a harder time adjusting to his death than those with distant or troubled relationships. On the other hand, having a close relationship generally freed these daughters from the guilt or remorse that many of the other daughters had to endure.

How well the daughter deals with her father's terminal illness or his death partly depends on how they have handled communicating about the situation. For example, spouses and family caregivers were more stressed when the terminally ill parent did not talk with them about the illness or impending death.[126] In contrast, adult children felt closer to their parents when they openly discussed the parent's diagnosis of cancer.[127] Interjecting humor into some of these conversations also helped bring parents and adult children closer together and helped everyone cope better with the parent's illness. As the stories in Box 8.3 illustrate, a father's terminal illness and impending death can be catalysts for enriching his relationship with his daughter.

More Americans with terminal illnesses are now living longer than ever before due to advances in medical care for the terminally ill. Inevitably then, more father-daughter relationships are affected by his long, slow decline and their awareness of his impending death. For some, their close relationship eases the pain and sadness at the end of his life. For others, their distant or troubled father-daughter relationship leave them both with lingering feelings of anger, remorse, confusion, sadness, and grief.

Review Questions

1 What are the differences among racial groups in respect to income, incarceration, education, and non-marital births?
2 What factors are linked to childhood poverty and how many children in each racial group are living in poverty?
3 How is poverty defined in terms of income and how do poverty rates in the U.S. compare to other developed countries?
4 What are some of the myths about poor, unmarried fathers refuted by the research?
5 What might account for the high incarceration rates in America?
6 What obstacles weaken incarcerated fathers' relationships with their children?
7 What are some of the most common myths about incest and what data refute them?

8 What percentage of parents are alcoholics and in what specific ways does their alcoholism affect their children?

9 How are daughters affected differently than sons by their parents' alcoholism?

10 What are opioids and which parents are the most likely to be addicted? How does this affect their children?

11 How and why are military and civilian fathers' relationships with their children different?

12 What unique situations do daughters with gay fathers often encounter and how does this affect their relationship or the outcomes for the children?

13 How common is it for children to be raised by gay fathers and how do gay men usually become fathers?

14 Who are most of the single fathers raising children and how do these children's outcomes compare to those of children from single mother families?

15 What are some of the issues involved in being a sperm donor or the child conceived through anonymous sperm donations?

16 For LGBTQ daughters, what special issues or concerns should their fathers keep in mind?

17 What are most parents likely to die from and how do sons and daughters seem to be affected differently by their parents' deaths?

18 Which factors or situations discussed in this chapter present the greatest challenges to father-daughter relationships and why?

Questions for Discussion and Debate

1 What could be done to maintain father-daughter relationship when the father is in prison?

2 Which fathers and daughters discussed in this chapter do you feel sorriest for in respect to the problems confronting their relationships? Why?

3 How might our society reduce the incidence of fathers' abusing their daughters physically or sexually?

4 If you suspected an adolescent daughter was being sexually or physically abused, what steps would you take?

5 How do you feel about "repressed memory therapy" for daughters who may have been abused by their fathers or stepfathers?

6 If you were dating a woman who had grown up with an alcoholic father, what concerns would you have about your relationship with her and how would you deal with those concerns?

7 If you were the daughter, which of these situations do you feel would have the most negative impact on you: growing up with an alcoholic father, having a father who divorced your mother because he is gay, or having a father who died when you were a very young girl? Why?

8 If you were a gay father or a lesbian daughter, what would you most worry about in terms of your father-daughter relationship?

9 How do you feel about gay fathers adopting or conceiving children through sperm donation with a surrogate mother?

10 Why do you think daughters are usually more accepting than sons are of their father being gay?

11 How do you feel about children being conceived through sperm donation to a single mother or to two lesbian mothers? Should the father be involved in his daughter's life? If so, how? If not, why not?

12 What benefits might there be for father-daughter relationships when the father is in the military?

13 Which daughter do you feel will probably be most damaged in the long term by her father's death, given the way he died: an extended illness, suicide, murder, drug overdose, alcoholism, or military service? Why?

14 How do you imagine your relationship with your dad might change when he is elderly or in the last year or two of his life?

15 What information in this chapter was most unsettling or most relevant to you?

References

1 Alston P. *Report of the special rapporteur on extreme poverty and human rights on his mission to the United States of America.* New York: United Nations Human Rights Council; 2018, May 4.

2 Guzman G. *Household income in the U.S.: 2016.* Washington, DC: U.S. Census Bureau; 2017.

3 Census Bureau. *Population Estimates in United States.* Washington, DC: U.S. Department of Labor: Census Bureau; 2017.

4 McClanahan S. Outcomes for children in fragile families. In: England P, Carlson M, editors. *Changing families in an unequal society.* Palo Alto, CA: Stanford University Press; 2011. 108–134.

5 England P, Edin K. *Unmarried couples with children.* New York: Russell Sage Foundation; 2007.

6 Haney L. *The mass incarceration of fathers.* Los Angeles: University of California Press; 2018.

7 Department of Justice. *Prison inmate population by race and gender.* Washington DC: U.S. Department of Justice; 2018, March 24.

8 Bureau of Justice. *American Indian and Alaska Natives in local jails.* Washington, DC: Bureau of Justice Statistics; 2017.

9 C.R.C.W. *Parental incarceration and child wellbeing in fragile families.* Princeton, NJ: Center for Research on Child Wellbeing; 2013.

10 Wildeman C, Western B. Incarceration in fragile families. *The Future of Children* 2010; 20: 157–177.

11 Pierce M. Male inmate perceptions of the visitation experience. *Prison Journal* 2015; 95: 370–396.

12 Cotton G. Father-daughter dance in Indiana prison strengthens family bonds. *Corrections Today* 2015; 77: 50–52.

13 Wax E. A father-daughter dance in jail. *Washington Post*, March 20, 2013.

14 Burgess A, Huebner B, Durso J. Comparing the effects of maternal and paternal incarceration on adult daughters' and sons' criminal justice system involvement. *Criminal Justice and Behavior* 2016; 43: 1034–1055.

15 Gottlieb A. Household incarceration in early adolescence and risk of premarital first birth. *Children and Youth Services Review* 2016; 61: 126–134.

16 Bryan B. Paternal incarceration and adolescent social network disadvantage. *Demography* 2018; 54: 1477–1501.

17 Besemer S. A systematic review and meta-analysis of the intergenerational transmission of criminal behavior. *Aggression and Violent Behavior* 2017; 37: 161–178.

18 Forster H, Hagan J. Maternal and paternal imprisonment and children's social exclusion in young adulthood. *Journal of Criminal Law and Criminology* 2015; 105: 387–430.

19 Luther K. Examining social support among adult children of incarcerated parents. *Family Relations* 2015; 64: 15–21.

20 National Institute of Alcohol Abuse and Alcoholism. *Alcohol facts and statistics*. Washington, DC: National Institute on Alcohol Abuse and Alcoholism; 2018.

21 Erickson C. *The science of addiction*. New York: W.W. Norton; 2018.

22 Rothenberg W, Hussong A, Chassin L. Modeling trajectories of adolescent perceived family conflict: Effects of marital dissatisfaction and parental alcoholism. *Journal of Research on Adolescence* 2017; 27: 105–121.

23 Kelly R, El-Sheikh M. Parental problem drinking and children's sleep. *Journal of Family Psychology* 2016; 30: 708–719.

24 Ackerman R. *Perfect daughters: Adult daughters of alcoholics*. Deerfield Beach, FL: Heath Communications Incorporated; 2002.

25 Livingston J. Etiology of teen dating violence among adolescent children of alcoholics. *Journal of Youth and Adolescence* 2018; 47: 515–533.

26 Haverfiled M, Theiss J. Parents' alcoholism severity and family topic avoidance as predictors of stigma among adult children of alcoholics. *Health Communication* 2016; 31: 606–616.

27 Cho, B. Associations of father's lifetime cannabis use disorder with child's cannabis use, alcohol use and sexual intercourse by child gender. *Substance Use and Misuse* 2018; 14: 2330–2338.

28 Drapkin M. Alcohol specific coping style of adult children of individuals with alcohol use disorders. *Alcohol and Alcoholism* 2015; 50: 463–469.

29 Kelley M. Mother-daughter and father-daughter attachment of college student ACOA's. *Substance Use and Abuse* 2008; 43(11): 1559–1570.

30 Windle M, Windle R. Parental divorce and family history of alcohol disorder: Associations with young adults' alcohol problems, marijuana use and interpersonal relations. *Alcoholism Clinical and Experimental Research* 2018; 42: 1084–1095.

31 Henry K. Fathers' alcohol and cannabis use disorder and early onset of drug use by their children. *Journal of Studies on Alcohol and Drugs* 2017; 78: 458–462.

32 Stanley L. Predicting an alcohol use disorder in urban American Indian youths. *Journal of Child and Adolescent Substance Abuse* 2014; 23: 101–108.

33 Nadel E, Thornberry T. Intergenerational consequences of adolescent substance use. *Psychology of Addictive Behaviors* 2017; 31: 200–211.

34 N.I.H. *Substance use in women*. Washington, DC: National Institutes of Health; 2018.

35 A.S.A.M. *Opioid addiction 2016: Facts and figures*. New York: American Society of Addiction Medicine; 2017.

36 Hedegaard H, Warner M, Minino A. *Overdose deaths in the United States, 1999–2016*. Hyattsville, MD: National Center for Health Statistics; 2017.

37 U.S. Department of Health and Human Services. *What is the U.S. opioid epidemic?* Washington, DC: U.S. DHHS; 2018, March 6.

38 Seth P, Rudd R, Noonan R, Haegerich T. Prescription opioid data. *American Journal of Public Health* 2018; 108: 4–28.

39 Davis M, Lin L, Liu H, Sites B. Prescription opioid use among adults with mental health disorders in the United States. *Journal of the American Board of Family Medicine* 2017; 4: 407–416.

40 Peisch V. Parental opioid abuse: A review of child outcomes. *Journal of Child and Family Studies* 2018; 27: 2082–2099.

41 Austin A, Shanahan M. Prescription opioid use among young parents in the United States: Results from the National Longitudinal Study of Adolescent to Adult Health. *Pain Medicine* 2017; 18: 2361–2368.

42 Edelman M. Children and the Opioid Crisis. *Huffington Post* 2017, January 7; 1–2.

43 Quast T, Storch E, Yampolskaya S. Opioid prescription rates and child removals: Evidence from Florida. *Health Affairs* 2018; 37: 134–139.

44 Tucker W. *The child welfare impact of the opioid epidemic*. Raleigh, NC: North Carolina Child; 2018, June 1.

45 Sacco L. *Unspeakable: Father daughter incest in American history*. Baltimore, MD: Johns Hopkins University; 2009.

46 National Sex Offender Public Website. *Raising awareness about sexual abuse: Facts and Statistics*. Washington, DC: U.S. Department of Justice www.nsopw. gov; 2018.

47 Deblinger S, Mannarino A, Cohen J, Runyon M, Heflin A. *Child sexual abuse*. New York: Oxford University Press; 2015.

48 Finkelhor D. *Childhood victimization: Violence, crime and abuse in the lives of young people*. New York: Oxford University Press; 2014.

49 Loftus E. *The myth of repressed memory*. New York: St. Martin's; 1996.

50 Kuehnle K, Drozd L. *Child custody litigation: Allegations of child sexual abuse*. New York: Routledge; 2006.

51 Stroebel S, *et al.* Risk factors for father-daughter incest. *Sexual Abuse* 2013; 25: 583–605.

52 Hamilton R. *Father-daughter incest*. Cambridge, MA: Harvard University Press; 2007.

53 Finkelhor D, Turner H, Shattuck A, Hamby S. Prevalence of childhood exposure to violence, crime and abuse. *American Medical Association Journal of Pediatrics* 2015; 169: 746–755.

54 Pullman L, Sawatsky M, Babchishin, K. Differences between biological and sociolegal incest offenders: A meta-analysis. *Aggression and Violent Behavior* 2017; 34: 228–237.

55 Seto M, Babschisin K. The puzzle of intrafamilial child sexual abuse: A meta-analysis. *Clinical Psychology Review* 2015; 39: 42–57.

56 Blaisure K. *Serving military families: Theories, research and application*. Routledge: New York; 2015.

57 Hall L. *Counseling military families*. New York: Routledge; 2016.

58 Wadsworth S, Bailey K, Coppola E. U.S. military children and the wartime deployments of family members. *Child Development Perspectives* 2016; 11: 23–28.

59 Lipari R. Examination of veteran fathers' parenting and their adolescent children's substance use in the United States. *Substance Use & Misuse* 2017; 52: 698–708.

60 Gewirtz A, DeGarmo D, Zamir O. Testing a military family stress model. *Family Process* 2018; 17: 415–431.

61 Nicosia N. Parental deployment, adolescent academic and social behavioral maladjustment and parent psychological wellbeing in military families. *Public Health Reports* 2017; 132: 93–105.

62 O'Neal C, Mallette J, Mancini J. The importance of parents' community connections for adolescent wellbeing: An examination of military families. *American Journal of Epidemiology* 2018; 61: 204–217.

63 Walsh T. Fathering after military deployment: Parenting challenges of fathers of young children. *Health and Social Work* 2018; 39: 35–44.

64 Yablonsky B, Bullock L. Parenting stress after deployment in Navy active duty fathers. *Military Medicine* 2016; 181: 854–862.

65 Chesmore A. PTSD as a moderator of a parenting intervention for military families. *Journal of Family Psychology* 2018; 32: 123–133.

66 Coles R. Single father families: A review of the literature. *Journal of Family Theory & Review* 2015; 7: 144–166.

67 Ellis R, Simmons T. *Coresident grandparents and their grandchildren: 2012.* Washington, DC; Census Bureau: Population Characteristics; 2014.

68 Goldscheider F. Becoming a single parent. *Journal of Family Issues* 2015; 36: 1624–1650.

69 Ziol-Guest K, Dunifon R. Complex living arrangements and child health. *Family Relations* 2014; 63: 424–437.

70 Hawkins D, Amato P, King V. Parent adolescent involvement. *Journal of Marriage and Family* 2006; 68: 125–136.

71 Clarke-Stewart A, Hayward C. Advantages of father custody and contact for the psychological wellbeing of school-age children. *Journal of Applied Developmental Psychology* 1996; 17: 239–270.

72 Lee S, Kushner J, Cho S. Effects of parents' gender on children's achievements in single parent families. *Sex Roles* 2007; 56: 149–157.

73 Goodfellow A. *Gay fathers, their children and the making of kinship.* New York: Fordham University Press; 2017.

74 Rivers D. *Radical relations: Lesbian mothers, gay fathers and their children in the United States since World War II.* Chapel Hill: University of North Carolina Press; 2013.

75 Ward B, *et al. Sexual orientation and health among U.S. adults: National health survey, 2013.* Atlanta, GA: U.S. Department of Health & Human Services; 2014, July 15. Report No.: 77.

76 Newport F. Americans greatly overestimate percent gays or lesbians in U.S. *Social and Policy Issues* 2015; May 21: 1–5.

77 Goldberg A, Allen K. *LGBT parents' families: Innovations in research and implications for practice.* New York: Springer; 2013.

78 Blake L. Gay fathers' motivations for and feelings about surrogacy. *Human Reproduction* 2017; 32: 860–867.

79 Golombok S. Parenting and adjustment of children born to gay fathers through surrogacy. *Child Development* 2018; 89: 1223–1233.

80 Boykin D. *Beyond the down low: Sex, lies and denial in Black America*. New York: DeCapo Press; 2006.

81 Carroll M. Gay fathers on the margins. *Family Relations* 2018; 67: 104–117.

82 King J, Hunter K. *On the down low: Straight black men who sleep with other men*. New York: Three Rivers Press; 2005.

83 Mezey N. *LGBT families*. Newbury Park, CA: Sage; 2014.

84 Lavner J. Gay parents with foster children. *Journal of Orthopsychiatry* 2012; 14: 4–10.

85 Farr R. Microaggressions, feelings of difference and resilience among adopted children with sexual minority parents. *Journal of Youth and Adolescence* 2016; 45: 85–104.

86 Garner A. *Families like mine: Children of gay parents tell it like it is*. New York: Harper; 2005.

87 Regnerus M. How different are the adult children of parents who have same-sex relationships? Findings from the New Family Structures study. *Social Science Research* 2012; 41: 752–770.

88 Tornello S, Patterson C. Adult children of gay fathers. *Journal of Homosexuality* 2018; 65: 1152–1166.

89 Blake L. Gay father surrogacy families. *Fertility and Sterility* 2016; 106: 1503–1509.

90 Tornello S, Patterson C. Gay grandfathers: Intergenerational relationships and mental health. *Journal of Family Psychology* 2016; 30: 543–551.

91 Coulter R. Sexual orientation differences in alcohol use trajectories and disorder in emerging adulthood. *Addiction* 2018; 113: 1619–1632.

92 Russell S, Fish J. Mental health in lesbian, gay, bisexual and transgender youth. *Annual Review of Clinical Psychology* 2016; 12: 465–487.

93 Reid C, Iglesias H. *His hands, his tools, his dress: Lesbian writers on their fathers*. Binghamton, New York: Harrington Park Press; 2004.

94 Aranda F. Coming out in color: Racial differences in sexual identity disclosure and depression among lesbians. *Cultural Diversity & Ethnic Minority Psychology* 2015; 21: 247–257.

95 Rossi M. Coming out stories of gay and lesbian young adults. *Journal of Homosexuality* 2011; 57: 1174–1191.

96 Ryan W, Legate N, Weinstein N. Coming out as lesbian, gay or bisexual. *Self and Identity* 2015; 14: 549–569.

97 Centers for Disease Control. *Assisted reproductive technology success rates: 2015*. Atlanta, GA: U.S. Department of Health: CDC; 2017.

98 Hertz R, Nelson M. *Random families: Genetic strangers, sperm donor siblings and the creation of new kin*. New York: Oxford University Press; 2018.

99 Vanderschueren D. A systematic review of sperm donors. *Human Reproduction* 2012; 19: 37–51.

100 Nelson M, Hertz R. Pride and concern: differences between sperm and egg donors with respect to responsibility for their donor conceived offspring. *New Genetics and Society* 2017; 36: 137–158.

101 Jadva V, Freeman T, Kramer W, Golombok S. Sperm and oocyte donors' experiences and contact with their offspring. *Human Reproduction* 2011; 44: 4–44.

102 Cha A. Children of sperm donors find their half siblings and demand change. *The Washington Post* 2018, September 13.

103 Kramer W. *Donor sibling registry*. New York: Donor Sibling Registry; 2011.

104 Kramer W. *Finding our families: A first of its kind book for donor conceived people and their families*. New York: Avery; 2013.

105 Hertz R, Mattes J. Donor shared siblings or genetic strangers: New families, clans, and the internet. *Journal of Family Issues* 2011; 32: 1129–1155.

106 Mroz J. *Scattered seeds: In search of family and identity in the sperm donor generation*. San Francisco, CA: Seal Press; 2017.

107 Paul M, Berger R. Topic avoidance and family functioning in families conceived with donor insemination. *Human Reproduction* 2007; 22: 2566–2571.

108 Provoost V. No daddy, a kind of daddy: words used by donor conceived children. *Culture Health & Sexuality* 2018; 20: 381–396.

109 Blake L, Casey P, Radings J, Jadva V, Golombok S. Daddy ran out of tadpoles: How parents tell children they are donor conceived. *Human Reproduction* 2010; 25: 2527–2534.

110 Belgrave F, Jennings P, Kramer W. Offspring searching for their sperm donors. *Human Reproduction* 2011; 26: 2415–2424.

111 Wyverkens E. The meaning of the sperm donor for heterosexual couples. *Family Process* 2017; 56: 203–216.

112 Zadeh S. The perspectives of adolescents conceived using surrogacy egg or sperm donation. *Human Reproduction* 2018; 33: 1099–1106.

113 Zadeh S, Jones C, Basie T. Children's thoughts and feelings about their donor and security of attachment to their solo mothers in middle childhood. *Human Reproduction* 2017; 32: 868–875.

114 N.V.S.S. *Deaths by age, race and gender: United States, 1999–2015*. Atlanta, GA: National Vital Statistics System; 2017.

115 C.D.C. *Alzheimer's disease*. Atlanta, GA: Centers for Disease Control; 2018.

116 Gelman C, Greer C. Children in early onset Alzheimer's disease families. *American Journal of Child and Adolescent Psychiatry* 2018; 26: 29–35.

117 Bastawrous M. Factors that contribute to adult children caregivers' well-being: A review. *Health and Social Care in the Community* 2015; 23: 449–466.

118 Lin F. Adult children's support of frail parents. *Marriage and the Family* 2008; 70: 113–128.

119 Byers A, van Doorn C, Kasl S, Levy B. Paternal attachment as a risk factor for depression in older women. *Journal of Mental Health and Aging* 2003; 9: 157–169.

120 Darden M, Gilleskie D. Affects of parental health shocks on adult offspring smoking behavior and self-assessed health. *Health Economics* 2018; 25: 939–954.

121 Marks N, Jun H, Song J. Death of parents and adult psychological and physical well-being. *Journal of Family Issues* 2007; 28: 1611–1638.

122 Burrell L, Mehlum L, Qin P. Sudden parental death from external causes and risk of suicide in the bereaved offspring: A national study. *Journal of Psychiatric Research* 2018; 96: 49–56.

123 Mangione L, Lyons M, DiCello D. Daughters, dads and the path of grieving: Tales from Italian America. *Psychology of Religion and Spirituality* 2016; 8: 253–262.

124 McMullen M. *Every fathers' daughter: 24 women writers remember their fathers*. Kingston, NY: McPherson & Co.; 2015.

125 Secunda V. *Losing your parents, finding yourself*. New York: Random House; 2000.

126 Hirooka J. End of life experiences of family caregivers of deceased patients with cancer: A nationwide survey. *Psycho-oncology* 2018; 27: 272–278.

127 Harzold E, Sparks L. Adult child perceptions of communication and humor when the parent is diagnosed with cancer. *Qualitative Research Reports in Communication* 2006; 7: 67–78.

128 Funderburg L. *Pig candy: Taking my father south.* New York: Free Press; 2008.

129 Merkin D. The public father. *The New Yorker* 2000, March 20: 58.

Index

Printed in Great Britain
by Amazon

64891328R00142